FRANCIS STUART: A LIFE

GEOFFREY ELBORN

Raven Arts Press/Dublin

Francis Stuart - A Life
is first published in 1990 by
The Raven Arts Press
P.O. Box 1430
Finglas
Dublin 11
Ireland

ISBN 1 85186 075 4

Raven Arts Press receives financial support from The
Arts Council (An Chomhairle Ealaíon), Dublin ,
Ireland.

Cover design by Susanne Linde. Portrait of Francis
Stuart by Edward Maguire, reproduced by
permission of the Hugh Lane Gallery of Modern Art,
Dublin. **Francis Stuart - A Life** is designed by
Dermot Bolger & Aidan Murphy and printed in
Ireland by Colour Books Ltd., Baldoyle.

For Madeleine
as promised
and
John Crampsie and Peter Rowlands

Stuart as a young man

INTRODUCTION

In his *Postscript* to the American edition of Francis Stuart's *Black List, Section H,* Professor Harry T. Moore writes "...the future biographer who works on Stuart's life in detail will find much in it that offers a challenge; so far, a good deal of that life remains rather obscure..."

Black List, Section H was my introduction to Stuart's work, and led to my approaching him in the hope that he would agree to my writing his life. We met in the Shelbourne Hotel in Dublin with his wife Madeleine, and spent the next few days in the Stuarts' home discussing the possibility of such a project. During the conversation I was immediately struck by Stuart's integrity.

For my part, I explained that if I should write about Stuart, I would not expect it to be vetoed by him in any way, and he agreed without hesitation. He made no attempt to hide the difficulties I would experience if we agreed that a biography would be written. When I came to say "goodbye" to Stuart and his wife, before returning to England, I was handed an envelope which contained a letter of authorization to proceed with a biography, and which requested the full co-operation of anyone I might approach for that purpose.

Stuart's anticipation of the problems proved to be correct, and confirmed Moore's speculation of a "challenge". Many of Stuart's papers and letters were lost, including those of the war years. Some of his friends felt unable to co-operate in the writing of this biography. Repeated pleas by letter to the late Sean MacBride, for example, with the assurance he could speak as freely as he wished, ended when he telephoned to say that "Francis Stuart treated Iseult disgracefully, and I will have nothing to do with you or your book."

Attitudes such as MacBride's were disappointing, but many believed certain myths about his part in the war in Germany, and his fourteen year absence from Ireland, while knowing none of the actual facts. One person in London, who has known a close friend of Stuart's for some years, maintained resolutely that Stuart had stomped through the Dublin pubs just before the war, wearing a Nazi-type uniform and jackboots. This, like much else that was alleged to be common knowledge, proved to be nonsense.

Although some refused to co-operate, the help I did receive, often came from those from whom I least expected it, such as Samuel Beckett whose views regarding his privacy were well known. We met in Paris, and I realised how it was possible for two men of differing viewpoints to remain friends, a friendship which was renewed when they met in Paris in 1987. Beckett typified those who were loyal to Stuart, and who did not hold preconceived judgments.

It is ironic, that because of the scarcity of material, the biography of an egocentric writer should centre almost exclusively around Stuart himself, with few other characters.

Much of the material for this book at least began through frequent conversations with Stuart and his second wife Madeleine. Iseult Stuart, his first wife, used to call him by the nickname "Grim" and although it was for reasons other than his tall, rather gaunt appearance, it seemed to describe Stuart very well. That is, until Stuart would relax out of his extreme shyness and apparent severity, into an exceptionally warm friendliness and tenderness, often noticeable when he would pause to stroke his rabbit or cat.

For one who has written novels which deal with chaos and revolution, Stuart is a man of ordered habits, always replacing a book when finished, and allowing no piles of untidy papers to gather on his desk. During my many visits it was obvious that those friends who came to see Stuart understood and accepted how he and Madeleine, more than others, needed the assurance that their home was "The Ark", where after years of storm, they had to feel secure.

Madeleine would be careful to exclude the literary-lions that Francis Stuart would otherwise have attracted, and this would ensure afternoons of serenity and happiness. Madeleine, whose exuberance complemented her husband's reserve, saw the beauty in much that others would overlook, and would make a walk around the garden, a memorable experience.

During conversation with Stuart's daughter, Kay Bridgwater, she asked me why I thought her father's life had followed such an apparently wayward direction. I suggested it was his "search for truth", which this biography attempts to explore.

To avoid cluttering the text with distracting references, these have been omitted, but will be supplied to anyone who approaches the publisher.

Stuart as a baby

Stuart as a young child

CHAPTER 1

During the night of 29 April 1902, when Francis Stuart was born in Townsville, Australia, a bat flew into the room, an incident that in earlier times might have been considered an ill omen. When his father Henry Irwin Stuart, dutifully registered the birth a month later, it was his last known act of responsibility, for on 4 July, he was admitted to Callan Park Asylum, Sydney, apparently suffering from melancholia and delusions, and displaying suicidal tendencies. In the early hours of 14 August 1902, he took his own life there, believing himself to be a "great criminal."

The Stuarts were an Antrim family who traced their descent from the late seventeenth century. Ballyhivistock, their estate near Dervock, was not particularly prosperous. By the nineteenth century most of the eight sons had to earn an income. Like many other Ulstermen of the time, previous generations of Stuarts had emigrated to Australia, as had one Samuel McCaughey, who went there in 1856 and built up a number of large sheep stations.

McCaughey returned to Antrim in 1871, looking for managers and partners, and invited James and Henry Stuart, younger twin brothers, to form a partnership with him in Queensland. Lacking capital they refused the offer then, but three years later, aged twenty one, they sailed for Melbourne with the help of a loan.

The brothers worked extremely hard in difficult conditions, and in 1882, bought a station called Rockwood which they developed into a prosperous town.

In 1898, Ballyhivistock, passed to Charles McDaniel Stuart, and Henry returned to Antrim.

Two miles from the Stuart house, were lands owned by the Montgomery family, where John Montgomery lived at Benvarden House. His father, Captain R.J. Montgomery had died of alcoholism according to W.B.Yeats, but as a "much loved figure", his death was announced in the local newspaper as due to "a complication of diseases."

Domestically, Benvarden was run by John Montgomery's sister Janet, who lived there with her younger sister Elizabeth, known in the family as Lily. Both were educated at home by governesses, but were completely opposite in nature. Lily, born in Dublin in 1875, was quiet and retiring, while Janet who was assertive, smoked a pipe and wore men's tweed trousers. Despite the family's long and loyal military tradition, Janet was a fervent Irish Nationalist, and later converted to Catholicism, as did Lily.

When Henry Stuart called at Benvarden as a family friend, it was the twenty-three year old Lily he particularly sought. Two years later when he was forty-seven, they married on 28 January 1901 in Derrykeighan Parish Church, Dervock, and shortly after left for Australia.

The voyage from London to Brisbane was uncomfortable, with another long journey to be covered by rail from Townsville, before arriving at Rockwood. Lily was welcomed by other members of the Stuart family already there, and the estate workers showed good will toward the couple, presenting them with a heavy silver fruit dish made by a Melbourne silversmith.

A year later Lily was pregnant, and after enduring the three hundred mile journey to a nursing home in Townsville, Francis Stuart was born.

Nothing is known of the circumstances which drove Henry into a state of mental imbalance, but he had tried to cut his throat early in June at his own home. A document signed by his brother George, who was with him in Australia, testified that Henry had been insane for two months, that there was no history of madness in the family, and that Henry was not dangerous. George noticed that his brother's appearance and health had so deteriorated that in a few weeks he no longer looked sane. Worse still, Henry began to hate his relations. There may have been other family problems before this which persuaded George to send for his eldest brother, for Charles arrived in Australia in mid August. Meanwhile, George took Henry to Sydney for medical advice rather than Brisbane, a strange choice, given the longer distance from Queensland.

When Henry tried to stab himself with a table knife during dinner in the Sydney hotel they were staying in, George had his brother examined by two doctors from the Sydney equivalent of Harley Street. They reported that he was suffering from an extreme persecution mania. Henry imagined he had committed some wrong for which he was going to be punished and from which suicide was the only release. With Lily's consent, George had Henry committed to a private asylum, Callan Park in Sydney, on July 4 1902. Henry made several more suicide attempts, but after opium treatment, he seemed to brighten a little by the first week of

August, although still under the constant scrutiny of the attendants.

On the night of 13 August, his night warder, a Herbert Laidlaw, noticed that Henry was in bed with the covers pulled over his head, and in the early hours of 14 August, that he was asleep. A quarter of an hour later, Laidlaw heard a noise, and hurried in from an adjoining room, to find Henry had hanged himself with a rope made from a bed sheet. With the help of another attendant, Laidlaw released Henry, who was still alive, and telephoned for two doctors. After over a half hour delay, the doctors arrived, too late to save Henry's life.

However deep his despair, Henry had been capable of calculating the right moment to outwit his attendant. The next day, a jury heard these circumstances, and brought a verdict that death was caused by self inflicted strangulation.

The asylum was negligent, but whether Henry could have been cured can never be known. Oppressed and haunted by his imagination, Henry had gained his own peace.

Lily did not attend the family funeral in Waverley Cemetery in Sydney, either by convention or because of the distance, but an unusually sympathetic vicar allowed Henry a Christian burial, and a headstone which read:

Sacred
to
The Memory of
HENRY IRWIN STUART
Who departed this life
14th August 1902
Aged 49
"Out of this darkness into His marvellous light"
Peter II, 9.

There was now no reason for Lily to remain in Australia, and with Francis, Nellie Farren his nurse, and Henry's brother in law, James-Stewart-Moore, she began the long voyage home in December 1902. When Stewart-Moore returned to Antrim, he told his daughter Nancy that Lily was devastated on board the ship, and seldom left her cabin. Suicide and madness were shameful, and perhaps Lily was simply in a state of shock. But once in Ireland Lily's attitude to her husband was strange. She never contradicted the rumours that he had shot himself in Townsville, which her family believed, despite the fact that a paid obituary notice in a Belfast newspaper recorded that he had died in Sydney. Instead of living in Antrim, Lily went with her son to Shallon in County Meath in the South, to stay with her sister Janet. Lily never again referred to Henry, nor revealed the circumstances of his death to her son. The Montgomerys and Stuarts too, never spoke of Henry in front of Francis Stuart.

In rejecting the memory of Henry, Lily also rejected her son in so far as this was possible. For the rest of her life, her attitude would be one of indifference towards him. When Stuart stayed with any of his father's brothers, it struck him many years later that Lily had never been invited with him, a fact that raises the question that her husband's family may have held her at least partly to blame for her husband's insanity. Henry may have suffered from sunstroke due to a severe drought, but it is possible that Lily, who was attracted by younger men, had an affair which the older Henry discovered.

Fortunately for Stuart, he was very much loved by his nurse, Nellie Farren, who was a mother to him in all but name, and whom he called "Weg" after a doll in a story. Lily was happy to leave her son with the nurse, which was not unusual for such a family. Despite his mother's kindness when they were together, Stuart felt extremely lonely as a child, for reasons he tried to write of in an early unpublished draft of his novel, *Black List, Section H:*

> His sense of precariousness came not alone from the meagreness of his family ties, but because he longed to belong to a different one.
>
> He wanted Weg his nurse for a mother. This she might be in all but name in the years he spent with the three women at the old white washed house set sideways to one of the leafy lanes of Meath where his widowed mother had returned from Australia to live with her sister. But H was obscurely conscious of the fragility of the relationship without natural and recognized roots. It made him cling to her all the more urgently. H's mother never came between them. She too was searching for devotion in her modest way, with men younger than herself, and from what then was called an inferior station.

Nurse Farren was very much on Stuart's side, but did not spoil him. She understood his sensitivity which he showed by long periods of silence, and a preference for the company of animals over adults, or children of his own age. As Stuart grew older, it was Lily who would indulge him. She read to him at night, and when he began to tell her his own stories, it was Lily who wrote them down.

Materially, Stuart lacked nothing, and his early photographs show him rather stuffily and formally dressed in clothes that were typical of his class, and with a favourite dog or pony.

In searching for happiness in the company of younger men who were not in her own social class, Lily may have felt some insecurity about her own background, and her doomed visit to Australia may have been an effort to escape from it. She may have reacted against having had an older husband, but remained remote from her son.

The days spent in Meath, in his aunt's house were, as Stuart noted, "intensely absorbed and happy", as long as Nurse Farren was there. But in 1909, when he was seven, Janet Montgomery returned to Benvarden, to look after her brother John, who had married unhappily, and Lily moved to Monkstown, near Dublin. Nothing altered much, for when Stuart was sent to a day school, his nurse was waiting for him to return home. Although he missed the Meath countryside, he spent long periods in Antrim, either at Ballyhivistock, or in the other houses which belonged to his paternal uncles, or those of his mother's family.

The world the young Stuart grew up in was limited to his school, and the restricted circle of neighbouring country houses, many of which belonged to relations. The shooting season dictated the pattern of Stuart's uncles' lives, but their houses, packed with sporting implements, held no interest for Stuart. He hated the stuffed animals on the walls, which he would have preferred to have found shelved with books.

During the summer, there was tennis and games with his cousins, but Stuart was particularly haunted by a memory of a winter dance which typified the aimless existence of his family. Driven in one of his uncles' cars, the side curtains were drawn against the gaze of the curious, and when they arrived, Stuart did not dance, but stood around the floor, shy and awkward.

The young boy was accepted as a member of the Stuart family, but as a moody and introspective child, he did not belong. Gradually he was aware of a sense of alienation, which only increased when at ten he was sent, in the autumn of 1912, to Bilton Grange, a Warwickshire preparatory school for Rugby. Stuart recalled that time, when:

> Without warning all was snatched away. He was in an
> unknown town...H's defences were inadequate to deal with a
> situation he'd been unable to foresee in spite of his nurse's
> attempt to forewarn him... All he could do was to make
> himself believe in a last minute change of fortune, that
> instead of being left at Bilton Grange... they would set out on
> the journey back to Ireland and Shallon.
> It was shortly before the carriage was due at the door to take
> his mother and H the few miles to the school that he gave up
> hope... Drowned in convulsions of weeping, blindly clinging
> to Weg's hand till the last moment, he was dragged away...
> The world was sinister and grotesque...

The shock of Bilton Grange was Stuart's first intimation
that even his Nurse whom he loved and trusted, could not
prepare him for the shock of the unknown. At school, Stuart
deliberately made himself ill with nerves, so that he could be
taken to the sanatorium. There he chanced to overhear the
matron remarking to a doctor that he was a moody boy and a
daydreamer, which only increased his misery.

Despite Lily's apparent indifference towards her son, she
found it more comfortable to agree with him than to argue.
When he wrote to her that he was miserable at school, she
simply allowed him to leave. He was overjoyed when Nellie
Farren took him away in her brother's car. The pattern
repeated for two more schools, one in Broadstairs and the
last in Conway Bay which Stuart hated more than the
others.

During these unhappy school years, Lily married her first
cousin, Henry Clements, in Chester on 4 July 1913, eleven
years to the day since Stuart's father was committed to the
asylum. Like her first husband, Clements was older, and was
immediately disliked by Stuart. He disapproved of his step
son's removal from his schools, and decided that Stuart not
only lacked the guidance of a father, but was pampered by
too many women. Stuart was a milksop to be so devoted to
his nurse, and he insisted that she should be retired.
Clements was determined to make a man of Stuart, and he
taught him to hunt and shoot. Stuart's cousin, Jack White,
also a cousin of Henry Clements, left a description of him in
his memoirs:

Henry... had been a cowboy in Texas and Mexico and looked it. He was a pleasure to look at, a greater pleasure to listen to. He added to the civilized detachment of the Clements in general, the wild and whimsical detachment of the prairie. His attitude to the solemnities of life was one of simply manly reverence suddenly illuminated by simple blasphemy. He was the quarry *par excellence* to stalk in the middle of family prayers. Not a muscle of his face twitched, but by whimsical allusions to the incident he could keep you laughing for a week.

The "cowboy" image was precisely what Stuart detested about Clements, and he never remembered the humour so admired by White.

Clements did not own a house, and Stuart went with him and Lily from one rented house to the next, either in North Wales, Bournemouth or Brighton. Clements who was an alcoholic had only a small income of his own, and drank a great deal of Lily's money, which he tried to recover through stock-exchange deals. Wherever they were staying at the time, telegraph boys would arrive almost daily, with news from various brokers, usually announcing his latest financial failure. Clements once hired a coach to drive round the coast of North Wales. As the only passengers were Clements,(who was drunk) his wife and Stuart, the flamboyant gesture was a ridiculous waste of Lily's money.

Stuart believed that Clements was homosexual and although Clements never made advances to his stepson, he told him there was nothing better than a cold bath, which on a few occasions they shared. Clements' efforts to make a man of Stuart may have been a reflection of his own guilt and determination to conceal the true nature of his sexuality, but in any case he botched his efforts to be the father figure that Stuart needed.

Lily did not seem to care about Clements' drunkeness, and while she was not happy, she settled down to a "kind of contentment." She had a small pug dog called Snuff, memorable for its heavy breathing, and her devotion to it was one of the few signs that she was capable of sincere affection.

With Farren retired, Stuart had no-one to confide in. The Montgomery and Stuart families, so united by inter-marriage did not realize that Stuart was suffering, as he guessed much later, from a kind of neurasthenia. Stuart's

Stuart as a young boy

Stuart at Bilton Grange

unhappiness was only intensified by the unsettling shunting from one house to the next at the whim of his stepfather.

Aunt Janet Montgomery who was rational and had an sense of economy, confronted Clements with his dissipation of her sister's money. Soon afterwards the Texan cowboy left Lily to spend his last years living in the Grosvenor Hotel at Victoria Station in London, taking with him a maid from Portrush, the home of George Stuart. Janet Montgomery coerced her nephew into writing a lengthy letter to Clements in London, stating they knew that he had swindled Lily. It was a cruel letter which Stuart was not proud of writing, but as he never had the slightest feeling of affection for his step-father, he was relieved that he had gone out of their lives. The Montgomerys despised Clements, but neither their hostility to him nor his eventual departure disturbed Lily. Near financial ruin, she showed no emotion and shed no tears, perhaps grateful that Clements had been unable to touch her income from capital held in trust.

The unpleasantness of the preparatory schools soon led to the rigours of Rugby in January 1916. Now aged thirteen, Stuart was placed in Michell House. In September, he was joined by John Sutro, whom he remembered as one of the few fat boys there. They would later share some acquaintances with Evelyn Waugh, but at Rugby they were never friendly. Stuart shared a study with Trevor, the son of Arthur Tooth, the London art dealer, but was closer to a Pole, Roderick Biernacki, whom he swam with, and discussed their mutual loathing for Rugby.

As these were the First World War years, there was a strong emphasis on military training, and Stuart, as a member of the OTC, hated the exercises and particularly the obsession with neatness and the fussy preparation of the uniform and equipment.

No longer a milksop, Stuart was good at all games, particularly squash, but academically, made little progress. When he came to leave Rubgy, Stuart had absorbed very little, and had failed hopelessly at French, Latin and Greek.

He did better at Geography and Art, but the future writer was only praised once in an English class. An essay he wrote on Sohrab and Rustum, read aloud for its insight, was the only scholastic triumph Stuart enjoyed during his school career.

Like most other subjects, English seemed to have no relevance for him, and he remained apathetic to everything

Iseult Gonne

academic.

Stuart was grateful for the number of poems he had to memorise, for it stimulated an interest in verse. A lifelong interest in astronomy was fostered by a master, but in general, school was a failure because he lacked motivation and had no idea what he was aiming for.

Nellie Farren had been forcibly retired, but Stuart was able to spend holidays with her in Bournemouth, and staying there during his first Easter vacation from Rugby, he heard of the Rising in Dublin which made a strong impact on him. His nurse's sister was apparently shocked by the photographs of the 'rebels' in the newspapers. One evening when Stuart went to her room to say goodnight, she asked him to remove the papers there, remarking, "Don't leave those terrible photos in my room overnight; those criminals." Stuart wondered "Were those criminals?" for to him, they were "wonderful." The rebels were a group he could identify with because this respectable woman disliked them. Although Stuart did not know that his father had believed that he was a "great criminal", he had by now, either gathered from hints, or had convinced himself that his father had committed suicide as an alcoholic. Stuart had probably amalgamated in his imagination, the fate of his maternal grandfather who had died an alcoholic, with some vague details he had gleaned about his father. By refusing to even mention Henry, Stuart's family had unwittingly forced the young man to create his own image of his father.

Stuart felt alienated from his school and his family, but to have felt anything else would have seemed a betrayal of his father, with whom he shared rejection. This concept of Henry, formed without substantiated facts, was one of the most important influences during Stuart's adolescence. His father was for him, a hero that justified and validated the notion of the "outsider", reinforcing some ideas he only half understood about himself and society, which he considered responsible for his misery. Henry had somehow died in disgrace, but his son would both consciously and subconsciously try to atone for the ignominy thrust on his father by an apparently uncaring family, who interpreted Stuart's own behaviour as that of a spoiled child.

He never felt on sufficiently intimate terms with Lily to ask about Henry, despite the fact that his father increasingly obsessed him. Stuart may have had a protective instinct not to demand the truth for fear of destroying what he had built in his own mind. Had he known the facts, it is unlikely that this would have altered anything, for the father figure who guided him, was his own conception of what a father should be. He was redeeming Henry's life by his own devotion, and coming to understand the pain of isolation which he felt was also his father's.

CHAPTER 2

When Major John MacBride was executed for his part in the Easter Rising of 1916, his death did not upset his widow, Maud Gonne MacBride. They married in 1903, had a son Sean in 1904 and were separated the following year.

W. B.Yeats was in love with Maud Gonne, but as she had remarked that she was not interested in marrying anyone, the news of the wedding had shocked him. Five years later, Yeats visited Madame McBride at her house in Coleville, France, and for a short time they became lovers. It was perhaps the memory of this, which encouraged Yeats to meet Madame MacBride in Normandy 1916. Now that she was free, he proposed to her, and was turned down.

Yeats first met Maud Gonne in 1889, when unknown to him, she had a lover, Lucien Millevoye who was a French political activist. Millevoye gave her a son in 1890 who died, it is believed, in 1893. Grief stricken, Maud Gonne consulted Yeats and George Russell about the fate of the soul of a dead child. Russell told her it could be re-born in the same family, but Yeats, seeing Maud Gonne's distress, could not bring himself to tell her that this theory was only speculation. Maud Gonne returned to France to meet Millevoye, and hoping to resurrect the soul of their dead boy, went down to the vault where their child was buried. There, Maud Gonne conceived a daughter Iseult, who was born on 6 August, 1894. For the sake of respectability, she was passed off by her mother as an adopted niece.

Millevoye's friendship with Maud Gonne ended in 1896 when he tactlessly brought his latest mistress to see her. His only known act of generosity was to buy the villa in Coleville in Iseult's name. In 1916 Yeats' familiarity with Maud's past life, did not deter him from remaining there with Maud Gonne and her family after his hopeless proposal. He decided to renew an old passion for Iseult. She had declared her love for Yeats when she was fifteen, but would not marry him. Iseult was now aged twenty-one and extremely beautiful, and from August 1916 Yeats employed her as his secretary. It was a difficult time for the family, as Madame MacBride was desperate to leave France to become involved in Irish politics once more. As she was considered a danger to Ireland, and not allowed to return there by the British Government, her constant grumbling about this and her ranting about politics, bored Iseult, who was grateful for Yeats' company. They read French writers together such as Peguy, and Iseult recalled later that Yeats had re-read "...Keats and Shelley and... thought it strange that he had ever seen anything in them." At this time, Yeats wrote two poems for Iseult, *"To a Young Beauty"* and *"To a Young Girl"*, but although he thought he was "managing Iseult very well..." she refused to give any answer to his proposal of marriage. Yeats returned alone to London where he wrote his essay *Per Amica Silentia Lunae*, addressing the prologue to Iseult.

At Rugby, Stuart was considered eccentric by his form master, who liked him the least of his class. Stuart preferred to live in the world of his imagination. The school at least helped him to endure physical hardship, something he recognised when imprisoned in Austria after the Second World War. Nevertheless, he ignored complaints that he was dreamy, and during the Easter term of 1917, was summoned to his House Master's study to be punished. St. Hill, the Michell Housemaster complained to Stuart that apart from his attitude to the school, his reports were at the best "fair to middling" and at the worst, simply "bad". Although Stuart had guessed for some time he was under threat of a birching, he had not prepared any story in advance to help himself. On impulse he told St. Hill that his behaviour was "Due to the war", explaining that a relation had been killed in action, flying an aeroplane in April 1917. The House Master assumed that this must be a brother to have affected Stuart so adversely, but the boy told him he had an older cousin, James Stuart, who had been like a brother to him. In fact the cousins were not particularly close, but St. Hill was impressed, and said to Stuart he understood that the war was terrible for everyone, which he had to accept, and try to do better in his work.

The homily made no difference to Stuart's attitude, and he

simply continued at school as defiant as before. The dreaminess, part of his imagination which had got him into trouble, had also saved him.

For Madame MacBride and her children, still stuck in France, it was a different matter. By August 1917 any remaining hopes of the family returning to Ireland evaporated when Maud Gonne heard that she could only be granted an exit visa for England. That alone, was infuriating, but if the family left France they might be refused re-entry there.

Madame MacBride could not decide what to do, but when Yeats arrived a few days after she heard the news, she eventually agreed to his suggestion that she should leave for London by September. Yeats had returned to France, determined to propose to Iseult before they left. The previous summer, he had noted in a letter to Lady Gregory that Iseult looked, "very distinguished and is now full of self-possession. She is beautifully dressed, though very plainly. I said 'Why are you so pale?' and she said 'Too much responsibility.'

A year later, worn out with the constant strain of her mother's company, Iseult was recovering from an illness which Yeats thought was caused by excessive smoking. From an intermittent diary of this time, although there is no mention of Yeats, Iseult seemed extremely disturbed emotionally. She was agitated and nervous, and wrote pages of her feelings, trying to come to terms with life in Normandy. Yeats could not get any further with her, and wrote to Lady Gregory on 12 August, "...Iseult and I are on our old intimate terms but I don't think she will accept. She 'has not the impulse.' However I will think the matter undecided till we part."

Despite Madame MacBride's uneasy relationship with the poet, she had not objected to him seeing her daughter. Iseult felt that although her mother was not a woman of much discernment, "...she had enough to know better than to marry Yeats, to whom she wasn't suited." When Iseult herself said to Yeats "You wouldn't say you loved me, would you ?" Yeats could not answer in the affirmative.

In mid September, 1917, Madame MacBride and her family travelled with Yeats from Paris to Le Havre for

London, and while they waited for the boat, a depressed Iseult burst into tears. She told Yeats she was ashamed of being selfish for not wanting to marry him, and unhappy that this might break their friendship. They arranged to meet at a Lyons Corner House tea room in London, where Yeats demanded a definite answer to his marriage proposal. Iseult finally turned him down, but he told her he would always be father and guardian to her, an attitude which would be important in the future. On the rebound, Yeats turned to his second choice, George Hyde-Lees and they married on 17 October 1917.

Yeats was haunted with a sense of guilt that he had acted selfishly towards Iseult, and in the first few days of his marriage, wondered if he should have waited in case Iseult changed her mind. Mrs Yeats was aware of her husband's doubts, which threatened their own relationship. She had already impressed Yeats by her gift of producing automatic writing, when strange messages apparently uncontrolled by her, appeared while she lightly held her pen over paper. Yeats believed his wife's hand was guided by spirits from another world and on 21 October, Mrs Yeats deliberately wrote the sentence, "What you have done is right for both the cat and the hare", pretending it was automatic writing. As George hoped, Yeats interpreted the cat as herself, and the hare as Iseult, and was satisfied he had made the correct decision in his marriage after all. Unwilling to waste the allusion, Yeats represented his wife as a cat in the poem *Two Songs of a Fool,* and Iseult in this and other poems as a hare, because she was a fast runner.

Stuart spent some of the summer vacation of 1917 with his Aunt Janet Montgomery in Ballybogey, the lower house of Benvarden. On a visit to Dervock, Stuart chanced on a bookshop where he "discovered poetry for the first time." Another aunt gave him a volume of Rupert Brooke, which he liked, and would use a line of for the title of his own first collection of poems, *We Have Kept The Faith.* Later in the summer before he returned to Rugby, Stuart stayed in Bournemouth with Nellie Farren and her sister's family, and was "stunned" when he read some early poems of Ezra

Pound. Nevertheless, perhaps because of his own love of nature, Stuart was more drawn to the Georgian writers of Harold Monro's *Chapbook,* where he found his first imaginative allies.

While at Bilton Grange, Stuart had deliberately made himself physically ill through nerves, and back at Rugby, he put himself in the school sanatorium in the same way. While he was there the flustered matron announced to the boys that she had "terrible news".

This was the outbreak of the Russian Revolution, and the Tsar's abdication which Stuart and some of the others greeted with a resounding cheer. They felt that the revolution attacked the establishment the school was part of, and as Russia was an ally in the war, it might well spread to Great Britain. Stuart read Mayakovsky and Esenin, poets of the revolution with more excitement than understanding for he would not have supported Esenin's interest in peasant traditions and folklore. Stuart's interest in literature was formed independently of what he read at Rugby, but books were notably absent from his uncles' houses in Antrim. It was in his aunt Janet's bookcase, that Stuart discovered the second part of Tolstoy's *Resurrection.* The first of the two volumed set was missing, Stuart was nevertheless fascinated by the snowy Russian landscape, which seemed like the Antrim countryside. The servanted estates were reminiscent of his own background and he realized how the life of the Northern landed gentry paralleled the decline of the aristocracy in Imperial Russia.

On holiday from the confines of Rugby, Stuart fell in love for the first time, with a cousin Maida, daughter of his uncle James Stuart, and enjoyed a "harmless flirtatious relationship" with her. Two of his cousins had gone to the war, but it was in a largely undisturbed atmosphere that Stuart often cycled over from Portrush, the home of his uncle George Stuart, to some other relations's house at Coleraine for breakfast. From time to time he visited his second cousin, Captain Jack White, the only other rebellious member of the family.

White was the son of Field Marshal Sir George Stuart White, the Defender of Ladysmith, but unlike his father, was a staunch Republican. He had helped to found the Irish Citizen Army in 1913, and Stuart enjoyed hearing of his adventures. Stuart did not support White's social or political views, but in him saw how it was possible to successfully break from an establishment upbringing.

Stuart had bought a roll top desk for his study in Rugby which "enshrined my little world in the midst of an alien universe."

In the pigeonholes he kept the first love letters he received, from Maida who wrote from Ulster. He recalled that there was "no mention of love in them from beginning to end. But I knew and she knew, that they were love letters all the same." In his desk Stuart also hid drawings of the boglands of Antrim he had made, always imagining it to be evening there, the bog water tinged with red from the reflections of a red sky. He was painfully homesick, and prayed that he might return to Ireland.

There was in fact, little point in Stuart remaining at Rugby for he was making no academic progress, and when he told Lily he wanted to leave, she did not object. His aunt Janet had other ideas and commented, "You can't leave just like that. We want you to go to Trinity and you are certainly not prepared." With the future unplanned, Stuart left Rugby in the summer term of 1918.

When he was older, Stuart recognized that he had survived his strange upbringing and school better than might have been expected:

I was lucky, if lucky is the word, that I came out of it as I did. It could have been quite disastrous. But I see in myself, or think I do, certain lacks, or certain disadvantages from it. It may also have had certain advantages...very definitely I would have wished for...some more enlightened guidance. I was totally without it, except what I found, in the end, in books and things for myself...

Free of school, Stuart had now lost the few friends he had there, and there was "nobody to whom I could revere or look up to."

With Iseult's welfare still at heart, Yeats met Sir Denison Ross, Head of the School of Oriental Studies, and pressed him to find her a post as an assistant librarian there. It seems that Ezra Pound, Yeat's friend and best man at his wedding also intervened on Iseult's behalf, for he wrote to Yeats, stating that the School of Oriental Studies would be willing to let her work there half time. Iseult took up the poorly paid appointment in March 1918, and from Pound's fragmented letters, he also considered employing her as his secretary. He could not pay much either, but concluded a letter on the subject to Yeats, with - " All things being considered, I do not think it well to refer to her as my 'secretary'...At any rate my poems are too Ithyphallic for any secretary of her years to be officially in my possession."

Meanwhile Madame MacBride back in Ireland, after leaving George Russell's house, was arrested on 17 May 1918 on the orders of Lord French, the Lord Lieutenant. The British Government trumped up a plot to remove potentially dangerous political activists, by falsely suggesting they were involved with Germany. As a result, Madame MacBride with seventy two others, was transported to London. She was locked in Holloway Prison without trial or charge, where she was kept for five and a half months.

Iseult worried about her mother's health, and their lack of money, for the St. Stephen's Green house in Dublin was only let to Yeats for a low rent. Iseult had to find a better paid job, and for a time she moved between Yeats' house in Woburn Place, and the Kensington flat which Ezra Pound shared with his wife. By July 1918, the problems of the "Ithyphallic" poetry had been overcome, for in a letter to his parents, employing his usual eccentric punctuation, Pound wrote that he had taken on Iseult as "... a typist three days a week so that I shall have less mechanical waste of time. & can use my lofty intelligence for more intelligent matters than swatting a Corona..."

It was probably shortly afterwards, that Iseult, then aged twenty-three, and Pound become lovers. Why Iseult lost her virginity to a man who was nearly eleven years older than herself, can only be partly explained. She belonged to a group of emancipated women who regarded sexual experience from an early age as a matter of course. Through Yeats she had met many of Wyndham Lewis's friends who considered chastity to be old fashioned. But as far as literature was concerned, women had little hope of being published unless they used a man's name. Iseult had been writing poems, and working on translations, and was referred to as "Maurice" by both Pound and Yeats. Her affair was perhaps a deliberate effort to break her mother's domination, for Madame MacBride who considered Pound to be "rather affected" was still in Holloway, and could not interfere.

Pound felt strongly enough about Iseult to ask her to travel with him to the Italian lakes, but Iseult refused because she was worried about her mother. The affair with Pound had ended, but he sent her letters long after she married making it clear that, like Yeats, he still cared for her deeply.

Janet Montgomery discovered Stuart had written some poems and secretly sent them off for the opinion of H.O. White, a tutor friend who later became Professor of English at Trinity College Dublin. White replied that the poetry was talentless and without any possible hope of improving. When Stuart accidentally found the letter, he felt even more determined to be a writer, undeterred by White's judgment.

When Stuart left school, he had few regrets, but now he was leading a pointless existence without any firm plans for the future. From what he had read he knew that alternative worlds to his comfortable background did exist, but although he wanted to change his own life, he did not know how to begin.

During his first summer away from Rugby, in 1918, he wrote a letter advocating Home Rule to *The Irish Independent*. His views were not particularly original, but he knew that the letter would be published because of his Antrim address. When the Stuart family, who were anti-Home Rule, read the letter, they declared he was unbalanced. Stuart had not deliberately invited such a response to his first public dissident act, but was pleased that what they said brought him a little nearer to his father. The letter also ended his life in Antrim. Arrangements were made for Stuart to be tutored in Dublin in preparation for

Trinity College by none other than H.O. White, and taking Stuart with her, Lily rented a house in Monkstown.

Used to the rather closed community of Rugby, Stuart took nearly a week to find the courage to take a tram to the centre of Dublin to see White. O'Connell Street still suffered the ravages of the Easter Rising (the Post Office was in ruins) but once he became familiar with Dublin, he was excited by the thought of meeting poets, and had no enthusiasm for his lessons.

Stuart had never lived alone with Lily before, and saw for the first time her inability to confront the truth if it was awkward, because of her desire to avoid scenes. She took no interest in Stuart's efforts as a poet, and paid little attention to the fact that he was absorbed by Bohemian Dublin and had stopped seeing his tutor. White realised that Stuart was simply wasting his family's money, and wrote to Janet Montgomery, suggesting she should come to Dublin to discuss the problem. Janet was met off the train in Dublin by White and they went to the Monkstown house for a meal with Lily and Stuart.

It was an awkward evening, for Lily seemed incapable of contributing to the conversation about her son's future. Janet had bought a copy of Joyce's *A Portrait of the Artist as a Young Man* at the railway bookstall on White's recommendation, and as a distraction, Stuart read part of it. Despite the fact that Stuart was living in Dublin where the book was set, he was not drawn to the novel. For Stuart the Joyce:

> was not visually evocative but had a direct impact on my nerves, or so it seemed. It excited me and made me feel uneasy as did some of the youthful sexuality I shared with one in particular of my girlfriends...

It was agreed that tuition was pointless, and White proposed that Stuart should stay on in Dublin alone, offering to find accommodation for him. As Janet was staying in Dublin for a week, White took her and Stuart to one of George Russell's social gatherings.

The night began badly when Stuart was introduced by

Russell as "Mr St. George", and he was disillusioned when the older poet passed round an album of photographs of the crowds at lectures he had given in America. Stuart was shocked because he had imagined all writers shared his own loneliness, and to be like his Russian heroes in spirit.

Later, a young woman arrived, strikingly beautiful, with a complexion that Emerald Cunard had described as the finest she had ever seen. Stuart overheard her introduced as Miss Gonne, and assumed he was looking at the same Maud who had inspired the early love poetry of Yeats. Stuart said nothing to her, but when he left the house with White and his Aunt, learned that the woman he felt attracted to was Iseult. White hinted that Madame MacBride was more closely related to Iseult than she could admit to the nationalist circles in which she moved.

Although Aunt Janet was difficult and bossy, she at least realised that Stuart was serious and intense, and cared about his future. She took him to the Municipal Art Gallery. He never forgot:

> some of the George Russells... fantasies... that appealed to me. There were others... Manzini: huge canvases, rather thick paint, portraits of figures. I don't know why they made such a strong impression on me. Also some of the French Impressionists... (the visit) made a great impact on me...

Lily and her sister returned to the North, and Stuart moved into a mews flat, near Fitzwilliam Street, which belonged to a Mrs Hester Travers Smith, a Dublin society hostess who was a friend of White's. Stuart lived a happy idle life, lunching with Mrs Travers Smith, and nibbling ginger biscuits spread with Nestle's milk at other times.

Sometimes Stuart was invited when she had literary company, and on such an evening met the young Lennox Robinson, secretary to the Abbey Theatre, and friend of Yeats. A Spiritualist, Mrs Travers Smith claimed that Sir Hugh Lane, had described to her his last few moments before he went down on the Lusitania.

Her society was artificial to Stuart who preferred to think alone in the mews where he was visited by a cat. Stuart found no Russian writers in his landlady's rather pretentiously furnished house, and the tittle-tattle he heard there, gave him a lifelong distaste for literary conversation.

Stuart decided that he was a poet, and wrote many poems in the mews. His contribution to Bohemian life was to meet, amongst others, Michael MacLiammoir and F.R.Higgins in a basement teashop called Sod of Turf, on the corner of Dawson and Anne Street. With "coleens" in green shawls serving strong tea and soda bread, the surroundings were just as unreal as Mrs Travers Smith's drawing room, but Stuart was accepted as a writer, and was happy.

He wanted to meet Iseult again, and was taken by a young medical student called Robert Faucett to Madame MacBride's house in St Stephen's Green. Stuart has provided an account of his first meeting with Iseult and Madame MacBride in his novel *Black List, Section H*. Although he later revised his view of Iseult, he never altered his opinion of her mother. From the first he regarded Madame MacBride as a sham because she was so certain of her ideals. Stuart's heroes were unsure of their mission, but driven to act by some compulsion they did not fully understand. Stuart maintained that Madame MacBride hypocritically wore widow's weeds for a husband she had hated and tried to divorce, but he probably knew perfectly well that the black was for Ireland. Madame MacBride's effusive conversation that evening, made the hypertense seventeen-year-old Stuart withdraw into himself. Awkward and gauche, he was aware that Madame MacBride hardly even noticed him.

When Stuart heard later that Madame MacBride and Iseult were living in a cottage near Glendalough in the Wicklow valley, he went on a walking holiday with Faucett. They called to see Iseult, who ignored the student, and when alone on a walk with Iseult the following day, Stuart handed her a volume of Yeats' poems and asked her to read from it.

The world of Yeats, which Iseult belonged to, now seemed one which Stuart could also enter. Once part of it, he thought he would be more acceptable to Iseult. This was a mistaken judgment, for it would have been better, as Stuart admitted later, if he had tried honestly to explain his own beliefs to Iseult, even if she considered them immature. He had not understood that even Iseult and her mother laughed at Yeats' foibles, but for the time being the Yeatsian world, and mutual love of poetry drew the couple together, and they fell in love.

Iseult was beautiful, and it is obvious on that level at least, why Stuart fell in love with her. More extraordinary was Iseult's attraction to Stuart. For apart from his handsome appearance and tall frame, he was seven years younger, totally inexperienced sexually and still excruciatingly shy in society; the complete opposite of Ezra Pound. Iseult was erudite, whereas Stuart had hardly even read the Russian poets he admired, drawn to them more as men of action than for their literary achievement. Iseult realised that she had little in common with Stuart, but was probably desperate to leave her mother. She was reckless in a different way from Stuart, and they both disregarded convention. Perhaps afraid of confronting their differences, they seldom spoke of their love to each other, but Iseult was perceptive enough to comment that it would not be she who would run away from Stuart. As she told him "I'm the willow rooted on the river bank and you're the black swan gliding past..."

Iseult would visit Stuart in his mews room, entering undetected by a door in the lane. She avoided meeting Mrs Travers Smith, who as an Anglo Irish supporter would have disapproved of Stuart's association with Iseult, and told Lily. Stuart still could not like Madame MacBride, as he came to know her better. He was embarrassed when she addressed Iseult as "belle animal" and winced when she was referred to as "my lovely niece".

Most of Iseult's meetings with Stuart were in secret, and Lennox Robinson lent Stuart his flat while he was away on business for the Abbey Theatre. Although homosexual, Robinson had fallen in love with Iseult, but did not stand in Stuart's way. One evening, Maud Gonne guessed that Iseult was in Robinson's flat with Stuart, (where they had spent a chaste evening) and stormed up the stairs accusing him of dishonourable behaviour. She was "shrieking like a fish wife" at him, and was only placated by Iseult.

Iseult ignored her mother's disapproval of Stuart, knowing

perfectly well that he was the antithesis of all she believed in, and what she wanted for her daughter. As late as November 1919, she was apparently uncertain what to do about Stuart. A letter from Yeats of 17 November suggests that Iseult had confided some of her difficulties to him, for he suggested she should marry Lennox Robinson, whose earlier proposal she had refused.

Because of Madame MacBride's disapproval of Stuart, he decided to elope with Iseult to London. Iseult was determined to avoid suspicion, and on 4 January 1920, she left one day before Stuart for London.

Stuart hardly knew why he was going there, but followed Iseult's lead. When they met, she showed him London, and after a few nights in separate rooms at a hotel near Euston, they took a furnished room above a grocer's shop in Tottenham Street, near Charlotte Street and Tottenham Court Road. Stuart dreaded returning to the room which only contained a single bed, for he had never made any sexual advance to Iseult. During conversation, he was shaken into a state of almost nervous collapse when she casually mentioned that she had been Ezra Pound's mistress. Stuart was hardly able to endure what she had said, but was compelled to ask for some of the details. Trying to hide his reaction, he hurried to an all night cafe, where he sat alone, and returned to Iseult early in the morning.

In fact as Iseult reminded him later, she had already told him about Pound when they were in Dublin, but he had totally failed to register the fact. His reverence for Iseult was such that he could hardly bring himself to touch her, and it was only during this visit that she called him "darling" for the first time. That Iseult was sexually experienced was beyond his understanding at seventeen, but worse, he recognized from the outset that while she could talk about sex, the physical act did not interest her, and this only increased Stuart's own lack of confidence.

Iseult told Stuart that John MacBride had made sexual advances to her when she was a young woman, and this may have contributed to the problems which became a serious obstacle to her relationship with Stuart. After three months in London, Stuart realised the visit was a failure, but convinced himself it was not. When letters from Helena Moloney, an old family friend, arrived stating how worried Madame MacBride was about Iseult, they returned to Ireland.

Stuart had more than strong hints from Madame MacBride that he should marry Iseult. A meeting was arranged between her and Stuart's maternal uncles from Antrim, who told Madame MacBride that their nephew had inherited his father's madness, even implying that it already showed in his decision to marry Iseult. They were strenuously against any marriage, but Lily who knew that Henry Stuart's mental instability was not genetic, said nothing.

Madame MacBride herself did not want Stuart and Iseult to marry, but as the couple had returned to Dublin, and were compromised, there was no alternative. Lady Gregory heard from Iseult that she was engaged, and wrote "...poor girl,- but it may be the beginning of a new life for her..."
The marriage was arranged for 6 April, a few weeks before Stuart's eighteenth birthday. Neither wanted it, and both knew that it was a mistake. As each sensed the other felt the same, it seemed pointless to speak of the wedding which now seemed an inevitability of fate.

Stuart had been content, writing his poetry, much of it inspired by his love for Iseult, and had even managed to paint a little, usually in water colour which he felt he managed quite successfully. One small oil-painting titled "The Empty Chalice", survives as a comment on Stuart's own state of mind. A peacock, as a bird of ill-omen, sits on top of locked double gates, behind which lies "the realm of poets". Outside, a shadowy figure representing the poet, is barred from entry, and his offering, an overturned goblet which symbolizes rejection, lies empty on the ground.

As Iseult was a Catholic, Stuart received instruction from a priest at the University College Chaplaincy, a few doors from his future mother-in-law's house in St Stephen's Green. There was no announcement in any newspaper of the ceremony, in Newman House Church, witnessed by Madame MacBride and Helena Moloney, and Lily and Aunt Janet, and the wedding was notable for the lack of celebration by

either family. Mr and Mrs Stuart had tea and cake in Helena
Moloney's house nearby, for she was always sympathetic, and
left Dublin to resume their hopeless life in London. On the
way to the station, they bumped into Lennox Robinson who
mentioned the encounter the following week to Lady
Gregory. With a pen for posterity, she noted in her journal for
13 April 1920 that of the marriage, Robinson, "... sees
nothing but disaster - the boy's father having died in a mad
house and he is but 18."

Stuart at Rugby

Stuart and Iseult in 1920

CHAPTER 3

The marriage had changed nothing, for life in rented accommodation in London did not improve the couple's understanding of each other. They were bored, and paid weekly visits to the cinema to watch serials, saw few friends and had no visitors. On the one occasion when a relation of Iseult's called, she hid in a cupboard, and nearly laughed aloud when she heard Stuart begin the conversation with "Are there many thunder storms in London?" They stayed there until the early summer, before returning to Ireland to live in a small gloomy two storey house in Glenmalure, County Wicklow. Called "Baravore", it was bought by Madame MacBride with the proceeds from the sale of the Normandy house, and featured in Synge's play *The Shadow of the Glen* with the stage direction "the last in the glen". Madame MacBride had attended the first night of the play at the Abbey Theatre on 10 October 1903, and walked out as a protest "against the intrusion of decadence" little realizing that she would eventually own the house of the play. The plot of *The Shadow of the Glen,* concerns a young wife, married to an old man and condemned to a life of loneliness, frustration, and monotony in the remote countryside. The bored wife elopes with a passing vagrant, but for Stuart and Iseult there was no such escape.

Glenmalure was approached by roads that were little more than tracks, and "Baravore" itself, finally reached by stepping stones across a stream, seemed inescapable to Stuart. While Iseult did not seem to mind their solitary life, he found it lonely and unbearable. He liked to be reclusive at will, and used to having his own way, realised he was caught in a marriage to which he was hopelessly unsuited.

One afternoon when frustrated and upset by his inability to cope emotionally, Stuart ran into the glen, sobbing helplessly. In a futile gesture of despair, he set fire to the gorse bushes, and as he watched the flames, jumped from rock to rock dislocating a knee. The situation was worsened when Iseult told him she was pregnant. Stuart had decided to leave her for a while, and the news was another unwanted burden of responsibility.

One morning in late July 1920, during an unresolvable argument, Iseult picked up a heron plaster cast he had made at Rugby. He told her that if she broke it, the marriage was over, and she threw it across the room where it smashed into pieces. The heron was one of Stuart's few school successes, and its destruction temporarily unbalanced him. In a blind fury he wrenched Iseult's clothes from the wardrobe, poured paraffin on them and set them alight. He then went outside and put a match to gorse, watching the smoke drift down the glen.

It was Iseult who made the first move, and came outside to take Stuart back into the house in silence, a gesture that suggests she was not angry, and understood his unhappiness. As often, where violence is provoked by passion, they embraced tearfully, both exhausted by the ordeal of the last few days. As the house was temporarily uninhabitable, they walked for miles in the rain for the Dublin train.

The incident brought to a head a series of quarrels that arose from unbearable tension, but their reconciliation could only be temporary for the Stuarts' problems had not been resolved. Iseult felt desperate enough to write to W.B.Yeats in Oxford, but only hinting at what had happened.

She also told her mother, who sent Yeats a more explicit account probably embellished with her own prejudice against Stuart. Yeats next received a telegram from Madame MacBride demanding his presence in Ireland.

On 29 July, Yeats mentioned this in a letter to Lady Gregory, declaring that he could not "...go into the details now but you can imagine with what a heavy heart I am setting out."

He appealed to her for absolute secrecy, "...anxious that no one should know I have interfered in the matter" and left for Dublin that evening, to fulfil his promise to Iseult to be her father and guardian.

Stuart had taken a flat in Dublin, and when Yeats arrived at Glenmalure, he spoke to Iseult and her mother. It was agreed that Iseult should spend a few days in a Nursing Home.

In arranging this, Yeats spent quite some time "interfering", and a letter to Lady Gregory of 1 August, lengthily detailed various allegations against Stuart. Iseult:

> has been starved, kept without sleep & several times knocked down by her husband who is mad. His father died in a lunatic asylum & his mother's father died of drink. He has never given her any money- he has an income of £365 I believe - & Iseult from pride or from some more obscure impulse has not asked for any. By a singular machination settlements were prevented. Iseult has £75 a year & when Maud who is very poor gave gifts - about £50 - to Iseult that she might have food enough, he got her to sign the lease for the flat & left her to pay the rent...

Other accusations came from a family who were paid by Madame McBride to look after the cottage when it was not lived in. The information Yeats passed to Lady Gregory was provided by Madame MacBride, whose imagination distorted the facts and exaggerated the crisis out of all proportion. She disliked her son in law, and probably hoped that defamation of his character would help to end the marriage.

There had been no violent scenes apart from the breaking of the heron cast and the burning of Iseult's clothes. Stuart was incapacitated because of his hurt knee, and his stay in bed because of this was defined by Madame MacBride as idleness. For the same reason, he was prevented from making meals, and he had not starved nor driven Iseult out of doors.

After consulting Madame MacBride, Yeats planned that after leaving the nursing home, Iseult should stay with Lady Gregory at Coole Park, where he would join her for a few days to discuss the future. Yeats did not ask to meet Stuart to hear his side of the crisis.

Iseult's loyalty to Stuart irritated Yeats ("She will defend her husband through all & minimize all his wrongs") but she had realized that any negotiations with Stuart's family over money should involve Yeats, and not her angry mother.

Stuart had to agree to new conditions if the marriage was to continue, and was to be told that Iseult would not come back to him unless he settled some of his income on her and the child. At the first sign of any scene, she would leave him forever. Still misled by Madame MacBride's version of the events, Yeats came to the extraordinary conclusion in his letter to Lady Gregory that , "The young man is I think a Sadist, one of those who torture those they love, a recognised lunatic type."

Obliged to write again to Lady Gregory two days later because he feared his previous letter had been lost in a raid during the Black and Tan war, he revised his opinion of Stuart after speaking again to Iseult and her doctor. Madame MacBride was presumably not there, and Iseult could speak freely,"There is just the chance that he is not mad, not a Sadist whose love expresses itself in cruelty," Yeats wrote to Lady Gregory on 3 August " but that he has never grown up..."

Yeats, well aware how unreasonable his former lover's tantrums could be, had listened to Iseult instead. She refused to leave Stuart, saying that "if he is mad he but needs me the more... what good was I doing with my life. I may as well spend it this way." Iseult would not let Stuart take all the blame, for as Yeats quoted her to Lady Gregory "'He has done me no injury - it is what is in my own mind that injures me' thus Griselda speaks."

Yeats was impressed that Iseult had "not once spoken with resentment, & the only untruths which I have detected her in have been to make things look better for him." She had also told Yeats that after "she had given in on something they were often happy for a few days", and told that Stuart has "Charm & certain gifts of poetical phantesy (sic)."

Yeats, as a writer, wanted to help Stuart practically, and probably had seen a periodical *Aengus,* which that month had poems by Stuart, and a short prose piece which referred to his own *Responsibilities.* Iseult had also published prose there as "Maurice Gonne", proof that she and Stuart were close enough together to share literary ambitions.

Continuing his letter to Lady Gregory, Yeats explained he had written to his wife asking if he could bring Stuart back to England, for,"If he comes to Oxford I believe I shall be able to find these (poetic) qualities & to keep them before my mind sufficiently to make it possible to become his friend. At any rate I see nothing else to do."

Nevertheless, the following day Yeats detailed the plan that was designed to startle Stuart:

> the greater the shock the more hope... Iseult would see her husband once only in the Nursing Home, during which he had to promise to avoid painful subjects, and if he wished to see her after she had recovered this would only be allowed after... he has consented to such settlements as will save Iseult & her child from starvation.

Yeats was prepared to meet Stuart "for purposes of negotiation", while offering the option of a lawyer or "Madame Gonne (whom he hates)" for the same reason. With Madame Gonne's agreement, Iseult was to be scared into believing that if she allowed a repetition of the events the child might die. The scheme confirmed Madame MacBride's refusal to take Iseult's account of the crisis seriously, preferring to believe her own imagined version that Stuart had been intentionally cruel to Iseult by trying to deprive her of sleep. Iseult had countered this by saying that Stuart was "...merely angry & went on from one thing to another." She explained part of the trouble was that Stuart wanted power over her, and was always trying to get her away from Ireland and her friends.

Stuart wanted Iseult away from the influence of her mother, for although he was an immature eighteen year old, he sensed that if the marriage was to work, they had to solve their problems without Madame MacBride. There was even less hope of this now than before, for Madame MacBride was likely to see Iseult more often to monitor her welfare.

All the discussion continued without him, and Stuart had no help in deciding what to do. He met Iseult at the Nursing Home, and at first agreed to the proposed financial settlement. Resenting the interference, Stuart changed his mind and wrote to Iseult that "he would never see her again." Yeats did not take the threat seriously, which was probably made to test Iseult's affection. She wanted to see Stuart again, but was not allowed to. Instead, she wrote to him at Antrim, where he had now gone to stay with Lily, explaining the new conditions. Madame MacBride had also written a detailed letter to his mother, and there was nothing to do but wait.

Iseult herself, after a "...long painful interview with Francis Stuart" told Yeats that she felt "strangely serene", and he hoped that she had found her own strength. She accepted they both were to blame for the breakdown, and defined Stuart's wish for power over her as more a form of selfishness. Yeats' conclusion that Stuart had "never grown up" was nearer the truth than the suggestion that he was "mad". Stuart had been protected financially but not emotionally all his life. When not ignoring him, Lily had nearly always complied with his wishes, and he expected his wife to do the same. Before his marriage Stuart suffered the consequences of his mistakes alone, but now he had new responsibilities which he had difficulty in confronting. Madame MacBride was a nuisance, but he disliked her partly because he was jealous of Iseult's closeness to her mother, which he never shared with Lily. He was understandably hurt that Iseult's bursts of affection were for Madame MacBride, and rarely for him.

Stuart could not gauge when to concede a point to Iseult, or when to stand his ground. He deliberately attacked the attitudes he disagreed with, and which he knew she would not alter, simply to demonstrate just how intractable she was.

In response, Iseult knew exactly how to goad him into a row, and judged him too much by what she wanted him to be, rather than for what he was. She was extremely sorry for Stuart's loveless upbringing, and in the early months of their marriage, had treated him too maternally.

Stuart wrote of the crisis in his autobiography *Things to Live For*:

> One day someone whom I loved and whom I had driven to frenzy took it up and hurled it on the floor. The despair and self pity with which I gazed on the poor fragments were so acute that I almost fainted. That crane was my last link with Rugby and now I think it was fitting that it should have been broken in such a way...

and recounted it in *Black List, Section H.* neutrally, blaming neither Iseult nor himself, nor mentioning the conclusion he came to in *Things to Live For.*

Stuart remained in the North for the rest of August. In the meantime Yeats returned to Oxford, where he had a letter from Iseult, now lost. From his reply of 1 September 1920, she was undecided about the future, but Yeats pointed out that there were:

> 'intitiatory [sic] moments' of great importance to a life, perhaps deciding its whole future. I was told some time ago that we were going through one & I knew it to be one of a type that begins with Venus and Saturn in conjunction and ends with Venus & Neptune in conjunction. I have looked up your dates. When you accepted Francis, Venus & Saturn were in conjunction & when you decided to go to the Nursing Home Venus & Neptune were in conjunction. This should mean that the worst is over and as the object of all such moments is to compel a too subjective nature into objective action & in the case of your phase into action implying practical expediency & prudence... it gives you some guidance also. To you it may mean the start of a new & stronger life. Take this too as certain, no fool, no person without a possible future of spiritual importance has ever had an 'initiatory [sic] moment'.

From Fitzwilliam Square, Iseult replied, explaining that she had been "...living all these days in a black mist over my eyes; and the effort to remain firm and not to let my nerves get the better of me reduced me to more practical incapacity than usual..." She would manage to earn her living to support the baby when it arrived, and in London if necessary. She did not want to go there, but was willing to give Stuart the chance to bring them together again. Lily had hoped in two friendly letters, that Iseult would join them in the North, and Stuart had finally written, asking her "...to come and forgive him.."

If the relationship was to survive, Iseult had to offer "... a mixture of generosity and firmness. Francis is selfish, but his selfishness, is not of a 'low' [nature] and he will be much

45

more likely to give in when he realizes that by not doing so he is using a rather mean advantage..."

Stuart wanted reconciliation, and to show Iseult he was serious about this, had to go to Dublin, for she would not see him in Antrim. She told Yeats that she would wait for a few days and if he did not turn up, she would then leave for London. New financial terms had been agreed, and there was fresh hope of success. Iseult hated the gossip and rumours about her marriage, and "...had to snub and put back in their places a number of people who tried to sympathize. That sort of thing drives me wild, but I am sure you understand that..."

Iseult refused Yeats invitation to stay with him and Lady Ottoline Morrell in Garsington Manor, and told Yeats they would meet in Dublin later that month, when he was due to have his tonsils out by Oliver St. Gogarty.

As hoped, Stuart met Iseult in Dublin, and determined to rebuild the marriage, took a holiday with Lily whose impassive presence helped to re-unite them. They returned in the middle of the Black and Tan war, to a new flat in Ely Place, where they led completely idle lives. Iseult disliked housework, and did less as her pregnancy advanced. Stuart had been accused of forcing Iseult to do the housework while he lay in bed in "Baravore", but now it was Iseult who moved from one room to the next leaving a trail of unmade beds. She smoked incessantly, often not bothering to dress, and passed the time playing chess and talking. A state of inertia had arisen because both were afraid to provoke scenes, and this new stage of their marriage was more like the early days of elopement in London, peaceful if not content.

Early in the new year of 1921, Stuart fell behind with the rent. He had accepted the responsibility of financing the home, and Iseult proposed he should sell a necklace which his family had given her on their marriage and which she never wore. Stuart tried in Dublin, and when he was not offered enough, Iseult suggested he could sell the necklace for more in London.

Stuart wanted to be alone, and was delighted to have the opportunity to have a break from Iseult. She welcomed the chance to stay with her mother, and in January, Stuart went to London where he quickly sold the necklace in Bond Street, at a better price than he had been offered in Dublin. He sent most of the proceeds to Iseult, then took an unfurnished room in Tottenham Court, where he stayed for three months.

One evening, when walking to St. Martin's Lane, Stuart came upon posters at the Coliseum, advertising a ballet, *The Life and Death of a Poet*. With music by Percy Grainger, the leading role was danced by Tamara Karsavina, and possibly drawn by the title, Stuart bought a ticket. He was completely overwhelmed by the mood and atmosphere of the ballet, and especially by Karsavina's beauty, and fell in love with her at once.

Later, Stuart returned to his room in a daze, and wrote a poem which was eventually published as *For a Dancer, II*

> *You were a young fountain, a mad bird,*
> *And half a woman, a secret overheard*
> *In a dark forest,*
> *Setting the trees alive, the leaves astir,*
> *You were my joy, my sorrowful you were!*

Stuart followed it with a longer poem, *For a Dancer, I.* (The poems were numbered in reverse order of composition), and in a romantic gesture, posted them to Karsavina. He attended several more performances of the ballet, and then left his name at the stage door for the dancer. He was surprised when Karsavina asked to see him, remarking that she was "touched" by his poetry. They walked down St. Martin's Lane towards Trafalgar Square, but Stuart who would liked to have taken her for tea at a particular hotel, had no money. Tongue tied, and embarrassed, he could only mumble goodbye, and returned to Dublin the following day.

Stuart had no intention of starting an affair with the dancer, even if he could have seen more of her. She was twenty years older, and his passion, a tribute in the best poetic tradition, haunted him for life.

In Dublin, Stuart hardly gave any account of his London visit to Iseult, who was not particularly interested in any case. She was more concerned about the approaching birth, which Stuart had felt obliged to return home for, and had moved into her mother's home, Roebuck House. One night, when Madame MacBride called goodnight, Stuart felt Iseult wince as she lay in his arms, embarrassed that her mother knew she was in bed with him. He was deeply hurt by her reaction, for he realized Iseult cared more about what her mother thought, than for his feelings.

When a daughter, Dolores was born on 6 March after a difficult labour, Stuart felt no affection for her, and ignored the child as much as possible. He did not go to the christening, unable to face the thought of Madame MacBride's effusive behaviour. Stuart's selfish decision, which hurt Iseult, was less a matter of hypocrisy than one of considering his own feelings before anyone else's, but he soon regretted not attending the christening, and wrote a poem for Iseult, *To Our Daughter* as an apology. Privately printed in an edition of less than six copies, without date or imprint, the poem began:

> *Today our child was christened, yet I was*
> *Elsewhere, in converse with the sky and grass.*
> *I half think I was amongst those who will have*
> *Most sway over Dolores when she grows*
> *To woman hood...*

Even imitating Yeats' *Prayer For my Daughter,* Stuart hoped that he would justify his absence from the christening to Iseult, by being the poet, and communing with nature. Iseult commented without jealousy or hurt, that she preferred the poems he had written for Karsavina. As a husband Stuart was a failure, but at least he was acceptable to Iseult as a poet. She wrote to Yeats for an astrological chart for Dolores, which he sent her on 10 April. He consulted Iseult's chart which he already had cast, and regretting he had none for her husband, did his best. "If I am alive when she gets to 17 or 18 we shall have a long consultation as to what is to be done to make her marriage lucky." Yeats does not include Stuart in this projection, but hoping for a son of his own, who was in fact born in August, Yeats continued, " Perhaps we marry her into my family. By that time I shall be very old and stern & with my authority to support yours, she will do in that matter what she is told to do. By that time you will no doubt have completed your studies & become a celebrated Bengali scholar..."

Iseult had more or less abandoned her pursuit of Eastern religion, an area of little interest to Stuart. Shortly after Easter, the Stuarts gave up the Ely Place flat to save money, and took Dolores to stay with Lily at a bungalow at Bettystown. While Iseult was occupied with Dolores, Stuart read Keats during the centenary year of his death, and in May, wrote a letter to *The Times Literary Supplement* about what he was sure was a misprint in a poem:

> "Teignmouth" an epistle to John Hamilton Reynolds. Line 75 of that poem has been printed in all the editions in which I have looked as "High reason, and the love of good and ill". I am vehemently certain as I think most will be who have understood anything of the poet, that in this context at least, he would not have written of the "love" of good and ill as never being his award, which apart from any other consideration, is a weak and uncertain phrase as to exact meaning in itself.
> Keats never saw this poem in print, and I think it is obvious that "love" is a printer's mistake for the more forcible and Keatsian "lore"....

Stuart's contribution to Keatsian scholarship was discussed at Coole Park, when Lady Gregory, commented in her Journal that Yeats found:

> some intelligence in Iseult's husband and says that he wrote to the Times Literary Supplement pointing out an error in Keats which had never been noticed but which S. Colvin at once accepted. The word that should be lore has always been printed as love and it just shows that poets are supposed to be unintelligible...

Stuart's behaviour must have seemed unintelligible to Iseult, for he had bought a motorbicycle with money he had saved by staying with his mother. Because of the Black and Tan war, he could not ride it until a permit arrived, but he tinkered with the machine instead, paying more attention to it than Dolores.

One morning when sitting outside the house, he was approached by a Black and Tan Auxiliary whose own motorbicycle had broken down. After pointing out the fault, Stuart gave the man some petrol from his own supply. Iseult was horrified at her husband's "treasonous" act of assisting the enemy, and he did not fully understand his own motive until he could connect it to something he heard of shortly afterwards. Some girls who had helped British soldiers were found chained to Church railings with their heads shaved. A notice with the word "Traitors" was attached to their clothing, and Stuart reflected that he could have been in their place. Far from being ashamed, he would have welcomed the chance to be on public display for his beliefs in supporting the outsider. Before he married Iseult, he had told her that a poet must be untainted by dishonour, and only by being an outcast, by rejecting all sides of society, could a poet be receptive to insights of any value. To take any side, such as in the Black and Tan war was to be identified with divisions of right and wrong, and Stuart who had reached his conclusion by intuition, nevertheless felt an identity with the Black and Tan Auxiliary and the chained girls, which he could not immediately reconcile. Iseult suggested that he had been influenced by his time at Rugby in having apparent British sympathies, but as he wrote in *Black List, Section H,* his reasoning was more complex:

> Hadn't he helped the Auxiliary because at that particular moment he was a despised and threatened person? There had to be an extreme flexibility of spirit and avoidance of all moralizing in order to associate with the losers at any given moment, who for the poet, were the only suitable companions. This meant never holding to any political, social, or moral belief, because that would put him on the right or justified side where he would be cut off from the true sources of his inspiration.

Whatever the beliefs to be questioned, Stuart would refuse to discriminate or form a judgment about what was right or wrong, or so he seemed to be saying. It was enough for him to recognize that, regardless of analytical questioning, he would automatically side with the outsider. Judgment simply was not to be considered for the sake of his own concept of what a poet should be.

Iseult was not interested in Stuart's philosophy, which in any case she did not understand, for she was worried about Dolores' health. The baby was sleeping badly, and gradually weakening. Iseult took her to Dublin by train to see a doctor, while Stuart remained with Lily, and the next day Iseult wrote to Stuart that Dolores was seriously ill in hospital with spinal meningitis. Soon afterwards, a telegram gave the news of her death.

Stuart's permit to use his motorbicycle had arrived, and he drove to Dublin to meet Iseult and Madame MacBride, who were already making the funeral arrangements.

In detailing the death of his daughter in *Black List, Section H,* the character "H" is deliberately depicted by Stuart as showing indifference to the tragedy, because it suited the fictional point he wanted to make. In reality, Stuart was not detached from Dolores's death, and his feelings are recorded in *Things to Live For,* where the infant becomes a boy:

> Already he felt a chasm widening between himself and the two or three of us around him in whom he had put his trust. He felt himself becoming alone, alone... He had only the love he had given and received. And he had faith in that love, believing that in spite of all, that love would somehow save in the end, at the last moment as it were...

Dolores was buried in Dublin's Deansgrange cemetery. Although Iseult never visited the grave again, Stuart returned thirty years later for the first time, and found it overgrown. Lacking affection for Dolores when she died, Stuart was increasingly pained as the years passed. For Iseult, the death was the deepest sadness of her life.

Writing to Lady Gregory, Yeats mentioned he had received "...a long letter from Iseult... very touching & heart broken - full of intimate little details such as the closing of the child's fingers about her fingers when it was ill...", adding that he blamed the doctors, especially a friend of Madame MacBride's, Dr Kathleen Lynn, who was "a violent woman". He concluded "...George said some months ago that it would not live...Perhaps it is well that a race of tragic women should die out", presumptuously supposing that the Stuarts would not have another daughter.

Rather than increasing the bond between the Stuarts, the death only forced them further apart. Stuart hoped that Iseult's attention, would now be given to him, but she felt that she had nothing to love, and withdrew deeply into a reclusive world which excluded her husband, and possibly even her mother. Madame MacBride, who was worried, arranged a long holiday in Europe for herself, the Stuarts, and for part of the time, Sean. She hoped the visit to Germany and Austria would distract Iseult and help her to re-adjust to life.

They arrived in Munich in late August, and after a few days Sean left for Dublin. He had only been there to buy guns which he hid in a recess cut into books, and posted to a safe address in Ireland. If Stuart could have left with him, he would have done so gladly. Madame MacBride, a devout Wagnerian, intended spending each evening at the Opera in Munich during the Wagner Festival. At the first night, Stuart was bored with the music, and during the interval, Madame MacBride met old friends who completely ignored him. He resolved to attend no more opera, but the following day in an Art Gallery, trailed behind Madame McBride, who rushed forward enthusiastically to describe every exhibit. The strain of being in the company of his mother-in-law and Iseult brought Stuart out in a nervous rash. A doctor confirmed this, but because of the beer Stuart had drunk, his frequent visits to the lavatory confirmed in Madame Macbride's mind that he was suffering from syphillis. MacBride had been syphilitic, and his widow, who wanted to morally categorise Stuart in the same way, made life intolerable for him.

Stuart could only think of staying in another hotel to avoid Madame MacBride, and told Iseult that he was going to take a holiday. When she naturally said that he was already on holiday he replied he wanted "a holiday from the holiday".

Avoiding Madame MacBride was not Stuart's only motive to be on his own. Karsavina was to dance in a Munich Theatre the following week, and he hoped to see her again. Unable to find words that would not hurt Iseult, Stuart moved to another hotel without leaving a message for her.

Now he had a little money, Stuart took Karsavina for a meal. Nervous at first, he relaxed in her company, and heard that she was to dance next in Prague. He determined that he would go to see her with Iseult, but not Madame MacBride, and later in the evening after he left Karsavina, walked to a fountain at the Karlsplatz. It was a favourite spot of Iseult's, and he found her waiting for him, as she explained, she had done every evening. They embraced, overjoyed they had met. Iseult, who understood why Stuart had absented himself, was not cross with him, and surprised him by remarking that she preferred his company to her mother's. Because of political unrest, the police had called to check their joint passport which Stuart had taken, and were unpleasant to Iseult. This inconvenience she brushed away as unimportant, and happily agreed to see Karsavina in Prague.

Against all expectations, the city was a disappointment. Although the ballet was a success, Iseult went back to their unpleasant and expensive hotel, leaving her husband to greet Karsavina. It was the last time he met her, and when he returned to Iseult, found her sobbing in bed, distressed at being in Prague. They took the train for Vienna the following morning where they planned to spend Christmas, and see out 1921.

According to one of Madame MacBride's biographers, it was on the Grand Tour, that Iseult, "Sensitive, impractical, aesthetic, insecure, guilt ridden, constantly striving for perfection" kept a notebook in which she wrote she hoped to:

> renounce smoking entirely for 9 days and handling cards entirely and letter games entirely. I make a vow for 9 days to bring to mind and accomplish as closely as can be, all duties big or small, inward or external and to have an outward serene manner...

The notebook cannot be traced, but the references to "smoking" and "cards" were only two aspects of Iseult's boredom which exasperated Stuart, and he may have pleaded with her to stop them. Vienna was a success for they both liked the city, and for the first time on the "holiday" enjoyed the atmosphere of sitting in cafes, and absorbing the architecture. Stuart wrote later that Vienna: "..never for a moment disappointed me.. And yet...nothing of any great moment happened to me there... It was an adventure of place and not of people". Stuart bought a second hand Daimler-Benz for a bargain price, and persuaded Iseult it would be cheaper to drive home than take the train. When the car was delivered on Christmas Eve, the tyres were bald, and it ran on only two cylinders. Stuart, unable to drive could hardly move the car out of the underground car park because of heavy snow, and when he took Iseult for a drive she was frozen. He had put up heavy curtains for warmth but then could hardly see out. A gust of wind ended the car's comic history, for the bonnet blew into the Donau Canal. The remains of the car were sent to London where they stayed, for Stuart could not afford to pick it up. An astrakhan coat bought for Iseult turned out to be a fake when it wore thin, and these domestic disasters suggested that the holiday had come to an end. Nevertheless, Iseult could not face their old life in Dublin, and delayed their departure to buy several pairs of love birds for her mother. These were so noisy that they had to be given away.

For a while Stuart had misinterpreted moments of genuine closeness with Iseult, as a return of their first love. She was apprehensive over the future, knowing the tour had not helped her deep depression. Stuart did not know how to help her, and tried to provoke some reaction, by eating steak tartare which he enjoyed, and she detested. His only consolation was writing poetry, the one way he knew to "lessen his isolation".

The car, the fur coat and the birds, providing an element of farce, unhappily symbolized the failure of the relationship. Before leaving Austria, Iseult noted:

I think of us both as moths who had loved each other on the flowers of the roadside, flowers tarnished by dust, then the wind rose and we were whirled in clouds of dust, each a different way.

Sketch done by Stuart in Tintown

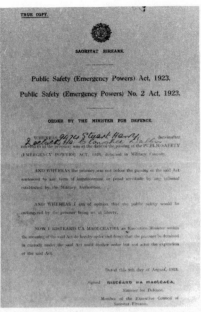

Order for Stuart's detention

Maud Gonne's house after Free State raid

CHAPTER 4

When the Stuarts returned in late March 1922, they stayed with Lily in Bettystown. Ireland was divided over the terms of a Treaty negotiated by Michael Collins and Churchill, to create a limited Free State, which was voted in by a majority of only seven. Cathal Brugha, a survivor of the Easter Rising and acting President of the Dail was against the Treaty, believing it "would split Ireland from top to bottom". It was a verdict that Madame MacBride agreed with, afraid of the violence that would follow.

When the Four Courts was shelled and Civil War broke out in June, Stuart and Iseult joined Madame MacBride to help in her house at St. Stephen's Green, which was set up as a hospital for the wounded. At first Stuart carried buckets and medical supplies, but as he was young and an unlikely suspect because of his Antrim background, he agreed to go to Belgium for the IRA to arrange a shipment of guns for Ireland. Stuart was encouraged by his brother in law, Sean, whose courage he admired when he watched MacBride throw a grenade in a hail of bullets during the Black and Tan war. Unlike MacBride, Stuart was never a member of the IRA but carried a card for identification purposes.

With only school French, Stuart completed his mission, and also brought back several guns he had hidden in his luggage. He also purchased contraceptives which he vaguely thought might improve his relationship with Iseult. She was closely involved in helping her mother and believed wholeheartedly in the cause, but Stuart hardly understood what the War was about. Despite this, he took part in fighting in Amiens Street and Talbot Street in Dublin, but there was little action. When men were needed in Cork, Stuart volunteered to join a unit of the Brigade there, and before he left, had inadequate training exercises in Roebuck House, using rifles brought out from under the floorboards. In Cork his unit had set up barracks at an old mens' home, and Stuart was astonished to find the Republican Army in uniforms left over from the 1916 Rising. The situation was unsatisfactory and a bored Stuart had other plans. He greatly admired Terence MacSwiney, the Mayor of Cork who had died during a hunger strike in Brixton Prison, and wanted to meet his sister Mary. With a note of introduction from Constance Markievicz, scribbled on a scrap of paper in case he was searched, Stuart set out to find her. Although he was unsuccessful, this purpose was of more importance to him than fighting. Despite his admiration for "the man of action", Stuart was no soldier, even if he imaginatively thought he was. This had nothing to do with cowardice; he simply did not have a fighting nature. MacSwiney was the prototype of the hero with honour, along with Ernie O'Malley, whose example had encouraged Stuart to become involved in the Republican cause.

Stuart rejoined the Brigade, and half heartedly operated a machine gun in the middle of the night. Despite practising in an old timber yard, his bullets went wild, and he realized his presence was futile. Nevertheless, it was not until he was helping to hold up a train at New Ross, that the whole question of his political beliefs struck him abruptly. Stuart recalled that when he and others were searching a carriage for Free State soldiers:

> some of the passengers were terrified but I remember going into one of the carriages where there were a couple of girls and they shouted 'Up de Valera'. Somehow that suddenly stopped me. I said to myself 'Are we really fighting for de Valera, for his puritanism and a thing I didn't personally believe in, his ultra-Catholic Gaelic state?'

During the early evening of 9 August, Stuart helped to capture a train with Free State ammunition at Amiens Street station. Unexpectedly he was arrested by a Free State lieutenant and taken prisoner. He had thrown away his gun, but not the bullets which were produced when he was searched and taken before Captain Corry at the Wellington Barracks. Stuart was lucky not to have been wounded as others were, but he was exhausted and disillusioned. A few days later, he was driven with other prisoners in a lorry to a train from Kingsbridge station, which was to take them to

Maryborough Prison. They rounded a corner, hidden for a moment from a lorry of soldiers that was guarding them from the rear. Several prisoners rolled off as this lorry lagged behind, but when it caught them up, the soldiers immediately opened fire.

Stuart was urged by Noel Lemass who jumped, to do the same, but he deliberately did not. Had he escaped, he would have returned to all the problems with Iseult and her mother. Although he had no idea what was facing him in prison, he welcomed a break from his marriage. Stuart had not long to wait for a foretaste of prison life, for as the prisoners boarded the train, they were struck on the face with revolvers by CID men.

The authorities refused to treat the inmates as political prisoners, and a few weeks after Stuart arrived, a protest was arranged to provoke sympathy and a change in status. On 29 August, Commandant Joe Griffin led the prisoners in setting fire to the main block, fuelling it with broken furniture and ripped mattresses. They then trooped out to the exercise yard and waited for a response.

President Cosgrave received a telegram from the prison Governor, which read "Entire East Prison set on fire today at 2pm. By prisoners. Still burning, but staff getting fire under control". In fact the Dublin Fire Brigade had to be called out to help the local forces, for the fire raged until the following day. The soldiers thought the prisoners were escaping under cover of the smoke, and fired shots to frighten them. Stuart and the others suffered rain and the cold for twenty hours in the yard, part of it through the night. Some slept in a coal shed and many fainted and had to be held up, but when they returned to the cells on the afternoon of 30 August, the walls were still warm from the heat, and dried off the wet clothing. The prisoners refused to sign an undertaking not to destroy bedding, and consequently were not given fresh supplies. They constructed makeshift hammocks from blankets threaded with wire and attached to the gas pipes. Stuart shared a cell with one other prisoner, Basil Blewett, whose hammock was next to his. By co-incidence, both men were sent identical copies of Dostoevsky's *The Brothers Karamazov* in their food parcels, and spent days discussing the book. As a background, Stuart thought that "no surroundings could have been more suitable" for in it he saw "the realization of sanctity in the midst of a cruel and sensual world..."

Dostoevsky profoundly influenced Stuart's personal philosophy, his views on the writer in society and his own particular definition of imagination. He could have read the book several months earlier, at Iseult's recommendation, for she was certain he would appreciate it, but Stuart stubbornly refused precisely because the suggestion was hers. To justify this he had even persuaded himself that the plot absurdly concerned Siamese twins who were separated by lightning during a storm.

Iseult understood Stuart far better than he ever realised, and sent the novel, for him to consider without the acrimony he would have had discussing it with her. Books apart, there was little comfort in the prison. The only news came from the latest batch of prisoners to be admitted, for papers were forbidden, as were visitors.

At least there was a change in February 1923, when after eight months, Stuart was moved to Hut No 2, Tintown, in the Curragh Internment Camp. Conditions were no better than at Maryborough, but Stuart read poetry, some of which was sent to him by James Stephens, and wrote some poems himself, including *Opium River* in April 1923. But it was the enthusiasm Stuart felt for Dostoevsky which inspired him to begin a novel in which he incorporated his recollections of Vienna. One morning the prison authorities marched in early, always a sign of trouble, and a lieutenant ordered Stuart to show them what he was writing. They made nothing of the manuscript, and when it was finished, Stuart posted his novel to Edward Garnett of Jonathan Cape. Garnett sent it back with a letter explaining that while the work showed promise, apart from faults of construction, Stuart should learn to spell. He had titled the novel *The Sweat of the Matyrs*.

Stuart spent his twenty first birthday at the end of April 1923 in prison, and was still denied visitors. His mother had gone to live with Madame MacBride at Roebuck House, for the St. Stephen's Green House had been wrecked the previous year by "Staters", but the two women had little contact with each other. Madame MacBride tried to call Stuart's mother "Lily", but soon lapsed into "Mrs. Clements". It would not have occurred to Mrs. Clements to call Madame MacBride "Maud", and she deferentially addressed her as "Madame".

Despite their lukewarm feelings for each other, "Madame" understood Lily well enough to prevent her from making yet another unsuitable marriage. Lily had fallen in love with an ex-prisoner called Timmins who was sheltering at Roebuck House and was much younger than her. When Madame MacBride found a letter Lily had written to Timmins, arranging a hotel room for them both, she suspected his motives were mercenary, and talked her out of it.

Temperamentally the opposite of Madame MacBride, Lily was isolated and lonely. She was impatient for Stuart's return home which seemed nearer when de Valera issued a "Cease fire" order to the Republicans on 24 May 1923. It was pointless detaining Republican prisoners, but because many, including Stuart had not even been sentenced, they were given no release date.

Apart from the rare occurrence of extra food rations or alcohol sent from outside, and the occasional boxing match, there was little to break the daily monotony. The arrival of a prisoner called Jim Phelan changed that for Stuart.

Phelan had fought in the Black and Tan war, and from a working class background, had none of Stuart's romantic notions of war and life. Blunt and direct, Phelan discussed the death of Collins, whom he considered was not a "pure" but a corrupt hero, because he had betrayed the ideals he once held. This was close to Stuart's own idea of the "poet without dishonour", and when Yeats received the Nobel Prize for literature, Phelan remarked that if he had been truthful in his poetry, he would have been hanged instead of honoured. Stuart understood from Phelan that there was only one truth, and that was to be "countercurrent" to conformity. Rather than experience life secondhand through literature, life itself had to be lived fully and then re-created imaginatively through poetry or fiction.

In the autumn, the Republican prisoners prepared for a

hunger strike to attract attention and sympathy for their release. They ate as much as possible in a last meal, and when the strike began, Stuart flavoured hot water with salt and pepper to convince himself it was soup. He doubted the value of possibly starving himself to death for a cause he did not believe in, and gratefully ate a biscuit that was smuggled to him by another prisoner. Meanwhile Madame MacBride pleaded for his release in a letter addressed to someone influential as "Dear Friend". Perhaps because of Madame MacBride's reputation a copy of the letter was shown to President Cosgrave who read:

> You remember Iseult Stewart (sic). Her little baby, always delicate from premature birth owing to English raids, died about the time your baby was born. Her husband we hear, is very ill in Tintown 2. If he is allowed to die, Ireland will lose a great poet, for he has more talent than any I have met since Yeats...

Madame MacBride also asserted that Iseult and Stuart had intended to study in Italy when war broke out, which, like the details of Dolores' death, was completely without foundation. The letter ended with a plea that Madame MacBride's correspondent should press her husband for a pass to let Iseult visit Stuart.

The hunger strike lasted eleven days, but despite or because of his hospitalization, Stuart was well. Shortly afterwards, a Christmas amnesty was announced and the prisoners were released in stages. His group were met at Newbridge Railway station by the Released Prisoners' Committee of the Women's Prisoners' Defence League, and a company of girl guides. As Stuart's family had no warning of his release, his arrival at Roebuck House in the early evening was unexpected. Iseult was there with a few friends, who welcomed Stuart enthusiastically, then left the couple alone.

Despite the letter, Madame MacBride paid little attention to Stuart, more anxious about Sean who had escaped from prison and was still in hiding. Iseult was glad Stuart was back, and for a while some of the past difficulties seemed unimportant. In the long term, Stuart's absence only prolonged the marriage which would have otherwise ended sooner than it did. Iseult thought he had fought for something they both believed in, not realizing that Stuart's suffering in prison had only confirmed how far apart their beliefs were.

Iseult was also proud of the success Stuart was enjoying with his poetry. A few weeks before his release, the American magazine *Poetry*, edited by Harriet Munroe announced that: "The prize of one hundred dollars, intended as a token of appreciation and encouragement for good work by a young poet, and offered by Mrs Rockefeller McCormick is awarded to H. STUART of Dublin, Ireland for his... Poems published in the April number." Iseult had sent off the verse Stuart had written in prison, and F.R. Higgins organised a collection of them in a small book called *We Have Kept the Faith*, which was published in January 1924. An advance copy was sent at Iseult's suggestion to Yeats, whom Stuart had not yet met, inscribed "For W. B.Yeats from Francis Stuart Xmas 1923."

Iseult took Stuart to a party in Fitzwilliam Street, given by her artist friend Cecil Salkeld, and there he met Liam O'Flaherty for the first time. Although they said little to each other, Stuart was impressed enough to arrange to see the older writer a few weeks later in a Dublin Club, where O'Flaherty said to Stuart "What's your poison?" a phrase unfamiliar to him then but which he would hear again, for the two men were to become lifelong friends.

The Stuarts had to find somewhere of their own to live. Although the Civil War was over, Roebuck House was still filled with hospital beds, and apart from Madame MacBride, was a hopeless place to re-start any marriage. Warnings that the marriage was still uncomfortable came when Stuart spent part of some money he had inherited from an aunt on a second hand car. When Iseult asked why he wanted one, Stuart replied, "to go to the races of course!". He could not stop deliberately provoking Iseult and could easily have said something else to avoid the row that followed. Nevertheless the car proved indispensible. The Stuarts called to see Joseph Campbell in Glencree, and when he pointed out that an empty cottage called "Ballycoyle" was available for a low rent, they agreed to take it. Just off the Dublin-Wicklow road, the cottage had a garden which Iseult wanted to cultivate. For Stuart the main advantage was that it was far from Roebuck House and Madame MacBride. With luck there was a slight chance that the marriage would strengthen without her. After installing some of Iseult's furniture, the Stuart's moved into the cottage early in the spring of 1924. Since leaving the Curragh, Stuart often thought of Jim Phelan, who was now dying of tuberculosis, Deeply shocked, Stuart was determined to make something of his own life and to live by Phelan's beliefs. The publication of *We Have Kept The Faith* gave Stuart credibility, and he must have felt pleased to have proved his Rugby masters and H.O.White wrong about his ability to write.

In March 1924, Stuart gave a lecture to Sinn Fein, *Nationality and Culture* (published as a pamphlet) in which he spoke of his hopes for Ireland. Although he was not quite twenty three, his ideas were now clearly formed, and no longer indecisive. The period of internment had changed that. Despite the failure of the Republican cause, Stuart was confident that it was still possible to build an Ireland which was not modelled on England. He resented that Dublin was being raised from the war ruins as "...an exact replica of an average English city. Personal and national needs and tastes are not being consulted..." Stuart wanted Ireland to be more European, and to consider the architectural ideas of Austria and Germany. Above all, not "...merely a tenth English delegate at the League of Nations, which means less than nothing - but a vital force in European and indeed in world culture which is the true test of freedom..."

English cheap fiction was to be countered with the best of Irish literature of the past and he hoped to find "our modern Irish poets and writers... side by side with what is best in foreign literature..."

There was no mention or encouragement for any Gaelic language books, an aspect of Irish culture that Stuart was not interested in, and considered retrogressive to any development of Ireland.

The Free State's lack of commitment to a national culture preyed on Stuart's mind. He had become friendly with A.J.

Leventhal, who ran a Dublin bookshop, and suggested Stuart should start a magazine to stir things up. After discussion with O'Flaherty, Stuart and Cecil Salkeld decided to launch a monthly literary magazine, called *Tomorrow*. Yeats, who loved controversy, was delighted when he heard of the idea. Stuart brought some of the other contributors to see him, and left Yeats "in high spirits", for he hoped *Tomorrow* would cause "an admirable row", as he wrote to Olivia Shakespeare on 21 June 1924:

> heard that a group of Dublin poets, a man called Higgins, and the Stuarts and another...were about to publish a review. I said to them, "Why not found yourself on the doctrine of the immortality of the soul, most bishops and all bad writers being obviously atheists."...
> I heard no more till last night when I received a kind of deputation. They had adopted my suggestion, and been suppressed by the priests for blasphemy. I got a bottle of champagne and we swore alliance... My dream is a wild paper for the young which will make enemies everywhere and suffer suppression. I hope a number of times, for the logical assertion, with all fitting deductions, of the immortality of the soul...

Stuart had already met Yeats after his release from the Curragh, and remembered "... the shock...when I realised that this strange and rather chilly figure with his eagle glance was talking about this little book" (*We Have Kept The Faith*). Yeats was almost certainly the 'friend' referred to in a notice of the book that appeared in Harriet Munroe's *Poetry*:

> After awarding our Young Poet's Prize to this Irish writer last November, we learned that we were correct in believing him young and of slight artistic experience. He is only twenty one and this ragged little book, which arrived in January, is his first. As an interesting biographical detail, a friend reports that he is the husband of Maud Gonne's daughter, a girl whose beauty has been famous in Ireland since his childhood.

The second paragraph is an obvious paraphrase of something Yeats sent the magazine.:

> Reading these fifty small ill-printed pages, I do not regret the prize. Mr Stuart has a caressing way with him in the handling of words and word-tunes and a poet's imagination in the invention of images. His music is slow and velvet-soft; slight and experimental as yet, of erratic quality...

If the authorship was easily identifiable, Yeats himself hoped the editorial he wrote for the first issue of *Tomorrow,* which appeared under the name of Stuart and Salkeld, would not be recognized as his. *Tomorrow* was published from Roebuck House at sixpence a copy, and there was no doubt whose voice declaimed:

> We are Catholics, but of the school of Pope Julius the Second and of the Medician Popes, who ordered Michelangelo and Raphael to paint upon the walls of the Vatican, and upon the ceiling of the Sistine Chapel, the doctrine of the Platonic Academy of Florence, the reconciliation of Galilee and Parnassus. We proclaim Michaelangelo the most orthodox of men, because he set upon the tomb of the Medici "Dawn" and "night", vast forms, shadowing the strength of antedeluvian Patriarchs and the lust of the goat, the whole handiwork of God, even the abounding horn.
> We proclaim that we can forgive the sinner, but abhor the atheist, and that we count among atheists bad writers and Bishops of all denominations...

Yeats had also given a poem *Leda and the Swan,* (for the second issue) and although Stuart was flattered, he had timidly suggested that in trying to create a radical and revolutionary periodical "it was not part of our purpose to appeal to traditional Catholicism against supposedly dissident Bishops..." Stuart realized if they were doing their best to be rebels "...this was something that Yeats was very definitely not. He was ever at pains in his confrontation with authority to show that it was he who supported tradition and the true Establishment..."

Paradoxically therefore Yeats' poem had a troubled passage into print. Previously offered to the *Irish Statesman,* the editor, George Russell (AE) thought the poem would be misunderstood and declined it with an excuse. Yeats' own typist had burst into tears and refused to copy *Leda and the Swan.* Nevertheless it was not the Yeats' contribution which caused trouble, but a short story by Lennox Robinson called *The Madonna of Slieve.* Denounced as blasphemous, it caused the first issue of *Tomorrow* to be suppressed. The story was about a simple girl called Mary, who ignorant of the facts of life, becomes pregnant as a result of rape by a drunken vagrant. She has had visions in the past, and remembering the tramp shouting "Jesus Christ", believes she will be the mother of Christ for the Second Coming. Mary gives birth to a girl and dies, while the tramp returns to drunkenly brag of his previous visit.

Lady Gregory considered the story an attempt to "pervert the nation", while Mrs George Yeats believed her husband's poem would be seen as something "horribly indecent" because of its association in print with the story. Lady Gregory noted with relish that the Provost of Trinity judged both to be "very offensive", and that he was also offended by a story by Liam O'Flaherty. In Lady Gregory's words "one must speak plainly - it is about the intercourse of white women with black men..." and added "Yeats has advised the Stuart's to appeal to the Pope as to the morality of L.R.'s story." The Stuarts did not, but Yeats later defended the periodical in the American magazine *The Dial* and earlier in the *Irish Statesman:*

My friends who started *Tomorrow* believe in the immortality of the soul...the purpose of this paper is the overthrow of the unbelievers...the question is the gravely serious one of the freedom to believe...

Robinson was obliged to resign his position as advisor to the Carnegie Trust in Dublin because of the scandal his story created, and found the "...whole thing inexpressively painful. It alienated many of my Catholic friends and with some the breach will never be healed."

Salkeld withdrew as co-editor of *Tomorrow,* and Stuart wrote the editorial for the second issue which was as remarkable as Yeats' was for the first. In it, he commented on the scandal the paper had caused, and in defence, reaffirmed Yeats' assertion that "The belief we had set ourselves as a star by which this paper was to be guided was belief in the immortality of the soul." In the first number of *Tomorrow,* Stuart had contributed a note on the seventeenth century German Mystic, Jacob Boeheme's *Threefold Life of Man* with whom he dissented. His editorial *The Hour Before Dawn,* enlarged the ideas he expressed in the Boeheme note, and are detailed in a later chapter, but concerned the apparent paradox of the sacred and the profane. The theme would preoccupy Stuart all his life. Although he had first formed his beliefs intuitively when he was younger, he had now developed sufficiently to substantiate them with philosophical references.

On a more mundane level, Stuart was pleased with "the admirable row" which helped to sell the paper, but not enough to let it survive. Natalie Barney was amongst others from Paris, who optimistically ordered a year's subscription, but the September issue of *Tomorrow* was the last.

Stuart had more to preoccupy him than *Tomorrow.* In the week after the annual Dublin Horse Show in August, there was a revival of a Celtic Festival, the Tailteann Games. Yeats persuaded the Royal Irish Academy to sponsor awards for Irish writers who had recently published work which conferred "honour and dignity upon Ireland". George Russell, Lennox Robinson and Yeats, selected Stuart's *We Have Kept the Faith* for such an award, and invitations were sent out in Yeats' name for presentation at the Royal Irish Academy at 3pm on 9 August 1924.

Among those who accepted were Iseult, Madame MacBride and Cecil Salkeld, but neither Lily nor Janet attended what *The Irish Times* described as "the novel ceremony of crowning with wreaths of bay..." G.K. Chesterton received a Gold Medal on behalf of Stephen McKenna who had declined to be there, then Yeats introduced Stuart, rather surprisingly as "Harry Stuart". Although he was known as "Harry" in his own family, Iseult called him by his second name "Francis", and his name appeared on the title page as H.Stuart. Of the poems, Yeats continued:

> though one finds no perfect poem one finds constant beauty of metaphor and strangeness of thought and so no lucky accident but a personality. Will his expression clarify, his music grow strong and confident, or will his promise remain unfulfilled ? That will probably depend on his critical capacity, upon his intellect, and of these we have no means of judging. His genius, if genius it be, is the opposite of Dr. Gogarty's...

whom Yeats went on to praise. Stuart himself, "felt little of that touch of the ridiculous that Yeats' solemnity could so easily evoke, in having to go up to a dais and kneel while he placed a laurel crown on my head", as he recalled in a broadcast about Yeats in 1965, but in *Black List, Section H* he states:

> At a whispered word from an usher, H stepped onto the dais and knelt down, while Yeats, enveloped in one of the clouds that seemed occasionally blown across his path, was groping around the laurel wreath that, with the others was lying on the table in full view of everyone else...

Madame MacBride deplored Yeats' politics, and warned Stuart not to address him as "Senator" in his acceptance speech. This would not have occurred to Stuart, but with the thought in his head, he may have done so. Because Madame MacBride would not be associated with Yeats the Senator, she went home. Stuart, Iseult, Yeats, crossed the road with G.K.Chesterton and a Major Cooper to a restaurant for some afternoon tea. The awkwardness of the ceremony continued. Yeats, Cooper and Chesterton were dressed in morning coat and top hat for a Garden Party at the old Vice-Regal Lodge. Discussing this, Chesterton mentioned his bulk, and remarked that often at gatherings he overheard people saying "Meet me at Chesterton". Nearly everyone at the table laughed, but when Stuart noticed that there was not the slightest sign of amusement on Yeats' face, he did not

smile either. Less impressed by the Yeatsian world than at
the time of his marriage, Stuart would not yet be disloyal to
its originator. He had however betrayed Phelan's views in
accepting an award, and worse, from one whom his friend
had despised.

Whatever justification Stuart found for this, at least he
was credible as a writer to Madame MacBride and Iseult,
and honoured on terms they accepted, even if he did not.
Iseult told Stuart that "Willie thinks you are a genius" and
such a blessing from Yeats was probably both a help and an
encouragement for complacency. There was no pressure to
earn money in any other way than writing, and as Iseult was
unworldly they managed domestically, with a little help from
Lily who contributed her keep when she came to stay. On the
surface, Iseult and Stuart seemed content. Because he still
could not evoke personal warmth from her, he became
absorbed in intensive reading in an effort to make sense of
his own frustrated desires. This was all very well, but Stuart
knew he could only feed his interior world for short periods,
and when restless, would drive alone to Dublin to seek the
anonymity he preferred. During the Second World War,
Stuart remembered "that sweet atmosphere of Glencree and
our cottage, those happiest years of my life," although he
added in parentheses that they were not "the best years".

Stuart at Laragh

CHAPTER 5

In August 1925, Stuart fulfilled a long held ambition and bought a race horse from the Bloodstock sales in Ballsbridge. In early newspaper interviews he used to claim with some truth that "Racing is in my blood", because his Montgomery ancestors had trained racehorses in Ayr in Scotland.

The county sporting tradition of hunting and shooting never appealed to Stuart, but from an early age he was taken to race meetings by his uncles, which he enjoyed, and placed his first bet of a shilling at Bellewstown.

Stuart was excited by horses because of the power and mystery they evoked as animals, but this later developed into a personal mystique. In some of the most vivid passages of his autobiography, *Things to Live For*, Stuart wrote that on the day of the Bloodstock sale, he rose early and walked several miles to catch the Dublin bus, knowing he would buy a horse and confident that it would win races, and make him rich.

He knew a former English jockey, Mick Gleeson, who had become a trainer, and they arranged to meet at the sale. They judged each animal that was led into the ring, and particularly noticed a yearling with a rather hollow back. Both men thought that although rather small, she had potential. Stuart bought the filly for forty guineas, nearly all the money he had, but Gleeson offered to share some of the expenses. The animal went to Cork to be trained, and Stuart returned to Glencree to explain what he had done to Iseult. In *Things to Live For*, Stuart notes that Iseult called the filly Sunnymova, but in *Black List, Section H*, where the incident is fictionalised and recorded at a later time than when it took place, Stuart takes credit for the name, unwilling to tell it to Iseult because he anticipates that she will say "Why ever that darling ? What on earth does it mean?"

Whatever the truth, Iseult was not interested in race horses. To her they only represented extravagance, for she had not been consulted about the sale, and grew to despise Stuart for constantly betting at meetings.

"To have a 'good day' on an Irish course", he wrote "is the best way of spending an afternoon enjoyably that I have yet discovered", not with Iseult, but with friends such as O'Flaherty and Lord Glenavy, who would not spoil the day talking about literature. As a national Irish pastime, Stuart's interest in racing might seem unexceptional, but in it, he found the first expression of a need for contrasting elements which were to dominate his life; adventure and the mystical quest, both of which were fulfilled later in different ways.

Despite Iseult's complaint about his betting, Stuart was not a gambler in the sense of placing large bets recklessly, and usually followed his own advice of only betting when he could afford to. As far as Iseult was concerned, that was never, but for Stuart it was the 'risk' which mattered, because it put his whole psyche on a knife edge. The race track where, "...all normal values are upset" brought everyone to the same level, and there, he "watched with delight the spectacle of eminent men of letters and famous surgeons and judges become mere nobodies...". The race course reflected an alternative life in microcosm, where some emotions, moods and action which would take time to be fulfilled elsewhere, were concentrated and brought to fruition in a pitch of intensity. The excitement of the 'risk' included the knowledge that the afternoon would bring failure and despair, or success and elation. On the second deeper level, the uncertainty was part of the tension Stuart enjoyed, akin to the often conflicting emotions of religious experience.

In his imagination, Stuart felt the racing was a ritual which combined both primitive and mystical elements, which he particularly expressed in the second stanza of his poem *At the Races*:

> *There falls upon this air of June*
> *The hollow clap of hooves over the grass.*
> *The rider's colours brighten through the light.*
> *Only in love the mind finds such wild peace,*
> *Stirred but by beauty's flight: there falls a hush,*
> *The heart half stops, as under a full moon*
> *We see but the faint stillness of midnight*
> *In light's continual rush.*

Just as he had initially refused to read Dostoevesky because the suggestion was Iseult's, so too Stuart ignored several books on mysticism in her bookcase. When chancing on Evelyn Underhill's *Mysticism* he later recognised the book made "... a greater impression than any other has on me, opening up a whole universe when I first read it...". Underhill's ordered study of mysticism identified more fully than anything Stuart had previously read, certain states of mind which he recognized in himself. From his study of Boeheme, Stuart had insisted that only through the recognition of the opposing forces of good and evil, could there be any understanding of spiritual truth, which it was the writer's task to reveal. Boeheme had influenced Yeats, who wanted:

> to get beyond good and evil. He wanted not only to redeem the contraries from their distorted state as Good and Evil in materialistic, rationalized religion, but also to show the way to a knowledge of the real ground in which the contraries in human life would be seen as creative rather than destructive; and that ground was the imagination that connected man with God.

In an attempt to reconcile the contradictions, and to give them universal understanding, both Blake and Yeats used complex symbolism. Stuart wanted to express his ideas through personal experience, and to come to some understanding of spiritual truth through observations of certain events that might appear outwardly mundane, but which he saw as significant.

Had the experiences in *Mysticism* been confined to the Saints, Stuart would not have been interested. The constant emotional and spiritual struggle of those who seemed as "delinquent" as he, and who were not remote from this world, supported Stuart against what others defined in his behaviour as moody and erratic. After Underhill, Stuart studied the lives of the Saints, and especially women such as Catherine of Siena, and most important of all to him, St. Thérèse of Lisieux. Her life was to him "... the record of the greatest adventure of modern times. Outwardly nothing. A girl who became a Carmelite and died in her convent at the age of twenty-four..." and who "staked everything, body and soul, not on human love but on Divine." Stuart understood St. Thérèse's gratitude for becoming a nun when young, because as she wrote in her autobiography, "If I had remained in the world I would have been burnt up with human love, I would have committed every act of madness and finally ended Gods knows where..." Stuart speculated that if St. Thérèse "had not been a nun what a lover she would have made..." This interpretation formed part of the foundation for Stuart's belief that the search for fulfilment through women, was part of the same longing for a passionate relationship with God. When his novels were published in the nineteen thirties, Stuart defined the results of reading and contemplation in them, but in the mid nineteen-twenties, Iseult suggested he was attached to various Saints who were women "...with a sort of spiritual love. And you love God because of them. But no, it's really life you're in love with all the time, whenever you find it at its most mysterious, its most romantic."

Stuart's interest in women, religion and racing was experienced on two levels; initial attraction followed by a more intense involvement which he hoped would extend his consciousness, and from these apparently diverse experiences, achieve enlightenment through the pain they might bring. He knew that at times his experiences were only on a shallow or what he termed "outward level", and when this failed to give him "inner" satisfaction, usually after a period of obsessive indulgence, he would withdraw.

Stuart was incapable of only slight involvement in his interests, and always took them to the extreme. This upset Iseult, who considered he was selfish, and wasted money. She told him when he was twenty four that:

Whatever you don't react against violently, you come under the spell of. There's nothing between, no detatchment, no balance, nor perspective...You suffer and you find that an adventure too. But that's because you don't know the worst suffering when everything seems dead, and yourself dead, and adventure and romance and joy are empty words.

When Stuart asked what he should do, Iseult replied that it would be pointless for her to say then, but possibly in ten years "...after you have made a proper mess of things. When you are a little humble...I'll tell you what it would be no use telling you now."

In *Things to Live For* written when he was thirty three, Stuart acknowledged the truth of what Iseult had said, but in general terms, his refusal to accept that she understood him underlines one reason why their relationship failed. He expected to dominate women, including Iseult, but far from submitting, she made allegations about his character which he did not want to hear, but which events proved to be correct. Unfortunately Iseult was smug in delivering her attacks, and relied on intellectual argument rather than emotion to make her points. Unable to mould Iseult into the desired ideal woman, he could not accept what she said about him until he either discovered his mistakes for himself, or proved a theory by his own experience.

The arguments became less frequent, when Stuart ordered a hut which was erected in the garden. It was the perfect hermit's cave where he retreated to study religion and mysticism, although he later regarded it as a rather immature period. Stuart went through what he considered his Tolstoyian phase, where he gave up eating meat, and made his own sandals. Despite Iseult's criticism of his methods, she did not object to his absorption in religion and philosophy. She suggested he would achieve nothing without prayer, and for a short while, Stuart walked the five miles daily to the Church at Glendalough for Mass. As a Roman Catholic, Stuart's beliefs were unorthodox, for his interpretation of the Gospels was selective and personal, and in his reading of them, Christ was the ultimate outsider who symbolized the suffering victim such as Stuart's father and hero.

However individual the conclusions Stuart came to, he was making a concentrated effort to understand the mysteries that had haunted him for years. He expanded what he had written about Boeheme and called it *The Only Happiness*. In 1897, Yeats wrote that Boeheme was "the greatest of the Christian Mystics since the Middle Ages and none but an athletic student can get to the heart of his mystery...". Iseult sent the unfinished essay to Yeats, and although he praised Stuart and urged its completion, Stuart destroyed *The Only Happiness* which he thought too derivative.

On the personal level, Yeats was probably aware that Stuart's relationship with Iseult was more settled, but in 1926 wrote two poems which reflected his own protective attitude towards her, and which the past had not altered. The first, *The Death of the Hare*, written in January 1926, continues the image of the hare for Iseult which he had introduced in *Two Songs of a Fool*.

> *Then suddenly my heart is wrung*
> *By her distracted air*
> *And I remember wildness lost*
> *And after, swept from there,*
> *Am set down standing in the wood*
> *At the death of the hare.*

In response to an editor's query, Yeats explained that "... the poem means that the lover may, while loving, feel sympathy with his beloved's dread of captivity..." The second poem concerning both Stuarts, germinated from a remark Yeats' daughter Anne had made about an unpleasant boy at a party. On telling her father that the boy had "lovely hair, and his eyes are as cold as a March wind", Yeats' response was "The cry of every woman who loves a blackguard". In the resulting poem *A Woman Young and Old*, Yeats imagined Iseult defending Stuart.

> *She hears me strike the board and say*
> *That she is under ban*
> *Of all good men and women*
> *Being mentioned with a man*
> *That has the worst of all names:*
> *And therefore replies*
> *That his hair is beautiful,*
> *Cold as the March wind his eyes.*

Yeats implies from both poems that Iseult required protection from "a blackguard" i.e. Stuart, and the reference to him in such terms raises the question of their personal and literary relationship. Yeats' marriage was happy, but he often wondered what kind of life he might have had with Iseult. On one unspecified occasion Yeats remarked to her, "If only you and I had married." It seems likely that Iseult had been talking about her own marriage problems, but she told Yeats "Why, we wouldn't have stayed together a year." Unlike most people who knew Yeats, Iseult was not intimidated by him, and found him easy to talk to. Aware of his foibles, she once wrote to him that "Those revelations from your spirits are certainly very curious and interesting but... May I speak frankly? I can hardly attach much spiritual value to them."

During the summer of 1926, Stuart and Iseult were invited to spend a few days with Yeats and his wife in their house in Merrion Square. As Stuart always felt uncomfortable with the poet, he dreaded the visit, but for Iseult, who was expecting a child in October, the break was a welcome change. The Stuarts were given Yeats' own bedroom, with a note pinned to the door reminding him that it was "Francis and Iseult's Room".

Yeats knew he made Stuart nervous, but was unable to relax the strain he created. Stuart recalled that "There was little or no ease in the talk" and at night, he hardly slept, lightheadedly imagining fantastic conversation to regale his host with the next day, knowing he would say none of it. During this and other visits to Merrion Square, Stuart noticed that when Yeats was carried away on "one of his more improbable drifts of conversation, George Yeats would sometimes wink across the dinner table at me, for... she saw through her husband's posturing."

It was left to Iseult to move the conversation to a lighter level, but Stuart remained silent. In the future, he tried to avoid being alone in the same room as Yeats, for whom he never felt any sense of the "friendship or even affection that a much older man can sometimes inspire in a young one."

It was only after Yeats' death, that Stuart suspected how "unfulfilled and lonely he had been in the latter years." The younger man had "awe, admiration and a certain respect for

Yeats" but his chief grouse against Yeats was that he:

> failed to merge his life and his art (the classic intellectual situation, perhaps) but the style of his living was so formal and unspontaneous that it was in constant opposition to the increasingly disreputable spirit that was inspiring much of his later poetry.

Nevertheless, Yeats knew his own dilemma well, for he wrote "A poet is by the very nature of this a man who lives with entire sincerity, or rather, the better his poetry, the more sincere his life...we should understand..."

In nearly all his comments on Yeats, Stuart emphasises the more ridiculous aspects of Yeats' personality, rarely referring to the poetry itself. When he does, the love poems are "banal and lacking in sincerity", a statement prejudiced by the knowledge that many were written for Maud Gonne. As a whole, the poetry "...so wonderful in texture, detail and artifice, lacks an inherent unifying vision of man..."

Stuart was unable to "formulate an abiding impression of Yeats" without "remembering him apart from his work...[which] was not the expression of a deep personal faith as it was say, for Rilke, Wordsworth or Blake." Where he has any admiration for Yeats at all, it is in the last poems, and especially for the sincerity of *"The Circus Animals' Desertion"*.

All Stuart's comments on Yeats highlight how their philosophy and attitudes differed. But he understood Yeats' stance as a writer, which was similar to his own. That "Yeats was really only interested in, or absorbed by, what was of use to his own work, what he could, in often strange and oblique ways, stimulate and inspire him" equally applies to Stuart himself. Particularly apt to his own position, Stuart commented that Yeats "had little interest in writers who, however good, were too far away from him to have this effect."

Unlike Stuart, unable to separate the poet from the man, Yeats judged him as a human being, and kept his personal conclusions apart from the impression he formed of Stuart's novels and poems. A few days after his marriage in 1917, Yeats wrote *Owen Aherne and his Dancers,* and in the last line referred to Iseult, and his hopes that she should "...choose a young man now and all for his wild sake'." Such a man was the opposite of the fifty two year old respectable poet, who had already created in his imagination the kind of man Iseult should marry, with a particular nature he sensed she needed.

Yeats' involvement in the early marriage crisis must have confirmed that Iseult had found such a man in Stuart, but because of Yeats' preconception of the kind of husband he thought she should have, possibly anyone who married Iseult would have been termed "wild", and a "blackguard". As long as Yeats admired her, he would keep his early promise of protection. Independently of this, Stuart wrote, "Yeats...got on [Iseult's] nerves with his formal and deliberate ways, while H [Stuart] with his quiet and deliberate delinquency, still attracted her..."

When Yeats visited the Stuarts at Glendalough in June 1932, he acknowledged in his poem *Stream and Sun at Glendalough* that his proposal to Iseult had been a mistake, or "Some stupid thing", presumably because he considered the couple were happy. However the most controversial reference Yeats made to Stuart was in *Why should not old men be mad?* written in 1936:

> *Some have known*
> *A girl that knew all Dante once*
> *Live to bear children to a dunce.*

Iseult herself told Professor A. Norman Jeffares that Yeats was "extremely fond of the Dante edition illustrated by Doré which she owned" and although not cited in print, Jeffares has since confirmed that he was told by Mrs Yeats that her husband identified Iseult as 'the girl' and Stuart as the 'dunce'.

Because Yeats wrote extravagant praise of Stuart's novels, and admired his essay on Boeheme, the use of 'dunce' seems inexplicable, unless reference is made to that fact that Yeats was reflecting on the past and not the present. To him Stuart was perhaps 'a dunce' in marriage, but 'dunce' was not his first thought, for his first version of 'fool' was sacrificed for the sake of the rhyme. This too may have been influenced by the first poem Yeats wrote for Iseult, *To a Child Dancing in the Wind,* with the lines:

> *Being young you have not known*
> *The fool's triumph, nor yet,*
> *Love lost as soon as won.*

Yeats himself disliked the suggestion of particular names in the poems where he did not explicitly identify them. From later evidence, Yeats considered that in Stuart the writer, he found an expression of some of his own ideals. Stuart the man puzzled and fascinated him for years.

Cartoon of Stuart

CHAPTER 6

Iseult had a son in a Dublin Nursing Home, while Stuart remained in Glencree. He immediately liked the child who was born without complications on 5 October 1926. Called Ion, after one of Lily's brothers, he was baptised on 14 October in University Church where his parents had married.

Lily came back with the Stuarts to help with Ion, initially for a few months, and returned occasionally to stay for longer periods. This arrangement worked well at the beginning, but Iseult concentrated all her love on Ion, as did Lily. Consequently, Stuart felt emotionally excluded from the household, and was aware that his wife would bury their marriage problems by absorption in the child. It was difficult to be alone with Iseult, although he could sleep and work in the garden hut. For nearly three years Stuart maintained a fairly reclusive life, and his excursions were so infrequent that Liam O'Flaherty called him "The Monk" on the rare occasions when they met. Nothing kept Stuart from race meetings, but he particularly looked forward to the time when Sunnymova was ready for her first run. In June 1927, she was entered for a five furlong race for two year olds at Phoenix Park. Both Gleeson and Stuart thought she had a good chance and after raising about £100 between them, backed her to win, at a price of about 100 to 8. Stuart felt the despair and anxiety of a lifetime, for the race was between his Sunnymova and Ballywirra. When they finished neck and neck, the judges' ruled in favour of Ballywirra.

The disappointment and loss of money did not deter Stuart, and he decided that when it was possible, he would buy another horse, and hopefully one with better prospects.

Lily was now living with the Stuarts for most of the time, and with the baby, the Glencree cottage was too small. They had to find somewhere larger, and Madame MacBride bought them an old blockhouse at Laragh, not far from Glencree in the Vale of Glendalough with the remains of Iseult's money from Colville. Laragh Castle was built as a British stronghold during the 1798 Irish Rebellion, and in the nineteenth century converted into a sham medieval castle by adding battlements. It was secluded and near the beautiful and historic St. Kevin's Church and the ruins of a sixth century monastic community.

Most of the rooms were small. Stuart recalled: "On the ground level, there was a kitchen, one very large sitting room, a back room where Ion would play and another small room. Upstairs, a large bedroom and two smaller bedrooms. We would spend our evenings in the sitting room which was the most comfortable room in the house, as it was comparatively easy to heat, but the rest of the house was cold and damp." Any romanticism of the house was lost when rats appeared, but this did not deter Lily who moved in permanently. Stuart was quite glad to have her there, but she often irritated Iseult who would take refuge in a small tower room, and eat roll-mop herrings which she shared with him.

Stuart now aged 27, and more responsible towards Iseult and his son, decided to make the best use of the ground they owned. Despite his dreaminess as a boy, he was practical, and after reading about all aspects of farming, he rejected the possibility of pigs in favour of poultry. Equipment arrived, including a new Peugeot with which to tow mobile laying sheds, and soon Stuart was as absorbed in the poultry farm as he had been in his study of mysticism. When his old hut arrived from Glencree, Iseult had already marked it as somewhere to eat, as nearer the kitchen than the dining room, and his days of contemplation seemed far away. Instead, he was only obsessed now with producing a high egg yield, and in achieving a particular dark brown egg with which he hoped to win a prize at an Agricultural show the following year.

The poultry farm gradually became profitable, for a lorry called daily to take away consignments of eggs to a fashionable Dublin shop, and as Stuart kept the same price all the year round, his order was assured.

Towards the end of July, Yeats stayed at the Royal Hotel, Glendalough, for a few days, and visited the Stuarts. He was fascinated by the hens and asked endless questions about their habits. Stuart was surprised at such interest, he was afraid that the hens, nervous of strangers, would be put off laying. The Stuarts supplied the Royal Hotel with poultry, and during dinner with Yeats, he was amused that they were convinced they were eating one of their own chickens. Yeats found Stuart "...silent unless one brings the conversation round to St. John of the Cross or a kindred theme."

The kindred theme was on Stuart's mind, for a few weeks later, a pamphlet he wrote for the Catholic Truth Society, *Mystics and Mysticism,* was granted the *Nihil Obstat Imprimatur* on 5 August 1929, although not published until November. Opening with the statement "The goal of our life is union with a personal god", Stuart stressed the importance of both bodily and spiritual suffering in the mystical life. It was a theme he developed later in his novels, as he did his belief that "Love...is the secret of the mystical life in all its aspects."

For Stuart, Mysticism was part of the everyday experience, and he suggested those who followed an interior life, would recognise the shabby values of society for what they were, and ultimately achieve personal redemption. Because the pamphlet was written for the Church, Stuart does not mention the artist, or a certain kind of criminal whom he also believed capable of such insight. Their enforced isolation would bring them heightened awareness, and closer to Christ. Twenty years later, Stuart thought his intense study of mysticism had been far too conscious, but he had partly recognized the need for practical therapy in the poultry farm.

By 1930, he was well enough off to employ an assistant from England, a Miss Hilda Burnett who eventually managed the farm for him, and in the Spring, he won a silver medal in the Department of Agricultural egglaying competition *For the Pullet non sitting breed having the highest winter record of First Grade Eggs*.

The Stuarts now more prosperous than before, took a holiday to France. Madame MacBride, who was going to Dax to take the waters there for her rheumatism left with Iseult in mid summer. A little later Stuart took a South American Liner from Liverpool for La Rochelle, and from there to Dax.

Remembering the visit they had made to Vienna nine years previously, Stuart was tempted to stay on the train. He thought unkindly that his mother in-law "...who had once inspired Yeats' love poetry now only asked for some amelioration of the aches in her joints".

He only spent a few days at Dax, short enough time to be polite to Madame MacBride, before taking Iseult to Lourdes. Stuart "fell in love" with Bernadette, and went back to Lourdes with a group from Ireland in 1928, believing that he would "find something of that so enthralling atmosphere, lyrical, romantic, joyous and yet suffering..." Lourdes remained the paradox of beauty and tawdriness, and Stuart became friendly with a doctor who had given up a lucrative London practice to become a chaplain. The man's fanatical devotion to his patients so impressed Stuart that he himself became a *brancardier* or stretcher bearer. For several weeks, he transported the sick to the baths, and formed a friendship with a Spanish girl who was dying of tuberculosis. Stuart was not physically attracted to the girl, but she fascinated him because through her suffering, they shared a similar psyche which he recognized "...could also be a mania for intense new perceptions". The Lourdes experience, confirmed Stuart's theory of enlightenment through suffering, but he did not unreservedly accept the apparition at the Grotto. Reality lay on several levels, and while Bernadette undoubtedly "saw" the Virgin Mary, for Stuart her experience validated the Gospels as something real.

On their way back to Ireland, the Stuarts met Madame MacBride in Arennes, and catching a glimpse of Paris on the homeward journey Stuart resolved to visit it alone.

Iseult was once again apathetic when she realised she was pregnant, and expecting a child in May. She gardened while she could, and passed bored days playing cards. She had given up writing, but encouraged Stuart to begin a novel which he called *Women and God*.

In it he used his Lourdes experiences, his unsatisfactory marriage, and even the farm appeared as a symbol of decay. The novel posed the problem of reconciling the conflict of the sacred and profane love, where the main character, like Stuart was "always lonely and unable to escape from the isolation of loneliness. Trying to escape through religion; trying to escape through women." Resolution comes through a sick girl called Elizabeth, who shows that through her suffering, she attains the love of God. She has a spiritual rather than a physical nature, and the love she has for one of the characters is derived from her love of God.

Stuart sent the novel to Cape, and as he had decided to visit Paris via London, he called to Jonathan Cape and Edward Garnett. They did not like the novel much, but because it was promising agreed to publish it after some revisions. During lunch, the conversation mainly centred around D.H. Lawrence, but with £50 advance Stuart did not care. He would spend the money in Paris and enjoy himself.

After a few bored days on his own, Stuart was befriended by some American women, and each evening for several weeks plunged into a hectic pattern of heavy drinking, sleeping off the hangovers during the day. One evening in the Cafe Dôme, one of the American women told Stuart that she knew James Joyce who was at a table in a corner of the room. Stuart, who was not a name collector, was indifferent about meeting Joyce, who remarked that he had read Stuart's poems in *Transatlantic Review*. As the poems had appeared in 1924, Stuart was surprised at Joyce's memory, and after thanking him, he returned to his own table. It was their only meeting, and so brief that Stuart was always to deny he had met Joyce.

Despite his heavy drinking, Stuart knew that this would end when he left Paris. But the effect of the alcohol shocked his psyche and disordered his senses in a way that was significant to him. Through his delirium tremens, he felt his subconscious reach out to some new understanding of his dead father, so that he identified with him in spirit. He also experienced other moments where "his imagination had escaped momentarily" and which convinced him he must deliberately place himself in situations where he would be disturbed, Only by avoiding the comfortable security that others wanted, could he extend his imagination.

Not long after, he returned to Dublin where a daughter was born on the 21 May 1931. Baptised Catherine, she was known to the family as Kay and she naturally occupied

Iseult's time. Stuart took up flying lessons. It may have been coincidental, but in both the case of Ion and Kay, Stuart absented himself as their births approached. Perhaps he could not cope with Iseult but when he was needed most, he was not there as part of the family. Paris had given him a taste for adventure, and by August *The Daily Express* described Stuart as an "experienced pilot."

There was something of Toad from *Wind in the Willows* in his nature; aristocratic but bored with it, reckless, uncaring what others thought, and seeking adventure which brought trouble. He took an apartment in Dublin and completed a second novel there, intending to send it to Cape as soon as *Women and God* was published in September. He lived wildly in Dublin, desperately trying to "get happiness out of gaiety", before returning to Laragh to read the reviews of his novel. Convinced they were favourable, he was appalled that they were all poor. *The Times Literary Supplement* complained that the miracle was not credible, and Frank Swinnerton, then influential, used the novel to attack all he thought bad about the younger generation of writers.

The reviews were justified, for Stuart was too close to his subject, and his romanticism did not suit the short sentences he had modelled on Hemingway. As a result *Women and God* sold badly, and Cape refused his new book. Stuart left it with an agent Curtis Brown, and waited for their decision.

Despite the obvious references to their marriage, Iseult liked the novel, and did not object to the publication of certain private details which Stuart had scarcely disguised. The autobiographical nature of *Women and God* set the method for nearly all Stuart's future novels, in which he used the "outward" events of his life, and appeared as "... a general, a bookie's clerk, a racehorse trainer, an aeroplane pilot. I live in my books the things I have not time to live in life", he wrote, although he added "And of course I always cut a much better figure on the printed page."

In his fiction, Stuart selected 'significant' moments in his life which might seem unimportant to others, and hated 'characterization'. "I don't care for what is called characterization... it's a tradition of a certain kind which becomes tedious. I'm not really analytical about these things, but a set of characters are bound to hold up the whole flow of the theme. If you get the theme really flowing strongly, the characters must be formed out of it in in some peculiar way. But not the other way round. That writers like Frank O'Connor or O'Faolain are praised for 'What characterization!' seems extraordinary to me." The new novel, *Pigeon Irish* was incomparably better than the first. Stuart wrote of what he knew, balancing the mystical and the adventurous and transforming his recollections of the Civil War into an imagined war of the future. The storming of the Four Courts had been: "instrumental in my taking part in the Civil War". And in *Pigeon Irish* a disguised O'Malley appears, where the execution of four members of the garrison, Mellows, O'Connor, Barrett and McKelvey forms one of the themes.

The quality of the book was recognised by a new publisher called Victor Gollancz, who published it in February 1932. Gollancz asked Stuart to approach Yeats to help with publicity, and he replied in early January that he no longer reviewed, but would read the book with pleasure, and send Gollancz "...a few lines upon it." *The Golden Treasury of Irish Verse,* had recently been published, and included some poems of Stuart's which Yeats found "once again most moving and beautiful."

Yeats was with Lady Gregory, who was dying, and wrote from Coole Park on 23 January:

> I send you an opinion of your book which may be what your publisher wants. If he wants a single sentence he can leave out everything before the word "cold". He had much better give the whole thing. I have tried to interest people in your personality, & I thought that would be a greater help than simple praise, especially as your publisher has on the wrapper praised your book with admirable courage. It is a great thing for a young writer to have found a man to believe in him so ardently.
> May be my desire to believe in your work - less for your own sake & Iseult's than for the sake of your theme, your doctrine which I too have so much at heart - makes me afraid of being deceived. I am so anxious to say "here is a new great Irish

writer" that I stop & say "we must not be deceived". You have very great powers, that much is certain...I will write in a day or so on certain matters of detail...

Gollancz kept all Yeats wrote and used it for his next novel and in advertisments:

Turning the pages of *The Golden Treasury of Irish Verse* a couple of weeks ago, I came on Francis Stuart's two little poems. They were not new to me, yet they so disturbed my imagination that they kept me from my sleep...*Pigeon Irish*...has the same cold exciting strangeness, attained less by beautiful passages, though there are such passages in plenty, than by construction, characterisation and a single dominating aim; and then what a lot this fanatical student of St. John of the Cross knows about chicken farms, carrier pigeons, parabellums, aeroplanes, Irish military, the Curragh races, and where did a man with a style so literary learn the points of a horse?

Yeats was not alone in his opinion. *Pigeon Irish* was praised on the first page of *The New York Times Book Review* and Compton Mackenzie wrote in the *Daily Mail* that the "novel swept me off my feet". Afraid his review might be considered unbalanced because of his enthusiasm, he contented himself with simply saying "the exquisite prose... has a quality like beaten gold-leaf." He wrote to Stuart on February 9 to send him "..a line for what to call 'pleasure' is ridiculously inadequate as a word to express what your book... meant to me." This began a long friendship with Stuart, who in reply said that the "spontaneous appreciation meant more than makes up for all the discouragement and difficulty I encountered before sending it to Mr Gollancz."

O'Flaherty warned Stuart not to have a "swelled head", for he had to bear in mind that his opinions:

about Western European civilisation, about Ireland or Christianity or any other topical question must be just as valueless as anybody else's, whether it be the Pope...or your wife, or myself. All these things will pass away and be forgotten and men will retain only beauties that are near permanent..things like *Rough winds do shake the darling buds of May*...in any case, three cheers old boy, and go to it. Now is the time to strike the iron. Get on before the price shortens...

Stuart visited London frequently during the 1930s, usually staying in O'Flaherty's flat off the Strand. He looked forward to these visits because there was "the sense of being 'on the eve' of some wonderful adventure" and remembered "Those first nights in London when no-one ever wants to go home. Talking, talking, in taxis, at restaurants, on greyhound tracks, in cars, in night-clubs, back at someone's house. All the schemes, all the plans for the future!"

This frantic life style ultimately gave Stuart little satisfaction. He later realised he could never live in London because "Life would become too unreal, too purely a game. Fantastic episodes would take the place with me of more difficult adventure." But during his early visits he was desperate for new experiences, and did not care how he found them. Although Stuart had friends who were Marxists, most of the company he kept were well connected and rich enough to enjoy a frivolous existence. They may have felt they were trying to see life, but in general their only unhappiness was broken love affairs, and their behaviour, shameful in a decade of poverty and unemployment. Evelyn Waugh, as much to blame, knew some of O'Flaherty and Stuart's friends, and thought Basil Murray, the son of Gilbert Murray, "satanic". Lady Ankaret Howard, a cousin of Murray's, particularly irritated Waugh. Of her he noted in his 1926 Diary:

think I like her... She 'shows off' incorrigibly - even in rather unimpressive ways such as drinking of spirits and jumping over chairs. She is so proud of knowing bookies and common men which I suppose is creditable considering her social position, [daughter of the 10th Earl of Carlisle] but she does not seem to realize that the only reasons why they like her is this same social position she is so triumphantly being independent of - or so it seems to me.

O'Flaherty described to Stuart a weekend in February 1932

spent trying to escape Lady Ankaret, who was by now married. "I love Ankaret more than anything in the world, but I'm determined to sit tight and lead my own life."

The older writer often stayed at Laragh, and despite the fact that he made a pass at Iseult, was one of the few friends of Stuart's that she liked. When his marriage to Margaret Barrington was breaking up in 1932, he appreciated Iseult's helpful advice over it and other complications with women. "Kiss Iseult's hand for me," he wrote to Stuart, "& thank her for telling me what to do. She will understand. She is a fine woman, Iseult, which is odd, as beautiful woman are generally pretty lousy bitches."

Iseult also knew that Stuart was having affairs with women in Ireland and in London, and only strongly objected when one such association appeared in a newspaper gossip column. His involvement with women was not serious, for he and especially O'Flaherty used women in a way which would now be considered chauvinistic. Iseult could not have stopped Stuart seeing women, except by being in London with him, but she hated society and refused to go when asked.

O'Flaherty was amongst the first to congratulate Stuart on *The Coloured Dome,* which was published in July, only six months after his last book. As neither men discussed their own work with each other, what he said was particularly sincere. "...in language and poetry it's a great advance on the Puritan Pigeons...it thrills me as in fact, all your work does. It's so beautiful. But then you have really a very beautiful soul." More like himself, O'Flaherty added "O.K.Chief- lay off the balony!"

Yeats, who had been unwell, stayed for a few weeks in the Royal Hotel at Glendalough towards the end of June. He dropped in and out of Laragh Castle, and on 26 June wrote his poem, *Stream and Sun at Glendalough.* Perhaps expecting to be stimulated by conversation with Stuart, especially after reading his *Pigeon Irish,* he admitted in a letter to his wife Georgie that he found "Francis Stuart alone rather flat...[he] always agrees with me or pretends to & that is very dull."

A few days later Yeats was feeling much better, but was

90

disturbed by noisy children in his hotel. Declining an invitation to stay with the Stuarts at Laragh, he told Georgie Yeats on the 13 July, "I should bore them & talk myself stupid. We have not enough in common to give back a splash when I drop a stone..." Instead Yeats invited the Stuarts to dine with him that evening, and he felt much happier. He had been preparing a lecture to give in America called *"Modern Ireland"*, and during the meal found "The conversation was profound and gave me great help..."

It was Iseult who made the difference, and the absence of a tongue tied art student who irritated Yeats at Laragh Castle for not opening her mouth. Yeats saw the Stuarts several times before returning to Dublin and the peace of his club. He wrote to Iseult from there, thanking her for "happy days" at Laragh, and was again full of praise for Stuart's work. He had:

> just said to Lennox Robinson, that if I was not afraid of being misled by my sensitiveness to a certain kind of mystic thought I would say that your husband had the most noble & passionate style of anybody writing in English at this moment. But I will not, because of that fear, say as much as that in public, or not yet. I enclose on a separate sheet of paper a sentence which should serve...

which was; "Francis Stuart has a style full of lyrical intensity, a mind full of spiritual passion...He has written a strange, profound, lovely book."

The Coloured Dome still haunted Yeats nearly a week later, when he urged Olivia Shakespeare to:

> Read *The Coloured Dome* by Francis Stuart. It is strange and exciting in theme and perhaps more personally and beautifully written than any book of our generation; it makes you understand the strange Ireland that is rising up here. What an inexplicable thing sexual selection is! Iseult picked this young man, by what seemed half chance, half a mere desire to escape from an impossible life, and when he seemed almost imbecile to his own relations. Now he is her very self made active and visible, her nobility walking and

singing. If luck comes to his aid he will be our great writer...

Angered that O'Flaherty's *The Puritan* had been suppressed, Yeats wrote to Stuart for his friend's address. He was trying to think of "any effective means of protest", and concluded that some literary institution was necessary to make a stance. Before Lady Gregory died, Yeats had discussed the idea of an Irish Academy of Letters with her and George Russell. In the summer of 1932, Yeats embarked on his last lecture tour of America to raise funds for the proposed Academy. From the talk he had written at Glendalough he mentioned Stuart as "...typical of the New Ireland...medieval and sceptical..."

O'Flaherty was in a Dublin street with Stuart when they bumped into Yeats, who spoke about the project. When he added that he was being helped by "George Shaw," both men at first thought of a jockey with the same name. More surprising to Stuart, was O'Flaherty's acceptance of Academy membership, knowing his friend shared his own distrust of such institutions. Under these circumstances, Stuart felt obliged to accept as well.

By September 1932, full membership of the Academy was offered to selected writers whose work Yeats considered to be "Irish" in theme, and they were sent a draft of the Academy's aims:

> We have at present in Ireland no organisation representing Belles Lettres, and consequently no means whereby we Irish authors can make known our views, nor any instrument by which action can be taken on our behalf.
>
> There is in Ireland an official censorship possessing, and actively exercising, powers of suppression which may at any moment confine an Irish author to the British and American market, and thereby make it impossible for him to live by distinctive Irish literature....

Yeats told a reporter for *The Observer,* that the Civil War had shaped certain writers "...Men like Liam O'Flaherty, Frank O'Connor, Peadar O'Donnell, Sean O'Faolain, and Francis Stuart, all of whom are remarkable novelists

... who in all probablity will shape the Academy and its policy." He was particularly pleased that T.E.Lawrence accepted Associate membership for "...few people have known that he is an Irishman." Shaw's wife Charlotte, had written to Yeats only a few days earlier on 4 September, incidentally praising *The Coloured Dome* ("What a fine book...") stressing that Lawrence had never even been to Ireland. The Academy was destined to be little more than one of Yeats' grandiose schemes, and its inaugural meeting on 18 September 1932 at the Peacock Theatre was scathingly recorded by the pompous and eccentric theatre-goer Joseph Holloway. According to him, Madame MacBride sat with the Stuarts, and heard Yeats ridicule the censors for banning *The Puritan.* Someone who had never heard Yeats lecture before, remarked it was all "so rambling and futile." Holloway concluded:

> All the carrion crows of Irish Litterature [sic] are on the list of Academicians...the cult of the ugly was lauded to the skies by Yeats. Realism was clearing the way for deeply religious literature. One felt as Yeats went on and on in his rambling remarks how little he was in touch with the real spirit of Ireland.

Several writers, including Joyce had declined to join, and Yeats was bombarded with complaints about the membership, including an objection that Lord Dunsany was only an Associate, whereas Stuart was a full member. Dunsany was not "Irish in his work", but Stuart himself regretted he had ever accepted. Nevertheless, he defended the Academy two months later in a letter to the *Irish Press,* against charges from a priest, that the works of the Academicians were "...far from being a faithful mirror of Irish life...". Stuart did not believe that writers should only confine themselves to writing of life in their own country, and cited Shakespeare as one who did not and "never lost the mark of his unique national character." He did not see why Gaelic should be the only language of national literary expression. There was a renaissance in Europe of Catholic writers, and Irish Catholics writers had to exert a wide appeal if they were to be noticed at all. It was not a view shared by Thomas McGreevey, who had written to Yeats in May that he had hated *The Coloured Dome:*

> that Dorothy McArdle kind of Catholicism in it is so contemptible...He is writing very well, I think but it is a monstrous crime for any Irishman to flatter Irish vanity at a time like this. Save Europe's soul indeed! If we could find a soul for ourselves to begin with we might be able to consider ourselves fit to associate with other European countries. I doubt that except modern Greece and Roumania there is any European country as ruined in its soul as we are - the Scotch [sic] of course.

O'Flaherty did not even trouble to attend the meeting of the Irish Academy, and was determined to settle down for a while and to leave women out of his life. He was also anxious that a colt called Galamac which Stuart had bought for 19 guineas was making little progress. Galamac was used as a private joke as a name for a Dublin Hotel lounge in *The Coloured Dome.* As far as the animal was concerned, Stuart thought Mick Gleeson pampered the horse too much, and removed him to train with someone else in Leopardstown. The change of trainer paid off, when the colt won the Dromskin Plate at Dundalk, beating the joint favourites.

O'Flaherty had completed his novel *Skerrett,* and invited Stuart to celebrate with him in the autumn. It was Stuart's first visit to Galway, and after an evening of drinking with friends, he woke up with a heavy hangover the following day. Compton Mackenzie had invited him to lunch in Dublin, 150 miles away, and after a difficult journey, Stuart collected Iseult and managed to arrive on time.

It was probably over the meal that Stuart told Mackenzie of *Try the Sky,* a novel he had written that summer. In any case, Mackenzie wrote a long foreword for it, stating the book "...will undoubtedly help those who recognise that humanity now stands at a crisis of evolution to consider one of the ways forward that the future offers...Francis Stuart has a message for the modern world of infinitely greater importance than anything offered by D.H.Lawrence."

Try The Sky was published in January 1933. Stuart used his own experiences of flying, to give his novel of "the machine age" authenticity. The main characters rebel against the real world of disillusionment and unhappiness by escaping in an aeroplane, where they find that spiritual illumination and love cannot be separated from their painful earthbound existence. Their flying is only a substitute for the mystical journey:

> Certain mystics have soared to unimaginable heights and have experienced the truth to at least some degree, but when they attempt to communicate it they have become almost unintelligible...One must be bold...be ready to sacrifice everything, if those heights are to be reached.

Stuart used some of his recollections of Austria to provide part of the background setting, but it is the only pre-war novel where he explicitly uses the word "Nazi", in the context of a pro-fascist violent demonstration. This is 1932, the year *Try The Sky* was completed but as it is reported from the past, Stuart intended the novel to be set in the future.

Mackenzie's praise was misplaced, for *Try The Sky* is a failure, as the elements of fantasy on which the book depends are unconvincing. Stuart was more absorbed with the urgency of what he wanted to say than in controlling its expression, and dialogue such as, "O Ireland ! O Carlotta ! O Love! I thought passionately. What little, little faith I have. Oh yes, it is true, it is true; this is heaven. You are my heaven, you three together!" was only embarrassing.

The problem of writing as a craft occurred in a play *Men Crowd Me Round* which Stuart wrote for The Abbey Theatre, and which was put on there in March 1933. His London experiences were not wasted, for the "smart set", was reflected with a cynical eye in the plot, which concerned a Republican who betrays his ideals for the sake of love and analyses his reasons for doing so. A critic from *The Irish Independent* thought Stuart had not yet learnt how to write for the stage, and his judgement was reflected in poor attendances. Mervyn Wall who was at the premiere, saw:

W. B.Yeats come in and occupy his usual seat... I had noticed a tall, spare good-looking young man in a polo-necked pullover, with an attractive, lively, young woman. She would jump up from time to time to greet and shake hands with people as they came in. I realised at once that the young man must be Francis Stuart with his wife. When Yeats entered, the young lady immediately ran over to him, taking his two hands, then ran back to seize Stuart and to lead him to Yeats, who did not arise on either occasion, but received each of them, in his usual, aloof, lordly way. I recognized the gaunt, weed-clad figure of Maud Gonne MacBride come in behind me. Iseult ran across and tried to drag her to where Yeats was sitting. Maud Gonne went all girlish, laughing and shaking her head determinedly. She broke from her daughter's hand and went to her seat...

Joseph Holloway went to The Abbey Theatre later to:

sample some of Francis Stuart's play, *Men Crowd Me Round*, which I heard had a very poor reception...only a few calling for the author - Yeats, Robinson and a few others. Last night the theatre was practically empty only a little over 300 in the house... Tonight was a little better, but wretchedly empty for the third night of a new play by a member of Yeats' Academy of Letters....The whole air of the play and the method of interpreting it had an air of artificiality that never for a moment ripened into real drama, and the amount of vulgar language the writer put into the mouths of the IRA without any effect was nauseating... the words should never have been given utterance to on a public stage..."A bloody English bitch". I record the vile words to show how far Stuart dared to go...

CHAPTER 7

Because Stuart always worked to a consistent routine when in Laragh, he was able to quickly follow *Try the Sky* with *Glory*. Published in August 1933, it was a more convincing attack on the machine age, and better handled.

Protesting against the dehumanizing elements of society, through the intrusion of an aerodrome on "sacred" land, those who crusade to protect the old values, are led by a recluse called de Lacy. He constructs a hut not unlike the one Stuart had brought from Glencree, and declares to the aerodrome builders, "... mechanical obsession is overshadowing the whole of life. Even human love is becoming a sort of mechanical relationship..."

Yeats' praise was now almost predictable, and *Glory* was "majestic, beautiful, all intellectual passion, perfect in structure, far beyond anything you have done hitherto - but sometimes vile in its grammar...", and he suggested Stuart should pay someone to read his work. The novel had Yeats up to three in the morning, a remark that can be regarded with suspicion since Stuart's poems had also "kept him from sleep." The unlikely theme of flying may have especially interested Yeats, for Stuart had introduced him to Mercedes Gleitz who was in Ireland for cheap flying lessons. Famous as a cross channel swimmer, she had met Stuart at an airfield, and one afternoon he took her for tea in Dawson Street in Dublin. Stuart was dismayed when Yeats entered the door and joined their table. Miss Gleitz had probably never read a poem in her life, and Stuart dreaded the subjects Yeats might bring up in conversation. Animated when she spoke of her adventures as a swimmer, he plied her with questions about the temperature of the water, and the grease she used to keep the cold out. This was a revelation to Stuart, who saw a hidden side of Yeats for the first time. He realised the poet yearned to be friendly with such uncomplicated women, instead of the literary ladies he knew such as Dorothy Wellesley. After Yeats left, Mercedes Gleitz asked who the charming old man was, and Stuart replied

"Just an amiable old eccentric we happen to know".

It was one of the rare occasions when Stuart saw a human Yeats, but he only published this recollection after portraying him as slightly ridiculous through his fictions. He accepted Yeats' tributes to his novels, yet privately could only think of him as a fraud. Such contradictory attitudes motivated Stuart's impulse to write. If an event was intense to him, it was valid reason to include it in his novels. He wrote of "mechanical obsession" convincingly, because he had taken flying lessons, initially for his own pleasure. The attack came later, when he realised flying was ultimately unsatisfactory, representing escapism and false values.

These conclusions were the basis for his two "aeroplane" novels, but while other writers might have described such experiences from imagination, Stuart scorned the Proustian cork-lined room as too remote from life (despite his admiration for Proust). He could only achieve enlightenment through pleasure first, convinced that hedonism was justified because it brought pain and understanding. Stuart could be no other kind of writer, but his approach was often self-centred, and hurt Iseult and his family.

The search for self understanding took Stuart to a Cistercian Monastery at Roscrea, where he spent a few weeks in retreat. Despite assertions in his autobiography, he did not seriously consider becoming a monk. In a conversation, possibly invented in *Things to Live For*, a monk tells Stuart he, "...will heap sin on sin and suffer and despair, but in the end, if you bow down, you will be forgiven..."

Stuart befriended a Spanish-American, José de Ruiloba, he met in Dublin, whose parents had sent him from America to Trinity. He was a compulsive gambler who never attended a race, and although talkative, Stuart liked him because he was a natural eccentric. He came to stay ostensibly for a few days at Laragh, and was popular with Iseult and the children. When he had money from betting, he bought the family lavish presents. His visit stretched into months, and neither Stuart nor Iseult dared ask him to leave. Eventually Stuart told de Ruiloba he would have to go, as they had packed for a holiday. Early one morning, Stuart went through the sham of locking up, and they all drove to Dublin where they dropped off their guest and returned to Laragh. During dinner, de Ruiloba reappeared, and after asking to see the children who were in bed, stayed on as if nothing had happened.

O'Flaherty and Stuart were dismayed when Fianna Fáil with de Valera came to power in the 1932 election. They drew up a document, protesting against establishment writers, the church and politicians. They advocated a conservative anarchy to create controversy, and sought support from other writers. De Ruiloba was referred to in the opening, "We Irish writers and our gallant allies...", but they could not gather enough support. Frank O'Connor was one who declined, and when Stuart tried to discuss his ideas with a sub-editor at the *Irish Independent,* he was asked to leave the office.

Although the "proclamation" has all the elements of farce, it was written with serious intent. Stuart especially disliked what he would later refer to as "the soft centre of Irish writing". This emphasis on parochialism, nationalism and writing to a formula to please the American Market, by writers such as O'Faolain and O'Connor did not represent the New Ireland. Politically the Free State was equally stale, and Stuart's dissatisfaction with this was shared by W. B.Yeats.

Neither believed in democracy, Yeats preferring what he called the "aristocratic principle" which Stuart interpreted as "an original and speculative way of thinking as opposed to what was then the incoming tide of popular and democratic concepts." According to Stuart, Yeats "...equally disliked the left-wing liberalism and rationalism that flourished in England between the wars."

Yeats told Stuart he had refused to sign a petition by English writers, protesting against the Reichstag Fire Trial in 1933. Yeats was not in favour of totalitarianism, but "carried his love of individual freedom further than most of the signatories; to the point...where he became suspicious of the smugness and collective self-righteousness which they seemed to him to embody." By any argument, Yeats' attitude was disgraceful, if apparent "smugness" prevented his helping individuals whose own freedom of life was at stake through Nazi injustice. It made a mockery of any "love of individual freedom," but the words were Stuart's, and it is obvious Yeats had his support.

Conor Cruise O'Brien wrote that Yeats was:

> generally pro-Fascist in tendency, and Fascist in practice on the single occasion when opportunity arose...(When he was briefly involved with O'Duffy, the leader of the Irish Fascist " Blueshirt" Party in 1933).

Stuart wanted nothing to do with O'Duffy, but like Yeats was, "...not alone in believing that at the moment of history, that the discipline of Fascist theory might impose order upon a disintegrating world."

O'Brien notes that "neither Yeats nor anyone else during Yeats' lifetime knew what horrors Fascism would be capable of. But the many who, like Yeats, were drawn to Fascism at this time knew, and seemed to have little difficulty in accepting, or at least making allowances for, much of what had already been done, and continued to be done..."

Stuart has said Yeats would have understood perfectly well the disillusionment which caused him to go to Germany. Both Yeats and Stuart only identified with aspects of Fascism, and would not support any regime which suppressed freedom of speech or the written word.

Stuart would not simply admire as Yeats did, a leader such as d'Annunzio. He wanted change and hardly caring how it was achieved, became involved in a ludicrous and unrealistic scheme to restore the Irish Monarchy. "Anything" he said "was better than the lot we had in 1921."

He had become friendly with a young T.D., Sir Osmund Esmonde, formerly the unofficial Spanish Ambassador to Spain, and a friend of Franco's brother. He had met Stuart shortly after reading *The Coloured Dome*, and told him that *Pigeon Irish* had inspired him with the notion of reviving the Irish Monarchy. For a man who had released a cage of canaries in the Dail to disrupt a speech by De Valera, nothing was too eccentric. Stuart occasionally borrowed an aeroplane from Esmonde and flew to Meath where friends lived at a house called Harbourstown. They had large fields on which Esmonde planned to land airmen, and details of the plot were discussed in Esmonde's Dublin flat. A flying Officer in the Flying Corps was to arrange for supporters to land at strategic points to organise the overthrow of the government. Once this was achieved, a descendant of the O'Neills was to be crowned monarch.

Mervyn Wall attended the inaugural meeting of "The Irish Monarchist Society" in a Mountjoy Square Hotel, more out of curiosity than commitment. The proprietor, announced that he knew the candidate who was to be offered the Irish Crown, but would not name him, and remarked that two members of the British Government had approved of the idea. The "Douglas Plan" was also mentioned, an eccentric system of economics that appealed to Ezra Pound and Hugh MacDiarmid for example, and eventually wrecked Alberta's economy.

The Restoration was not even attempted due to lack of expertise, but characterized the hopeless schemes Stuart took part in. It was all very well to be "countercurrent", but counterproductive when both the declaration against the establishment and the Irish Monarch scheme proved such a waste of time.

The poultry farm had been disposed of in 1931, and Iseult took over the space it had occupied for a vegetable and flower garden. Apart from a small annuity, Stuart had no constant source of income to support his family and needed money badly. He jumped at the chance to write a film script about London, but the result was so banal his work could not be used. This did not bother Stuart, who knew that if he was motivated to write for money, he could not produce anything of value. "I must only work to please myself, when and where I feel like it. And if I've no money, well and good."

If Stuart was not earning much from writing, his reputation was sufficiently distinguished for Jonathan Cape to commission his memoirs in Spring 1934 and published in October, when he was only thirty two. *Things to Live For*, is not a reconstruction of Stuart's life either chronologically or factually, but an accounts of the circumstances that shaped his philosophy and beliefs.

Patrick Campbell enjoyed *Things to Live For* because it was romantic, but Stuart disliked it later for precisely that reason, and because he had made himself "always right."

Raymond Mortimer the English critic realised the predicament of Stuart's approach. Suggesting he would no doubt "despise some of the persons I most admire as bloodless intellectuals", Stuart in common with other romantics, ignored "...the wild exhiliration to be derived from the intellect, when abandoning every interest, it fights its way to the discovery and exploration of truth."

Mortimer pin-pointed a dilemma that Stuart was also faced with in his novels. By dismissing the intellect as a means of questioning life, and only by relying on intuitive senses, he risked antagonising the reader who could argue that, not only was this approach too selfconscious, but produced a result that was effectively "too intellectual."

Nevertheless, Stuart's book appealed to those at the "grass-roots" level, for Jim Larkin's secretary, Jack Carney, not only read but bought the book, and in a lengthy letter to the author, noted that:

> My copy will go the rounds of the workers around Gloucester Street. They will gain in a greater hope in life.
> I am writing as maybe you know, with a vast experience of life. Thank you for your book...

In October, Stuart spent a few days in Cumberland mountain climbing with William and Ankaret Jackson. From their house, he found time to write an encouraging letter to Joseph O'Neill about his novel *Winds from the North*. Hoping O'Neill would "write more, for you certainly do for Ireland something like what Sigird Undset has for Norway", Stuart pressed Macmillan of New York to read the book. He then spent a long weekend as a guest of Enid Raffael and her family, where he ended an affair with Joan Haslip the biographer. She found this difficult to accept, and followed him to the railway station as he returned to Ireland. To her, he was "so firm and cold" but Stuart was determined not to be seriously involved with women at this stage.

At Laragh, he maintained a united front with Iseult and

always spent Christmas with her and the children. There was no difference that year, when the Stuarts returned to a large breakfast after early Mass, and the children opened their presents in the sitting room around the tree. Stuart used to tease each year with the same ritual question, "Which did you enjoy the most; the early Mass, the big breakfast, or opening the presents?", although he knew their answer very well.

From the few references to Kay and Ion in his books, Stuart shows how much he understood and entered their world. Kay recalled that he played wonderful imaginative games with them, and was always inventing endless stories. With few children's books, and no nearby library, they depended on their father for much of their amusement. But although Kay was too young, Ion who was eight, soon began to feel disturbed by the tension between his parents.

Two days after Christmas 1936, Stuart wrote again to O'Neill, with a detailed criticism of his new novel *Land Under England*. He did not like it as much as the first, perhaps because he was "...prejudiced in favour of a certain presentation of life..." but still read it with great interest.

Stuart also mentioned that he was working on a non serious novel, which became *In Search of Love*. Influenced by Evelyn Waugh's *Black Mischief* Stuart satirized what he knew of the film industry through the producer Brian Hurst. The book, which broke Stuart's rule about writing for money, was finished in six weeks, and was his only published attempt at comic fiction.

Stuart was in London from mid January 1935 where he spent much of the year. His lengthy visit was as much a trial separation from Iseult, as a convenient place to write. *The News Chronicle* and *Cornhill* magazine took serials and short stories, earning him time to complete a book called *The Angel of Pity* announced as "philosophy" but written as fiction.

By the early summer Stuart was back in Ireland, where he attempted to write a film scenario for Hurst, on Synge's *Riders to the Sea*. This failed, because Stuart was unsympathetic to Synge's writing, and by the time *In Search of Love* was published, the whole subject of films exasperated

Stuart.

His attack on the film industry, was hardly noticed in the reviews. One notice considered the novel "...all very absurd but highly amusing."

In thanking O'Neill for his comments on the book, Stuart was grateful for "...personal appreciation from someone like yourself" because it meant much more than the "impersonal praise of reviewers though these I suppose are to be welcomed from the point of view of sales..."

O' Neill's third novel *Day of Wrath* evoked the comment from Stuart that "It never seems to have occurred to anyone else to write a book about the next war in its effect on the civilian population as you have done...these good ideas seem so obvious *once someone has hit on them.*" (Stuart's italics.)

The Day of Wrath may have influenced the content of Stuart's *The Angel of Pity* published in November. The theme of war occurs in many of the novels, but *The Angel of Pity* is concerned with the aftermath of a future conflict. A woman who is destroyed by a mob of soldiers, is obviously identified as Christ on earth, and her death, resurrection and ascension offer hope and redemption from the war-ruins left by man.

Repetitive and poorly constructed, *The Angel of Pity* should have been a failure. The theme was not new, for a vision of Christ as Woman appears in *The Coloured Dome* but the later book is more memorable because of the views expressed by the first person narrator, which show Stuart was completely and deliberately at odds with most contemporary novelists. Both in Ireland and England many were suffering through unemployment and poverty. While Orwell and others were gaining a reputation for social realism, Stuart attacks such fiction by implication in *The Angel of Pity:*

> The Brothers Karamazov fulfilled no social problems but it...inspired thousands of beings separately by its grasp of a particle of that truth that has nothing to do with the conduct of a state or the betterment of material conditions, but has everything to do with the conduct of a man's secret, personal life.

More than before, he stresses the importance of suffering in achieving art of lasting value:

> Show me the being who has suffered most...I would know beyond doubt that he had gone further towards finding the eternal truth than anyone else whether as an artist, a lover, a saint, or in some other more obscure capacity...Lovers and saints remain for the most part unknown to the world. It is only artists of whom one can say: He is the greatest because he suffered most...it may be known from the quality of the artists' work...of those who have plunged deepest into the human tragedy, there will be an unmistakable quality that I can only call the tragic sense...

The fact that Stuart wrote that neither Dostoevsky's work, nor presumably his own, "fulfilled no social problems", indicates he knew he could be accused of irresponsibility as a writer, in ignoring the conditions of the poor. To mention the importance of art would seem ridiculous to a starving man, who could reasonably argue he might have the strength to consider such values if he could eat first. Stuart would not accept that both spiritual and physical nourishment was necessary to life, nor was the artist with insight any more an élitist than simple human beings whose first concern was survival. Others could write about that, but in his view, the human condition would only improve if the spiritual values were established first.

The Angel of Pity would have appealed to Yeats, who would have written a preface, if he had he not been ill. Praise came from Capt. Basil Liddell-Hart, the military historian in December who read "many books in search of truth and understanding. Few are worthwhile. Yours is. Thank you..." In thanking his correspondent the following week, Stuart mentioned that the book had a "rather cold reception by critics and the general public."

This was shared by Iseult, who detested the book, and who wrote to Stuart in 1953 that *"The Angel of Pity*...was all wrong. It nearly broke my heart that you had dedicated it to me." Stuart believed Iseult objected to the way he "took a religious theme and twisted it in a certain way which she didn't like." Iseult was not narrowminded in her religious beliefs, and as *The Angel of Pity* was one of the better books, her remark shows how far the gap between them had become. Stuart could not have realised this or he would not have dedicated the book to her.

The early weeks of January 1936 found Stuart in London to see a play he had adapted from *Glory*. Planned only to run for a few nights at the Arts Club Theatre off Charing Cross Road, it was enough, for *Glory* was not a success. Basil Liddell-Hart wrote sympathetically to Stuart, now back at Laragh, that:

> the message of that play is so well worthwhile that I hope you will not be deterred from making improvements and remaking its presentation...the margin that kept it from success was not large...Also don't forget that you promised to let me know when you are next in London. I look forward greatly to deepening our contact...

Stuart thought *Glory* had "...turned into a melodramatic absurdity on the stage..." and although he wanted to write more plays, *Glory* was abandoned. When next in London it was not to see Liddell-Hart, but to become seriously involved in a love affair.

Enid Raphael, who was staying with O'Flaherty when Stuart arrived, knew of his problems with Iseult for years. She thought he should find someone else, and introduced him to Honor Henderson, the daughter of Lord Kylsant, a former chairman of the White Star Shipping Line. She was divorced in 1930 after a miserable marriage that lasted three years, and after seeing Stuart on several occasions he fell deeply in love and wanted to marry her.

Stuart saw a solicitor, to establish if there were grounds for an annulment of his marriage. Whether Iseult knew about this seems unlikely, but the least objectionable reason would have been that Stuart had married under age before his eighteenth birthday, and as far as the Roman Catholic Church was concerned there was no marriage.

The solicitor asked Stuart for the name of the woman he intended to marry and suggested he should return in six weeks. During that time, Honor Henderson called to see Stuart at O'Flaherty's flat and unexpectedly announced that as their relationship would not work, they should not marry. Stuart told her that the news shocked him, but privately his feelings for the woman had cooled. When O'Flaherty heard the news, he took Stuart for a drink, and told him that there would be other Honors round the corner. For such a serious subject, Stuart treated the possible dissolution of his marriage with Iseult, with apparent casualness. Despite not really loving Honor Henderson, he would have married her simply to leave Iseult. He had reached a stage with her where he could no longer be rational about his marriage because it had failed completely.

The "Honor round the the corner" proved to be only too true. This time, Stuart was taken more seriously than he would have liked, by a young woman called Margery Binner, who played the principal girl in pantomine at The Palace Theatre near Victoria Station in London. She would have preferred more serious stage parts, and had played in Stuart's *Glory.*The theatre world was fairly new to Stuart who, while disliking aspects of it, wanted to know more. He should have ignored the warning signs, for Margery Binner loved the company of writers and the famous, and boasted that she rented a flat from an actress known as June, the estranged wife of Lord Inverclyde.

When she took Stuart there, to show him a novel inscribed by Aldous Huxley he was unimpressed, and embarrassed at her determination to marry him. His way of coping with this, as with Honor Henderson, was to treat the matter light heartedly, and he gave her ten pounds towards a ruby engagement ring without seriously considering his actions.

In a bid to force Stuart's hand, Margery Binner arranged what was ostensibly to be a quiet lunch for two in an expensive restaurant, which she claimed would cost nothing apart from the wine. She had however, also invited various society people, including the Turkish Ambassador, and a gossip columnist. In due course a newspaper noted that "Francis Stuart, the distinguished writer celebrated his engagement to Margery Binner in the company of..."

The report was nonsense, but a country neighbour of

Iseult's read the account and showed it to her. Stuart returned to Laragh to find his wife bitterly hurt, and accusing him of frittering away the money he had from his publisher on other women. He was ashamed of what had happened, but while he failed with Iseult, he still loved her.

Despite his unsettled life, Stuart wrote *The White Hare,* in 1936. It was his ninth book in six years, as well as two plays, but their sales did not match the quality of the reviews they received. With *The White Hare,* Stuart returned to a traditional Irish setting, and the book was quickly acclaimed. *The London Evening Standard* under the heading of *A Great Romantic Writer* chose it as their "Book of the Month". To *The Sunday Times* it was a "tender and very beautifully told story" and for *News Chronicle* "The beauty of this book is not to be set down in a few words; nor perhaps could it be caught by any other writer."

The praise would have been acceptable if *The White Hare* had been a good novel. Unfortunately it came close to the kind of writing Stuart himself disliked. It was full of Irish clichés, always popular in England, especially in the setting of the tumbledown house in a bog. Even the worst Stuart book has memorable qualities, and in this case, observations of Ion who shaped the character of Dominic make it interesting. More importantly it was in this novel that Stuart introduced for the first time, the hare symbol, which would recur in his fiction.

As a child, Stuart was fascinated by rabbits and hares as private companions, which were more than simply pets, and like the horse, stirred in him some deep and perhaps primitive response. At an early age, he had dictated his first story which was about a rabbit to his mother, who preserved it in an exercise book, and later manuscripts were often decorated with small drawings of the animal in the margin. At Glencree he had kept pet rabbits, when he returned to Ireland after the war he had several hares, and in Dublin, a much loved rabbit until it died in 1987.

Initially Stuart may have seen something of his own nature in rabbits and hares, sharing shy timidity with rabbits who prefer to live in isolation, and the wild fearless behaviour of hares in March, who take risks in the face of danger. He saw nothing of the 'hare' in Iseult, despite Yeats' symbolism for her and by an irony, "the hare' was a term he identified his second wife Madeleine with, and introduced in his post war novel, *Redemption.*

In *The White Hare,* the animal represents lost and unattainable love, but through the novel, Stuart admits he cannot fully explain why it was part of his own private mythology, "The White Hare! To him it was *'the'* not *'a'*, because it had become for him an almost mythical animal, without exactly knowing what he meant..."

The novel did not charm all the critics, and in one more realistic evaluation, the reviewer found it:

> hard to take such romantic unreality seriously... there is a pervading air of poeticized affectation which makes the stories subside uneasily between a stage-managed glamour and the distressing intrusions of poverty...

The White Hare began a decline in the standard of Stuart's novels. As sales dropped, he tried more desperately to include material he thought would give his work greater appeal. *The Bridge* published in 1936, was announced in a review as *Francis Stuart Turns Realistic,* exactly the kind of book which Stuart himself distrusted, and in the same vein, Collins published *Julie* the following year.

More satisfactory, was Stuart's short study, *Racing For Pleasure and Profit.* It was a subject he could not write badly about, and his enthusiasm carried through each page directly and simply.

Stuart's novels may have been more realistic, but they had none of the intensity of his best work, which was fuelled by the contradictions he found in adventure. He rarely went to London, as his group of particular friends, took their compulsive restlessness elsewhere. Even O'Flaherty was bored, and wrote:

> see nobody, as I hardly go to London. Enid telephones now and again. She has been to Berlin Vienna and Buda-Pesth...your friend Miss Haslip is, I hear, going to Mexico....One feels that a marvellous life is going on quite near, but that it is just as well to pay no attention...

Like a character in *Julie,* Stuart found Tottenham Court Road soulless, and as for Ireland, "its hushed beauty had in the end left her cold and dissatisfied."

London failed, but there was Paris which Stuart visited in 1937. He saw Beckett, and envied him his exile. Both were at odds with Ireland, but Stuart felt trapped there, and reluctantly began a historical novel about the time of the Rebellion. During his research, he discovered details of an eighteenth century race between a pig and a horse, which the pig wins.

It was one of the few amusing and credible sections of *The Great Squire* which suffers from an improbable and unconvincing plot. By its nature, a good plot was more important here, than in his previous novels which depended more on theme. Nevertheless Lord Glenavy wrote he felt for the first time " what Ireland really was like, and all that it was round 1780. I had always sentimentalized that time, but you must have seen it truly as no-one else has. But what a unity they had in those days...". In her only surviving letter to Stuart, Maud Gonne enthused that *The Great Squire* was "...a great book. Iseult is right about your genius..."

There could be no blurb on the wrapper this time from Yeats, for he had died in France in late January, 1939. Stuart felt no particular sadness on hearing the news, and remembered a shivering Yeats shuffling towards the door in carpet slippers the last time they met. Yeats' dissatisfaction with Ireland as well as his poor health, had driven him to spend more time abroad. All that Yeats had said about Stuart's work was ultimately disastrous, for his praise encouraged Stuart to produce so many novels, few of which were well written or expressed its theme convincingly. Stuart's own life had reached a limbo of complete staleness and deadness which he did not know how to break. The chance came unexpectedly, when in February, he was asked to go to Germany to lecture and give readings from his books.

CHAPTER 8

Helmut Clismann was head of the German Academic Exchange Service in Ireland, which arranged for Irish writers and teachers to visit Germany. He was a friend of Iseult's, who asked if such a visit could be arranged for her husband. She did not tell Stuart, perhaps because that would have been enough reason for him to refuse. Apart from the much needed money, Iseult wanted a break from the constant domestic tension, as much as Stuart did. Clissman explained the costs and fees would be paid by the Deutsch Akademie, for which he would simply give readings from his novels, and a talk on literature if required. There was nothing remarkable in the suggestion, except for the particular political climate of Europe and Germany. Hitler broke the Munich agreement and seized Czechoslovakia in March 1939, and there was talk of war. Stuart agreed to go, and arrived in Berlin in April.

Stuart's main publisher was Victor Gollancz, who as early as 1933, had published a book called *The Brown Book of the Hitler Terror*. Referring to it in a pamphlet, *What Buchenwald Really Means*, published in 1945, Gollancz recalled that although *The Brown Book* contained "a wealth of documentary and photographic evidence which allowed no denial," the book caused almost no stir at all. *The Morning Post* opened a review of the book with, "A blood curdling compendium of 'atrocities' alleged to have been committed under the Nazi regime..." and ended "Anything that is not corroborated up to the hilt from other sources will naturally be suspect, and the same reader will be predisposed to sympathize rather with Herr Hitler than with his accusers..." It was an extraordinary conclusion for a newspaper to reach. Stuart never read *The Brown Book*, but even if he had, preferred to see Germany and decide for himself. No informed person was unaware of what was happening in Germany, but even as late as 1939, Stuart was naive in his judgement of Hitler and the Third Reich. Whatever he felt about the well-publicised suffering in

Germany, it had to be irrelevant as far as his purpose was concerned.

Welcomed by Professor Schirmer, head of the English faculty at the Deutsche Akademie, Stuart was given a timetable for the cities he was to visit. He would be driven to Munich, Hamburg, Bonn and Cologne. Starting with Munich and Berlin, Stuart was well looked after, and wherever he went, treated with greater respect than in Ireland. Later, when lecturing in Hamburg, he was startled to see a highly decorated Gestapo Officer in the front row of the audience, who left half way through the talk. The General, Stuart was told apologetically afterwards, had hoped to hear Nazi propaganda. Remembering this when he returned to Germany, Stuart had "...very few illusions about receiving any support from the regime."

In the meantime, he went on to Bonn, where he met a young Nazi, Prince Biron Von Kurland, an Ace air pilot who was to die in the London Air Raids. He was a grand nephew of the last Kaiser, with an estate in East Prussia, which Stuart later visited, but watching him lead his squadron of the Luftwaffe flying low over the Rhine, Stuart felt exhilarated. He was convinced that this was preparation for some revolution which he had longed for all his life. In a letter to Iseult, he remarked that Prince Biron was "the only practising Catholic" that he knew at all well, and also "an ardent national Socialist...", adding no comment about the incompatibility of worshipping two gods.

As a guest, Stuart was shown attention and kindness which he had not experienced before. Ironically, he was aware he was not being fêted as a famous writer or for the quality of his novels. Unknown in Germany, he had only been invited because no British writer would have gone there. What Stuart spoke about was of little consequence, for his audience only wanted to hear English pronounced.

In Cologne, the Direktor of the Deutsche Bank, and a close friend of Von Ribbentrop, took Stuart for a meal, and allocated him a woman interpreter. Driven by the Banker's chauffeur, he visited several beerhouses sampling Bowle, a mixture of champagne and white wine. Such a carefree life, reminded Stuart of his old days in Paris but when he returned to Berlin in mid May, he explored the city on foot. In a letter he told Iseult that to earn enough money to send home, he had agreed to lecture and take English language classes at the University in early June. Of the Jews, there were:

> framed pictures and articles exhibited here and there in the streets depicting types of Jews and the writing dealing with their activities in the past and present. These are mostly pages from newspapers -especially *The Sturmer* the special anti-semitic one. Also I think from the *Schwarze Korps* the official paper of the S.S.
> Also I have heard something of the Jewish activities prior to 1933 here and in cooperation with the communists - they were in many instances appalling. As for the presence of Jews now: They are scarcely to be seen in this part of Berlin (central) or the West End. But in the East End - beyond Alexanderplatz - where I penetrated one day there are still a good many to be seen. It is an extraordinary thing to see the busy, fashionable streets of a big city, without Jewish faces. It is something one realises gradually...

In both *Julie* and *The Great Squire*, Stuart drew sympathetic Jewish characters who feature as 'outcasts'. But he distrusted those who were motivated by excessive greed for money, and if that group included certain Jews they were not exempt from his judgment. He did not examine the facts of Nazi persecution of the Jews, and as in other matters of the past, he had already made up his mind what the truth was. Dangerously gullible, he took the anti-semitic prejudice of the Nazi newspapers as factual evidence to confirm his uninformed conclusions. All free Europe thought war was imminent, nevertheless Stuart believed as others did in Berlin, that war was unlikely. Although he conceded that the differences between the Democracies and the Totalitarian countries were so great, that he could not see how they could be "pacifically settled..."

When Stuart completed his lecture tour he had a long talk with Professor Schirmer who unexpectedly invited him to return to the University of Berlin in the autumn, as lecturer in English and Irish Literature.

For most foreigners, any question of lecturing in Germany in 1939 would not even be considered. The brutality of Hitler's rise to power, the shameful episode of the Reichstag Fire Trial, as well as countless examples of Nazi ruthlessness would be enough to dismiss the suggestion as totally repugnant. Stuart was neither liberal nor Socialist, and not impressed by democracy. Individuals were more important to him than their identification with particular party politics, and he had been equally comfortable with Sir Osmund Esmonde, a Franco supporter, as Harold Stroud, who was a Marxist. During the Irish Civil War, Stuart was naive and vague about the political arguments of both sides. Any personal doubts about the moral acceptability of coming to Nazi Germany, were over-ruled by his hope that romantic and idealistic ideas which had come to nothing in Ireland, would be fulfilled in Germany.

As a failed revolutionary, Stuart was constantly frustrated by inaction in his own life. Changes he had hoped for in society, were only imaginatively realised through his early novels. Stuart was willing to passively condone the brutality of the Nazi regime by living in Germany, for he had already cast Hitler in the heroic mould, and saw him as:

> a kind of blind Samson who was pulling down the pillars of Western Society as we knew it, which I still believed had to come about before any new world could arise...I probably had certain other visions of Hitler, but I think my main one was of a great destructive force (not a constructive one), after which perhaps something would arise...

Stuart was not desperate to work in Germany, and it had not been his first choice. He wanted to support his family, and had applied unsuccessfully for a job with the London *Daily Express*. Had he been offered it, he would have accepted.

With no prospect of anything else, Stuart tentatively accepted the Berlin appointment in May or early June. He did not know how long it would be for, but hoped to earn enough to put his finances in order. In a letter giving Iseult the news, Stuart asked her to come to Berlin with the children, which she refused to do. He replied:

> If I had known that in no case would you all come here then I very much doubt if I would have accepted the position here. At any rate I would have made every possible serious attempt at some other solution...

Iseult apparently wanted to come to Berlin with the children for a short holiday, but Stuart was against causing extra expense, which would only delay paying back loans which Janet and the bank had made.

By June, he had not made firm plans about either remaining in Berlin, or returning to Ireland during the vacation. His decision was dependent on whether Iseult could be pressed to come to Berlin:

> Above all, I am anxious not to be cut off from you for too long...But otherwise, very lonely as it would be, I prefer to stay here if it makes it quicker for us to put our affairs right and all be together again....you should know that I am not here either now or even less in holidays to 'enjoy' myself. No, interesting as it in many ways is, I miss you all very much...

In any case, Stuart had to wait for his appointment to be officially confirmed and could not leave Germany until the contract was signed. The Ministry of Education had granted the necessary permission to the University for his appointment, but some delay prevented Stuart being paid. He could only draw his salary in Germany, as currency could not be sent abroad to Ireland. Iseult decided for the time being that she could not leave her mother, and when Stuart heard of this in a letter, he wrote at once to tell her that he would return to Ireland in the autumn. "...it is not really the question of the holidays that worry me so much as next winter. I don't much like the prospect of you all being at home and me here all that time..." He wondered if Iseult might come back with him after the autumn until Christmas, and then return to Laragh to be with Ion who would be home from his boarding school.

Stuart had promised to visit Dr Ruth Weiland, who was translating Madame MacBride's autobiography *Servant of the Queen*, and to check on her progress, but perhaps not surprisingly could not find time to fit the visit in. He had however gone to the Midsummer's Festival at the Olympic Stadium. It was, as he wrote Iseult on 12 June:

a most amazing thing. Such a spectacle and organisation! Thousands of the S.A. with torches. The Hitler Youth Movement in regiments circling the centre of the enormous arena that was floodlit, about 120,000 people there...As for the fireworks with which the celebrations ended, I have never seen anything like them. The explosions were terrific and at moments the whole place was as bright as day. The whole sky was filled with fountains of stars and streaming waves of all colours...At the end thousands of rockets burst and down from them floated huge Swastika flags from rockets...

Impressed by the outwards show of power and strength, Stuart outlined his views of the situation between Germany and the Western Democracies. War would:

be tragic, because the more one thinks the more one is convinced that war would be almost the supreme tragedy...What was hoped here was some ultimate reconciliation between Germany and England in face of communist danger. And this was strongly believed possible up till a year ago. Indeed up till then we Irish were not too popular here! Because they were very keen on this understanding with England. And for that I don't blame them - for the sake of world peace even an English-German alliance would to my mind have been welcome.

Stuart spoke from the Irish Nationalist stance, but he would not draw a parallel between the small size of his own country, and those relatively small threatened nations such as Poland and Czechoslovakia. He concluded, "...since I came here more than ever before I am convinced of the unimaginable terror and horror of war..."

Among the German intellectuals he had met, there were some "remains of anglophilism", but among the "active elements", such feeling was dead. The result was that "Ireland and the Irish get great publicity and are constantly in the news..."

Because of the delay in finalising the contract, Stuart decided to return to Ireland in July, for his return ticket had almost expired. When confirmation of the appointment finally arrived at Laragh in the late summer, Stuart discussed his move with Iseult. The marriage had now reached a stage of "mutual hostility". How seriously he had hoped Iseult would go to Germany is uncertain, but they both had to live apart.

On 3 September, when Stuart was writing in his room at Laragh, Ion ran upstairs to tell him that Britain had declared war on Germany. This only complicated, not prevented any return arrangements, for Ireland had announced a neutral stance.

Stuart did not change his mind, and on 21 September, wrote to Berlin that despite the war, he would accept the appointment. In November, he received a clumsily written letter from Schirmer's secretary, hoping Stuart would come as quickly as possible. Hans Galinsky who had arranged Stuart's appointment with Professor Schirmer had already gone to the front, but with a certain Teutonic efficiency which the war would not hamper, the secretary arranged for Galinsky to write to Stuart from there.

When organising his papers for Germany, Stuart applied for a new passport, to cover the evidence of his previous visit, but he needed an exit visa from London. He decided to plead he had to be in Switzerland for health reasons, and go from there to Germany.

A friendly doctor gave Stuart the necessary certificate which stated his lungs were in poor order, and after repeated difficulties he collected his passport.

Stuart had mentioned the growing publicity Ireland was receiving in Germany. In November 1939, Admiral Canaris, head of Abwehr, the German Military Intelligence, began investigating possibilities of landing German agents by submarine in the Republic of Ireland. Secret exchanges between the Abwehr and the IRA which had taken place during the preceding months, resulted in the first landing of a German spy in the Republic in January 1940.

Until war seemed imminent between Britain and Germany, the Abwehr had little interest in Ireland, and no information about the IRA. When it was declared, neither Germany or Britain had anticipated that the Irish Republic would take a neutral stance, a position which would constantly irk Churchill who had assumed that the British would be able to occupy vital ports in Ireland. He would have been furious had he known that the Abwehr had already taken steps to use the Republic to its benefit.

The German Intelligence had four departments, and the second, Abwehr II, was responsible for contacting discontented minority groups in other countries, a category the IRA obviously fitted.

Early in 1939, Abwehr II asked Oscar Pfaus, the head of their English language territories, to contact the IRA at their Dublin headquarters to establish if they would be interested in collaborating with Germany in the event of war. Pfaus agreed, and arriving in Dublin in 3 February, met Eoin O'Duffy, leader of the Irish Fascists or "Blueshirts" and a former IRA man. O'Duffy now detested the IRA, but introduced Pfaus to their inner circle. After extreme caution on both sides, arrangements were made for Jim O'Donovan a former member of the IRA, to go to Berlin as an emissary, with the possibility of receiving arms for his old organisation. It took him several visits to Berlin to arrange radio contact between the Abwehr and the IRA, which was managed just before the declaration of war.

In the event, the wireless transmitter was technically inadequate, and Abwehr II was annoyed by long periods of silence from the IRA. German Intelligence thought that the IRA's campaign of setting off small explosives in England as rather feeble, and wondered if the IRA was worth bothering about at all.

On 25 August 1939, a time bomb exploded in Coventry in the English Midlands, killing five people and wounding fifty others. The five suspects who were arrested pleaded innocence, but two were found to be guilty, and on 14

December, sentenced to death by hanging. The verdict provoked a surprise raid on the Irish Army's Magazine Fort in Dublin on 23 December, when thirteen IRA lorries carried away 1,084,000 rounds of ammunition without resistance. Abwehr II decided the IRA could be useful after all, and could not know that the arms were later recovered.

The poor transmitter used between the IRA and Abwehr II was unexpectedly seized by the Irish police on 29 December, and a better replacement became urgent. This could only be achieved by submarine, and an agent called Ernst Weber-Drohl, was sent to Ireland with the equipment. Trying to land during a gale, his small boat capsized, sending the radio to the bottom of the sea. It was only a matter of luck that he and the crew, were able to cling to the upturned boat and were washed ashore alive.

While finalising his travel plans, Stuart received a message from the IRA to go to Jim O' Donovan's house near Killarney. The two men waited there for the IRA Chief of Staff, Stephen Hayes, who arrived with a bodyguard and two cars. Stuart disliked the way the meeting was arranged, but agreed to take a message to an address in Berlin. The message was incomplete, and he guessed the rest had been already sent to Berlin. Nevertheless he surmised that it concerned a radio transmitter, and had to be hidden. Iseult sewed his part of the paper into the lining of a warm winter coat, and he was ready to leave Ireland.

In 1924, Stuart had imagined a foreigner arriving in Dublin by aeroplane, from England, and speculated if the visitor would know he was no longer there. He would see:

> the bookshops crammed with the latest English trash in the way of novels; he would hear the latest wireless English programmes while having his tea in his hotel. He might go to the cinema in the evening, and find he had already seen the film a few days ago in London. There would be the slums to remind him of the English slums and the uniform rows of suburban red brick villas... I will only say that that time must never come...

Fifteen years had passed, and little had altered. His

expectations of Ireland were unfulfilled, and the time had come when the stranger would still think he was in England.

Stuart re-affirmed these views in a polemical article headed *Ireland A Democracy? The Real State of Affairs Defined,* published in *The Young Observer* of 1 December 1939. If anyone had troubled to read it, they would have recognized Stuart had more faith in what he calls "The Authoritarian States" than the Democracies.

Declaring that "Freedom is the ideal of the Democracies, according to their public speakers, sociological and political literature and Press", Stuart cited examples of Irish freedom such as poverty and the limited choice of candidates, making "freedom", "blatant nonsense!"

Suggesting the counter argument would be "that at least the goal at which Democracy aims is freedom while that set up by the Fascist and other states is a different one," he continued with a paragraph which contained the essence of his opinion of Germany.

Here a strange fact emerges from the perplexing science of sociology. It is this: the maximum ultimate freedom, spiritual or material for the maximum number in a modern community can never be reached by the apparently direct method of 'laissez-faire'. A government whose policy is largely to "leave people alone" is simply leaving the weaker, the economically or mentally dependent, to the prey of the financially stronger and mentally louder. To in fact, big business and the Press.

I admit that in such a state, many who are favourably situated in the first instance, can achieve a great measure of personal freedom, but this is only at the cost of vast numbers of people being doomed to something the very reverse of freedom...

With such ideals, it is not difficult to understand, how Stuart, wary and apprehensive, looked for an alternative future in Germany, however misguided or mistaken this would prove to be.

Stuart felt particularly sad about leaving Kay behind. She had been with him on visits to the passport office, and too young to understand what was happening, thought it was all a game and an adventure. He had taken one of Kay's small bears with him on his German tour, and had written her amusing letters about it. This time, the bear remained behind.

After spending a few days together in Roebuck House, Iseult went with Stuart to see him onto the boat for London, and rather sadly told him that if he was unable to get the exit visa for Switzerland from England, and had to return, they could do worse than spend the war together. It was an unusual moment of closeness, for they still loved each other in a painful way. If Iseult had asked him not to go to Germany, he would not have left Ireland, any more than he would have spent so much time if London if she had pleaded with him to stay. Iseult had not cared enough, and it was now too late.

As they both walked towards the boat, Iseult chased a rat away. The incident seemed to Stuart, something of an omen, like the bat which had entered his room the night he was born. Nellie Farren who had told him the story, had just died. The only person who had given Stuart secure happiness in his life, had gone into the past.

On the boat to Holyhead, Stuart and the other passengers were questioned by British Intelligence officers, and after looking at Stuart's papers, one jokingly said to him, "I suppose you'll be going on to Germany!". Stuart laughed rather too heartily, but as Iseult had anticipated, he had difficulty in obtaining his Swiss visa in London. This was enough to make him unwilling to risk being caught with the message, and after unpicking the lining of his coat, he removed the paper and destroyed it, and went on to Switzerland. Stuart really thought he had left Ireland without attracting suspicion, but his movements had been watched by Irish Intelligence, who alerted the Ministry for External Affairs, suggesting Stuart was probably trying to return to Berlin. They received the reply "Remember we are neutral."

The University appointment began in early January, but to make the health excuse plausible, Stuart spent a few weeks ski-ing, at the expense of the German Embassy in

Switzerland.

He did not reach Berlin until the end of the month. The city was in total blackout, the sense of war far stronger than in London. It was also bitterly cold, and Stuart spent the first night in a hotel Anhalter Hof which he remembered from his earlier visit. He could only be given a couple of apples, as he had no ration coupons, but the following day he contacted the University who gave him the name of an agency who would find him a flat. Whatever difficulties Stuart faced now, they were not financial. Since he had signed his appointment for the University the previous summer, his salary had accumulated for seven months, and he was comfortably off for the first time in his life.

The agency proposed a large flat on the Nikolsburger Platz, owned by a couple who had had left Berlin in fear of danger. Stuart called there, to be greeted by a prosperous woman who showed him the two bathrooms and eight rooms, which were divided into two wings. Large flats, he was assured were easier to take than anything more modest, and showing him a drawer of silver cutlery, the woman remarked she supposed he would be doing some entertaining. The prospect struck Stuart as ludicrous, as food was already severely rationed, but he decided to take the place. Despite the expense, he still had enough money left to send home to Iseult at Laragh.

On 4 February, Stuart called on the German Foreign Ministry. Hempel, the German ambassador in Ireland had given Stuart a letter of introduction to Ernst von Weizsäcker, State Secretary at the Foreign Office, but his arrival which was unexpected, aroused some suspicion. Stuart hoped to be given a laisser-passer with which he could move freely around Berlin without harassment from the S.S. After a long wait, the Secretary received Stuart in an office, explaining he had been delayed by Von Ribbentrop, Hitler's Foreign Minister.

Weizsäcker was the only high ranking member of the Nazi regime that he would meet during his stay in Germany, and Stuart sensed that he was not a particularly convinced Nazi, but a crypto Anglophile, which later proved to be the case. Stuart was asked what his impression of the mood in London had been, and as he was there during the "phoney war", replied that he "hadn't noticed much of a mood at all." Weizsäcker then asked if he had ever listened to the broadcasts by William Joyce. In fact Stuart had heard him on the wireless at Laragh, often with Liam O'Flaherty. Both were delighted at the outrageous content of his talks, O'Flaherty once remarking that "Joyce was winning the war single handed for Germany."

This Stuart repeated to Weizsäcker, and the frivolous joke was noted down with due seriousness by a secretary. Stuart explained he spoke little German, was a neutral and was given the pass he wanted.

Later, Stuart went to a private house where he was asked for the message from the IRA. He replied he did not have it, but gave it verbally. "My main concern" Stuart told the authorities, "is that when you are in radio communication with the IRA if you would ask them to give a message to my wife to say that I have arrived safely in Berlin."

The officials were friendly but reserved, and indicated that they would have to verify Stuart's identity. He told them he knew an old archaeologist from Dublin, a Professor Fromme, a Nazi sympathizer, who was in Berlin and would vouch for him.

Stuart spoke at length about conditions in Ireland, and according to the Abwehr II Diary detailed the recent "Magazine Raid" and solved the mystery of why the first radio transmitter had been seized by the police:

The representative (ie Stuart) of the Irish agent... who arrived in Berlin at the end of January reported [that] ... Contrary to directions which had been given the transmitter delivered from the USA was not only being used occasionaly for communications with Germany but was also frequently used for internal propaganda purposes. In consequence, the authorities had no difficulty in locating it...

Stuart wrote a message for Iseult which he was asked to place on a grand piano and then left. Fromme, however, called later at his flat to explain he had been contacted about Stuart, and that all was well.

That might have been Stuart's only involvement with German Government authority, for as he experienced, they distrusted outsiders. However, public interest in Ireland about the fate of the two IRA men in the Coventry bomb case, also extended to Germany. At the end of January 1940 the Court of Criminal Appeal in London dismissed their petition, and despite intervention from de Valera, the men were hanged on 7 February, three days after Stuart visited Abwehr II. The New York Times noted on 5 February that "Opinion here is either that two innocent men will hang or that, it is the partition of Ireland and the British who forced these young Irishmen to perpetrate such outrages. Anglo-Irish relations could markedly deteriorate through the hanging of these men."

The same report carried a statement from a former IRA leader, Simon Donnelly:

> We know very well what outcome we want to this war. We want the enemy who has kept our people in bondage for 700 years and who continue to pour insults on us to be pitilessly vanquished. Until such times as the Irish Republic is established, Ireland's youth will continue to sacrifice itself. If the government does not bring foreign overlord-ship to an end, others must be entrusted with the task...

In Berlin the speech must have been read with great satisfaction, for it confirmed that certain Irish people could play a significant part in aiding Germany in the war.

Later in February Stuart was approached by the Ministry of Propaganda, at Fromme's instigation, and asked if he would write broadcasts for transmission to Great Britain and Ireland, and translate German news items into English. Stuart insisted he would not write anti-semitic material, and when told this was not required, he agreed. The British attitude of constant re-iteration in a moral tone that the war was waged according to Christian principles infuriated Stuart. No country with Christian values could possibly enter any war, and he saw the opportunity, rarely given to a writer then, to reach a wider audience than he ever could by his own fiction. Only later, did Stuart learn that his scripts would be read on the air by William Joyce, whom he did not meet until some time after that.

The German Foreign Ministry decided in February 1940 to inaugurate a series of secret radio stations, broadcasting from Germany to Britain, but which would seem to be run by a fifth column in Britain itself. This was an attempt to persuade the British their ideas of National Socialism were wrong, and that the real enemy was not Germany but Britain. The broadcasting centre, or Redaktion where this operated from was the Rundfunkhaus in the Charlottenburg area of Berlin, not far from where Stuart lived.

Joyce threw himself wholeheartedly into this "New Broadcasting Station", but Stuart's involvement there was very slight. When they did meet, contact was kept to the minimum, for Joyce disliked the Irish. For his part, Stuart never cared for Joyce, despising his heavy drinking, but in any case, most of his work for the Redaktion was re-writing news translations into acceptable English.

Stuart used to call at the home of the Irish Ambassador, William Warnock, to hear Joyce read the talks. As he wrote in *Black List, Section H:*

> When it was time for William Joyce's nightly broadcasts, H turned on the set and they heard the English voice with the snarl in it announcing (twice over): 'Germany calling'. The tone was that of retribution being pronounced on a proud and stiff-necked people who had got away for too long with the role of the chosen ones. Lord Haw-Haw's polemics left H cold.

Stuart had insisted in his *Mystics and Mysticism* and in his early fiction, that suffering was necessary for inner enlightenment; he now said "It wasn't the political or military events that concerned him but the possible inner revolution that he hoped the war might bring about...". Joyce was presumably unimpressed with Stuart's work, for he asked to write his own scripts.

Like many other foreigners in Berlin during the war, Stuart found himself in a privileged position, and was given the same value of ration cards as industrial workers. He could buy luxuries from the black market, and procured one of the last wireless sets that could be openly bought. He had only eight hours work at the University a week, and with his pass, travelled freely over Berlin.

Stuart gave a party on St. Patrick's day in a hotel, to which he invited various members of foreign diplomatic corps, Rilke's friend, Hauptmann, a news editor and others. Stuart also particularly asked Warnock, the Irish Charge D'Affaires, because he wanted him to notice that he was establishing his own identity, and knew quite well that Warnock would report his activities to Dublin. Warnock had an awkward relationship with Stuart who was closer to his secretary, Eileen Walsh. The three socialised together, and later in the summer, swam and played golf, but Eileen Walsh kept Stuart informed about Warnock's thoughts about him. Early in April, Fromme introduced Stuart to a Dr. Hermann Goertz, who the Abwehr were training to parachute into Ireland as a spy to contact the IRA. Stuart was extremely cautious when asked to help Goertz with details about Ireland, and was told very little of the actual landing plan. He gave Goertz an Irish pound note, which he wanted Kay to have, and some loose change, suggesting if he was in difficulty, he could contact Iseult at Laragh. Stuart particularly stressed this was to be only in the last resort. Goertz recalled in a statement later published in *The Irish Times* that he:

> quickly took a warm liking to Stuart. Unfortunately I only met him a short time before I flew off to Ireland. He had nothing to do with the Abwehr, he was no politician, he had no contacts with the IRA and not much knowledge about them. But he was a genuine Irish patriot and the prototype of those people who later became my friends in Ireland.

Goertz was a sensitive and kindly man, but a hopeless spy. During a long stay in England in 1935, he was imprisoned for noting aircraft details at a military base. This embarrassment now seemed unimportant to the Abwehr who had at the time complained that Goertz had been arrested because of his own incompetence. They thought he was qualified for his mission because he had spent a long holiday in Ireland. Now his brief was to "[1] Gain the assistance of the IRA in a possible German attack on Britain," and "[2] to enlist their support in severing Ireland's connections with the British Isles..."

On 5 May he left Germany and was flown over Ireland where he dropped in County Meath by parachute. A second parachute, carrying equipment including a radio, landed miles from Goertz who had to abandon his search for it. He was confused and uncertain where he was, and when he met a local man on the roadway, asked what country he was in. With a certain naivety, the man replied "You're in Ireland Sir, and welcome to it!" Goertz gave him Stuart's pound note, but he did not know that the British currency he carried, could then be spent in the Republic. Apparently penniless, he was faced with a seventy mile trudge to Wicklow. Rather than the last resort as he had promised, he decided to make Laragh Castle his first stop.

After discarding some heavy clothing, including his uniform, Goertz took four days to reach Laragh on 9 May. Iseult did not believe Goertz had known Stuart, and was "Not convinced till I tell her more about her husband. Then charming and completely ready to help..."

The spy spent the day in bed, while Iseult went to Dublin to seek advice, after swearing the children to secrecy. She met her mother, and they visited Switzer's, a large department store in Grafton Street, to buy clothes for Goertz. Pretending they were needed for a large invalid, Iseult selected various items including shoes, a lounge suit, and underwear, while Madame MacBride bought a canvas leather bound utility bag in another department. They then had afternoon tea at Roebuck House, where Iseult contacted Jim O'Donovan and all three went back to Laragh Castle.

Apart from the danger, it was pointless for Goertz to remain there, as it would have been easier to make contact with the IRA in Dublin. He was taken to stay with Stephen Held, an IRA member known to Berlin, until a servant became suspicious of various visitors and informed the police. As a result the house was raided and although Goertz escaped by hiding behind a wall, Held was arrested.

The Irish police found Goertz's parachute, his medals, some coded messages, and 20,000 dollars, which Held glibly explained away, claiming they belonged to an imaginary "Heinrich Brandy", a German relation of a dead friend. Meanwhile, Hempel, the German Ambassador in Dublin was quite unaware of Goertz's arrival in Ireland, and innocently reported to Berlin, a newspaper account of Held's arrest and the suspicion that an agent called Brandy had landed.

Hempel was considerably embarrassed when a representative from the Irish Ministry for External Affairs called with the news that Iseult Stuart had been arrested. The clothes purporting to belong to "Brandy", had been traced to her through Switzer's labels. The Irish Government suspected German Embassy involvement in supporting subversive activity against the Irish state, and as Hempel reported to the Foreign Ministry in Berlin he feared:

> a critical undermining of our position here, which is indicated among other things by an unsparing, though objective publication of all details. Since Stuart had friendly relations with us... my personal position is also seriously involved. I fear indiscreet statements in Stuart's letters...Brandy has apparently not been apprehended as yet...

On 23 May, while Iseult was drinking tea in bed, a daily help ran up to her room to say that the castle was surrounded by police. Iseult dressed and let them in, and as she was well known, her interview with the local police was awkward and embarrassing. She was then driven to nearby Bray and questioned for two days at the Police Station by a Superintendent O'Reilly, who was extremely unpleasant. O'Reilly explained to Iseult that she must answer certain questions "...in accordance with the provisions of the Offences Against the State Act, 1939", and the relevant sections were read to her. When asked for her name and address, Iseult replied with a certain humour "You know, don't you, it is Iseult Stuart."

O'Reilly then asked for "...an account of your movements from 10.am to 10pm on Thursday 9 May, 1940," the day she had bought the clothing, to which Iseult replied, as she did to nearly all the other questions, that she needed legal advice before answering. She was taken to Collins Barracks in Dublin on 25 May, where she saw her lawyer. In the afternoon, Iseult was again interrogated by O'Reilly. He showed her clothes which had been found in Held's house, and explained that they:

> were used to prevent hinder or interfere with the apprehension of a person at present unknown who committed the offence of having in his possession instructions, for utilising a means of secretly conveying, receiving or recording information, to wit, a Code or Cipher. This is a scheduled offence under the Offences Against the State Act, 1939. I therefore ask you for whom you purchased these clothes.

It was obvious to Iseult at once that her interrogators knew nothing about the identity of Goertz, and could honestly reply she had no knowledge of Held or his house. She had no idea for whom the clothes were intended, but bought them:

> because I have an account in Switzer's and an old literary friend of both my husband and mine asked me to oblige him by doing so... I did not know he had any political connection. When I realised from your questions on May 23 1940 that there was some suspicion attached to the clothing, I thought it would not be loyal to divulge his name.

O'Reilly pressed Iseult to name the friend, and when asked if she still refused, answered "I'm afraid I must."

Iseult admitted the "friend" had called to collect the clothes, but cleverly avoided implicating anyone else, by explaining that the car he was travelling in had not come up to the hall door because of a bad road and a hill. Certain papers were seized when Laragh was raided, probably brought by Donovan, whom Iseult refused to betray.

She was then charged on two counts. The first for "assisting to interfere with the apprehension of a person who had committed an offence under Section 5 of the Emergency Powers Act of 1939", and the second for having "...failed and refused to give all the information in your possession in relation to the commission by another person of a scheduled offence...", and driven to Mountjoy Prison.

Meanwhile, the children were worried when Iseult was driven off to Bray, and Ion telephoned Madame MacBride to explain what had happened. Unable to come herself because of illness, she asked Helena Maloney to take care of the children, who could be trusted because she had also met Goertz.

While Iseult waited in prison for her trial, set for 25 June, Aunt Janet replaced Helena Maloney at Laragh. Goertz himself was unaware of recent events, and tired of being on the run, turned up once more at the castle where he learned of Iseult's arrest. He remained there for a short while only, hidden in some gorse bushes where the children brought him food, and returned to Dublin where he was sheltered in Dun Laoghaire.

Because of difficulties in amassing evidence, Iseult was not tried before the Special Criminal Court until July 1. She had read statements from various witnesses, including Switzer shop assistants, and the experts who had examined the Code Books and the parachute found at Held's house.

As the trial was held in camera, and access to the records is still withheld, no details are available, but presumably Iseult managed to invent some convincing elaboration of the "literary friend". She was found not guilty and released.

Goertz was eventually captured and imprisoned nineteen months after his landing in Ireland, an extremely long time for a hunted man to be free in a small country. Perhaps the most poignant feature of Goertz's stay in Laragh was the effect he had on Iseult. It seems that she fell in love with him in the short time that they knew each other. They were perhaps drawn together by a common interest in literature and eastern philosophy, but nothing could come of her love, which was probably unrequited. After Goertz's capture, Iseult noted of the spy, "No voice has ever caressed my ears like one which I may never hear again, no smile has so inveighled me."

The hopelessness of the situation heightened Iseult's feelings of complete solitariness, for she realised that she could never have who she passionately longed for. Iseult recalled that when in Mountjoy she had said to herself, "I stand alone." It was bitterly galling to have fallen in love with a man who was now imprisoned, and if ever released, was already married. Stuart always thought Iseult incapable of passion, but he was unable to engage it.

Something of her attitude to Stuart, can be deduced from either a dream or a fantasy Iseult recorded in an undated entry in her diary. She imagined she was being married to Goertz in a Nurnberg Church they both knew well. Kay and Ion are present, as are Stuart and some woman he is clearly in love with. Madame MacBride and all those Iseult has cared for, alive or dead including pets were amongst the guests at the ceremony.

In his novel *Memorial,* Stuart quoted part of the entry, with Iseult as the narrator's dead wife, Nancy, but wrote "Let the identity of the hero of her last fantasy remain secret."

Apart from Iseult's love for Goertz, there is the suggestion that she needed the presence of those at the wedding to approve her action, and it is significant that Stuart is amongst them.

At a simplistic level, Iseult recognized her marriage with Stuart was over, but the guests are described in order of importance. Kay and Ion are first, followed by Madame MacBride, and then Stuart who "...stood quite close with a girl by his side, both tall and slim with grey-green eyes and long mouths, and knowing each others' thoughts without words." Knowing Stuart well, she could not imagine him without another woman, but this only mention of him in her diary is without bitterness or judgement. For herself she concluded, "The watchword is alone. ALONE...".

Iseult, Lily, Kay and Ion

Iseult in her garden at Laragh

CHAPTER 9

Before he left Berlin, Goertz mentioned to Stuart that he knew an Irish girl, a Nora O'Mara, stranded in the city, and half starved. She was working as his secretary, and Stuart met her a few days later in a fashionable cafe. Unable to order something because he did not have enough food coupons, Stuart was touched when Nora O'Mara gave him some of hers. When he saw her again, Stuart realised she was pregnant. Nora had been abandoned by her Ukrainian lover, and was miserably unhappy. Two elderly Russian ladies, let her sleep in their sitting room, but she could not return to the house until they had gone to bed. Nora told Stuart that she was adopted by General Sir Ian Hamilton and only knew that her own father was Irish.

Hamilton had taken a prominent part in the Dardanelles campaign in the First World War on the British side, and it seemed unusual that Nora had now taken a pro-Fascist stance. In spite of British loyalty, he supported Hitler during the thirties, and had brought his wife and daughter to meet him several times in Munich.

When Rudolph Hess landed in Scotland in the hope of meeting the Duke of Hamilton, Nora was certain that he was confused, and had really intended to meet her adoptive father, whom Hess knew rather better than the Duke.

Now that Nora was in such uncomfortable circumstances, Stuart offered her a wing of his flat, where they could lead independent lives, and after a few days she moved in. A few months after Iseult's trial, Nora went to a maternity home, where a girl was born, and returned to Stuart's flat. Restless and bored, she took on a babysitter who would also cook meals for Stuart and herself. With Goertz in Ireland, Nora needed a new job, and when Stuart suggested she could be his secretary at the Drahtlose Dienst, where he prepared the English translations of the news, she accepted.

As far as the war in Europe was concerned, nothing dramatic was happening and Stuart considered asking Iseult and their children to join him in Berlin until a friend in the German Foreign Office hinted that according to Hitler's plans, the "Phoney War" would not last. Unwilling to put his family at risk, Stuart wrote to Laragh to say they would have to wait. By now, Nora and Stuart had drifted into becoming lovers, and a visit by his family would have been impossible. Certain women, either Saints or in the Gospels had a particular personal significance to Stuart, and when he called Nora "Thérèse" after St. Thérèse of Lisieux, he saw in her at least part of the ideal woman he yearned for, one whose nature was both of the divine, and of this world. It had not taken him long to forget Iseult, who never was given such a place or name.

Stuart became friendly with several men who worked in the German Foreign Office. Clismann, who had arranged for Stuart's 1939 visit was now in Berlin, and through him Stuart was introduced to Kurt Haller. Haller called one evening in August 1940 and asked Stuart if he would be willing to sail to Ireland with a German sea captain, in a boat which would purport to be from Breton. Stuart would act as an advance link between the IRA and two Irishmen, whom he learned later were Frank Ryan and Clismann, and who were to be landed in Ireland. The idea did not greatly appeal to Stuart, partly because of the trouble he had taken to come to Germany in the first place, but he agreed because he did not want to be considered a stuffy intellectual, and also because he liked the idea of adventure. The plan was abandoned without explanation, but Ryan was taken in a submarine which nearly reached Ireland, but he refused to land when his companion, Sean Russell former IRA Chief of Staff, and also fleeing Berlin, died unexpectedly.

Frank Ryan had fought in the International Brigade during the Spanish Civil War where he was captured and imprisoned. After intervention by Haller, Ryan was released and brought to Berlin from Paris in early August 1940 to which he returned after his abortive submarine attempt for Ireland.

Ryan was in an impossible position. He had left the IRA to form a workers' revolutionary party, and his Communist sympathies were just acceptable while Germany was still allied to Russia. In Germany, he was considered the IRA representative as long as Stephen Hayes was its Chief of Staff, and given certain privileges such as extra ration cards. Haller told Stuart that Ryan wanted to see him, and after they met, a few weeks later he suggested Stuart should visit prisoner of war camps to find out how British and Irish prisoners were treated.

Taking Nora, Stuart travelled with a Major Rumpel, a friend of Goering, to a camp near Frankfurt. When they met an Irish prisoner from Wexford who wanted to meet Stuart, Rumpel, who was friendly and helpful, left the room with his attendants. The prisoner told Stuart that from what he knew of him from his books Germany was the last place he expected to find him in, and as fictionalized in *Black List, Section H*, suggested that the Nazis are "...the enemy of mankind, I mean of those very human and irrational attitudes and the freedom of thought that you're so committed to in your novels." Stuart explained that he wanted to be "in the company of the guilty that with my peculiar and... flawed kind of imagination" he belonged. The prisoner replied he understood this, if Stuart was at home with the defeated, but "surely not among these vicious brutes." Stuart had assumed Germany would lose the war and he would be with the "defeated", but he was struck by the possibility that if it won, he would be with the victors and on the wrong side.

More than the prison conditions had disturbed Stuart. On the way to the camp, he saw German officials ill-treating Poles. It did not occur to him that what he had seen might only be part of a larger scale of atrocities which he had heard rumours about, and could not accept to be true.

When Stephen Hayes was discredited as IRA leader, he made a written confession in which he claimed "Ryan was... working in conjunction with Francis Stuart doing propaganda work among the Irish soldiers in the British Army who were prisoners of war in Germany." This was completely untrue. Ryan and Stuart had visited a camp for Irish prisoners who indicated they wanted to join an Irish Guard. The plan came to nothing, and Ryan told Stuart he was sorry he had been there at all.

In late August, Stuart was disturbed enough to meet a

Colonel Van Stauffenberg, a relative of the Van Stauffenberg who tried to assassinate Hitler, and spoke to him of the poor prison conditions. He was assured they would be improved to conform with International Red Cross standards. "He is obviously highly intelligent and not one of the habitual prevaricators...." Stuart noted in his diary for August 1940, naively believing that changes would be made.

For his first few months as a stranger in Berlin, Stuart had plunged into a rather hectic life style, as he noted nearly a year later in his diary. He was repeating the pattern of heavy drinking which he had enjoyed in London, and his relationship with Nora had become difficult. There were violent quarrels, and Stuart found it hard to determine when Nora was being truthful, for he felt she often romanticized details of her past life. Their involvement in the war was for quite opposite reasons, and only stressed their incompatibility. Nora was bitter towards the British because she believed they had shot her real father.

While in Dublin, Stuart had made friends with Cudahy, the American Ambassador to Ireland. Transferred to Belgium he had entertained some German Officers after the occupation in 1940, and was dismissed by Roosevelt. He met Stuart in Berlin where he worked as a political correspondent, and they met one evening for drinks. Cudahy had interviewed Hitler, and told him that if he continued to torpedo American ships he would only please Churchill, who wanted America provoked into entering the war.

Stuart thought his remarks extremely incautious, and told Cudahy that if the British Intelligence Service heard of this, he would be in danger. Cudahy thought Stuart was living in the world of *Pigeon Irish* but he had spoken to Hitler about him, and asked if he could bring Stuart as a neutral observer to meet him. Hitler had agreed, and so did Stuart, for he had been drinking champagne. In the morning he was appalled at the suggestion, feeling that "By being taken along and granted an audience, for that is what it came to, I could lose some of what I still considered my spirit of independence as an imaginative writer, though some others might think I had forfeited that already..."

Stuart felt extremely nervous when he went to the

University, and because he suspected that Cudahy's telephones were tapped, did not dare to contact him. Shortly afterwards, Cudahy died in Switzerland, and Stuart was unable to discover how this had happened.

Before Stuart left Ireland, he had planned to translate a book on the life of Roger Casement, *The Forged Casement Diaries,* by William Maloney, who granted Stuart permission to do this. When war broke out, this permission was withdrawn, and instead, Stuart wrote about Casement, drawing heavily on Maloney. This was translated into German by Ruth Weiland, who had previously prepared other books of Stuart's for his German publisher.

Der Fall Casement: Das Leben Sir Roger Casement und der Verleumdungsfeldzug des Secret Service was only published in Hamburg in 1940 and never in English.

Following the theory that the Casement Diaries were forged, the book is unremarkable, except for the final paragraph:

> Casement's name is now immortal in the history of Ireland - raised high over the reach of the repugnant slander of English forgers...
>
> Perhaps one day, no longer lying far away, Irish and German soldiers will stand together before Casement's unmarked grave...to honour the great patriot who has done so much to further friendship between the two nations.

It is difficult to imagine circumstances in which Germany and Ireland could honour Casement's grave, then in a London prison yard, unless Great Britain was defeated by a Germany allied to Ireland. Stuart never saw the finished book, and believes that this final paragraph was inserted either by the translator or the publisher, for he rather ingenuously declared later, that he did not consider what would happen if Germany won the war.

Meanwhile, Iseult was in danger of creating a diplomatic problem. Stuart had not been paid his full salary, and consequently she was living on £15.00 per month. She complained to Hempel in the German Legation in Dublin, who telegraphed the Foreign Office in Berlin to pay Stuart's salary properly, and to ask Warnock to persuade the Irish Government to let the money through. Because of Iseult's part in the Goertz affair, Hempel stressed that Stuart must not tell Warnock he knew of the problems or his intervention with the German Foreign Office, for he did not want his Legation to attract embarrassing publicity.

With the complex personal and political circumstances that Stuart became involved in, the University seemed comparatively mundane. He had been lecturing weekly, apart from holidays, but from his arrival, Stuart refused to wear suits, preferring grey flannels and a fisherman's jersey. If his appearance was casual, the style and preparation of Stuart's lectures was not, for he emphasized that literature was not divorced from life, but should illuminate and enrich the dark interiors of the mind. Stuart read widely for his talks, but had realised that at the time his appointment was discussed, the German professors were anticipating a call-up. Male students were also almost totally absent for the same reason, and Stuart's classes were mainly attended by women.

He was particularly noticed by one student, Gertrud Meissner who was twenty four and who fell in love with the thirty seven year old Irish Professor at once. He had noticed the earnest but good-humoured young woman, who listened carefully to his every word, but although he found her attractive, he paid little attention to her beyond what was expected as a teacher. Later he was aware she understood what he was trying to express in his lectures, entering his interior world in a way no woman had before. Stuart introduced her to art and books she had scarcely heard of, and as they grew closer through shared imagination, they fell in love. Stuart was unable to say anything because of Nora, and for Gertrud who had never been in love before, their meetings were often tortuous. Impulsive and often incautious through enthusiasm, Gertrud longed to express her feelings directly, and was hurt by Stuart's apparent remoteness and detachment. It would take her a long time to learn reserve, and to understand Stuart's need for solitariness.

Gertrud Meissner was not German by birth, but was born

Geoffrey Elborn

in Kashubia in 1915, south of what was then called Danzig, now better known as Gdansk. The Kashubes, an old ethnic tribe were sneered upon, and considered by many Poles to be peasants. Gertrud's father left Poland in 1919 with his wife and four daughters for Lauban in Germany, and taught there until he died of tuberculosis two years later. After the First World War, the Kashubians were forced to accept either Polish or German nationality, and Gertrud's father opted for the German side. In 1929, the Meissners moved to a small suburb near Danzig until 1936, when they went to Berlin to find work.

Dark haired, lively and with a strongly independent mind, Gertrud did not want to teach, as her mother had wished, and planned instead to go to University. After a year on a secretarial course, followed by various unsatisfactory jobs, Gertrud agreed to enrol as a teacher after her mother made life impossible. As she had anticipated, she was bitterly unhappy there, and ran away after only a few weeks to stay with her eldest sister in former Poland near the Russian border. For once, Frau Meissner understood Gertrud's unhappiness, and agreed she could go to University only because she wanted her home. Like Stuart, she arrived at Berlin University for the first time in January 1940, but while the State paid her fees, Gertrud needed a job to pay for her keep. Fate seemed to have intervened in a doubly benevolent manner, when, in December 1940, Stuart offered her a job as his typist at the radio station.

With the routine imposed by the University and the news translations Stuart felt like an office worker, as his days were planned for him. When he had free time, he often played golf, or drifted in the evenings to parties. He had become friendly with the Hungarian writer Gunther Weissenborn and his wife, who entertained lavishly in their flat on the Nurnberger Strasse. One evening in April 1941, when Stuart and Nora were there, they met Lala Anderson of Lili Marlene fame, and also Lt. Harold Schultze-Boysen and his wife Libertas. Schultze-Boysen was a striking figure with long blond hair, and the grandson of the Grand Admiral von Tirpitz. He was attracted to the Left, but despised both Nazism and Communism. Unknown to Stuart, the couple were leading members of the Soviet Secret Service Intelligence, the Rote Kapelle. Schultze-Boysen had infiltrated Goering's research office, which specialized in tapping telephones, and set up a large espionage centre for Russia. He also planted friends in every ministry and military department in Berlin.

Stuart liked the Lieutenant because he was an idealist and had been inspired in his youth like Stuart, by revolutionary poetry. They exchanged addresses, which would have repercussions later. (Stuart has said that Libertas Schultze-Boysen surprised him by memorising, not writing down his telephone number, but she did note his address).

It was not until after the war that Stuart learned of his friends' secret life, but there may have been talk about Russia at the party, for he seriously considered leaving Berlin for Moscow at this time. He was finding life extremely complicated, sharing his flat with Nora, and also seeing Gertrud. Gertrud herself was driven to distraction by her feelings for Stuart, which she believed to be one-sided, and decided she could not work for him. Explaining she would find a job elsewhere, she had to be content with Stuart's plea that he needed her and she must not leave. He had always hoped to find a particular woman where spiritual union would be intensified by sexual fulfilment. He was almost certain he had found her in Gertrud, but he had thought the same about Nora, and was still guarded. At last on 28 May, during dinner, Stuart told Gertrud that he loved her.

(As Gertrud disliked her first name, after a time in her relationship with Stuart, she changed it to Madeleine, for their private use. For consistency, Madeleine is used from this point throughout, although it was not until the 1950s that the name was permanently adopted.)

Just how committed Stuart was to Madeleine at this point is uncertain. Undoubtedly he loved her, but with thoughts of moving to Moscow, he could not have taken her, as she was Polish as far as the officialdom was concerned. She would have found it difficult to leave her mother, and also her studies.

At the very least, Stuart was confused. He later ridiculed

himself for wanting to go to Moscow, but then he hardly stopped to examine the practicalities involved, or even his motivation. He would have found Russia unacceptable, but that was part of the reason why he wanted to go. Stalin was, to Stuart, a more powerful hero to replace Hitler with.

Stuart also taught English language at the Berlin Technical College, and amongst the students, were some young Russians who joined him for coffee or a drink after a class. Cautiously, he hinted about his idea of leaving Berlin, and was told he would be welcomed in Moscow. He was given a name to contact at the Russian Embassy, which was not far from where Stuart lived, and he called to make the initial arrangements to move. He hoped he would be given an appointment in Moscow University, and was told on a second visit that his application was in the last stages of being processed. When he was due to collect exit papers, Germany invaded the Soviet Union on 22 June, and exodus from Berlin even for an Irish neutral was impossible.

Stuart was not free of Nora, and as the relationship had at its best been very intense, he found it difficult to leave it easily. Madeleine now knew about her, and would not tolerate her presence in the same room without acute jealousy. They had occasionally met, and for Stuart's sake, managed to be polite. When they had to work together at the Redaktion, Nora once deliberately dictated too quickly to annoy Madeleine, which provoked a nasty shouting scene.

The situation was abruptly brought to an end, although not resolved, when Stuart returned unexpectedly to the flat. As he had no keys, he repeatedly rang the door bell. After a while Nora came to the door, and Stuart asked why she had taken such a long time. Nora seemed confused and asked if he really had been ringing. She made various excuses, insisting that Nadeshka, her child had been howling. Stuart was convinced she was in bed with a man he knew of, and challenged Nora with his name. Nora retaliated that he was "only saying this because you're tired of our relationship and want it to end."

To reflect on his problems, Stuart planned a holiday in Munich in mid-July 1941. It was an unsettling time for Nora who was trying to salvage something of her life, and according to Stuart, was considering a career as an actress again. She had enough money to have her daughter looked after, but dreaded any change, including Stuart's Munich visit. The night before he left, Nora clung to him sensing they would separate when he returned. When Stuart left, she was in despair.

Stuart too, was isolated and depressed in Munich. When a parcel arrived from Nora, containing a cake, and a copy of Mann's *Death in Venice* he felt momentarily relieved that the parcel symbolized the end of their affair. Compelled to go on to Vienna, where he had been with Nora in the previous year, he recalled the distant and painful memories of his visit with Iseult in 1921. After a day at a racecourse some miles from the centre, he returned to his hotel, where he felt intensely miserable. For the first time since he had arrived in Germany, Stuart forgot his own problems and began to understand the horror the war had for others, "... that the intensity of his own private life had kept him largely insulated from...".

In less than a month, Germany had begun the invasion of Russia under "Operation Barbarossa," with the intention of destroying the Soviet Army. When Stuart heard that innumerable Russians were marched off to Camps, he realised that they were deprived of compassion, and perhaps worse, were without hope. Stuart was honest enough to record his own slowness in recognising the significance of suffering in others, but it emphasises how he had to exclude what seemed irrelevant to him, in his obsessive concern with his own life and the way he managed it. He would not attempt to understand himself through the experiences of others, and could only achieve enlightenment through the intensity of relationships.

He had wanted Madeleine to join him in Vienna, but as her mother knew nothing of their association, she could not leave Berlin, and had to wait for his return in mid-September.

Once in Berlin, Stuart gave up the flat he had shared with Nora for she had moved elsewhere. New rooms in the Rankestrasse, gave him a sense of tranquility he had not known for some time, and after a few days, he and Madeleine became lovers for the first time.

Madeleine did not care what her mother said now. She had found Stuart, and would never look anywhere else for love. How much he had quarrelled with Iseult and Nora because they were strong willed, and refused to conform to his ideals can only be guessed. In Madeleine he had found one young enough to be responsive and so much in love with him that she was desperate to please and accept even his self centredness.

Since he came back from Vienna, Stuart had stopped his translating work for the English radio station, and was transferred to the Irish station in a new building. He worked with Madeleine for Dr. Hans Hartmann who was responsible for broadcasts to Ireland, and they were well paid. The money which accumulated was almost useless, as it could not be spent without coupons. As Stuart was not allowed to increase the amount he sent to Iseult, he used some of the money to buy a large ugly gold ring, in case of a future emergency.

The invasion of Russia had first awakened Stuart to the truth about Hitler. He was shocked by the anti-semitic conversation of Nazi officers he overheard in Berlin. Particular Jews he recognized, who had been forced to wear the yellow star, would later simply disappear, a situation which Stuart was slow to draw any conclusion from. At no time in any interview about his period of Germany, would he make a point of condemning Hitler for the atrocities of the concentration camp, beyond saying that he was disturbed by the photographs he saw in Freiburg after the war ended. However frequently he was asked to give reasons for going to Germany, Stuart was always consistent in his answer. When he was questioned by Emanuel Kehoe in 1978, "did he support the Nazis ?" Stuart replied that "it's hard to say. It's always difficult to go back and try to be honest about it... I saw Hitler as a... super dissident if you like, which he wasn't as it turned out. He was ultra-conservative, as I later saw. I mean he was a supporter of everything that we disliked most, leave out whatever atrocities came into question..."

Stuart had once believed the super-hero or super-dissident was Hitler. But Hitler who had proved corrupt, could never fit the pure heroic mould as defined by Stuart. He experienced unpleasantness first hand when early in 1942, the Gestapo arrested the Schultze-Boysens after penetrating their underground movement, and found Stuart's telephone number in a notebook. The Gestapo called round at his flat, questioned the doorkeeper, and left. Stuart tore the pages out of his earlier diaries in which he mentioned the Schultze-Boysens, in case the Gestapo returned to search his flat.

The first diary entry of Stuart's which survives, notes that in March 1942 he was "...asked to give radio talks to Ireland, speaking this time myself. This is better and for a time at least there are things I would like to say." The broadcasts Stuart made, would prove the most controversial action of his life, but in later years, he never defended or excused his actions.

It may be argued that Stuart was in a sense defending his own position in a review of Stephen Spender's *The Thirties and After* in October 1978, when he noted that between the wars:

> Nearly all the writers in English, except the outstanding ones, were committed to left-wing politics...Yeats, Lawrence, Pound, Eliot and, more ambiguously, Joyce, were distrustful of the principles of democracy because it seemed to them, not unreasonable, to promote and prosper mediocrity. None of them, I imagine, supposed seriously that dictatorships did not tend to do the same...Neither Fascism, nor anti-Fascism, Marxism nor Capitalism, has ever inspired any worthwhile writer. Leslie Fiedler pointed out... that when a writer starts taking specific 'anti' attitudes, no matter how morally justified, he compromises the interior vision in which his 'alternative worlds' are formulated. Nothing less than a total 'No!' is what he is impelled to give in rejection of all ideologies; institutions, consensuses, hallowed customs, general assumptions...

Inevitably, the name of Ezra Pound is often invoked with Stuart's, a writer who broadcast during the war from fascist Italy and was accused of treason. Any comparison suggests mutual political motivation, and without digressing into Pound's career, his confused understanding of economics led him into a naive alliance with Fascism which had nothing in common with Stuart's reasons for broadcasting. Stuart's own interpretation of the poet in a review, tells us how he eventually understood his own reasons for broadcasting to Ireland, if one substitutes his name for that of Pound.

I believe that Ezra Pound's violent involvement in political ideology was primarily a means, largely instinctive and subconscious, of deepening his alienation as an artist, he being the kind of writer... who requires isolation, even condemnation, from and by his society to reach the peaks of which he is capable... Pound was conscious of the over lapping of the concept of artist and criminal. He had an instinct that his poetic destiny involved social ostracism...It was Pound's subconscious urge to become an outcast, so seemingly irrational and self destructive that it takes another artist to recognise (as Sartre does in the case of Genet) which impelled him to churn out... his wartime broadcasts.

The nature of the "things" Stuart felt he "would like to say" were proposed in his first broadcast on St Patrick's Day 1942, which was preceded by an introduction by Hartmann, who began, "Tonight at 20.45pm. German Summer Time, that is to say at 9.45 pm. Irish time, the well known Irish writer, Francis Stuart will speak over our usual stations ..." Stuart opened his talk with:

I'm glad to have this opportunity of saying a few words...I want to make it clear that by speaking to you I'm not trying to make propaganda. You can hear as much of that as you want...you have a good idea of what is true and what is false. I, the writer, do not want to add to this sense of propaganda, if I'd wanted to I could have done so during the two years...here in Germany. But my only desire is to put before you very simply my idea about Ireland, a place in the world...

Much of the broadcast could not be monitored, possibly due to a faulty microphone, (as the Irish Intelligence Service noted on their transcription) but from the few detatched sentences, Stuart wanted to emphasize Ireland's place in Europe, rather than as part of Britain. Apart from the inaudibility, there was nothing particularly memorable about the talk and Stuart makes no comment in his diary about it, beyond noting that Madeleine had found what he said full of warmth.

When he broadcast on 5 April, he continued with the Irish Nationalist argument, hinted at in March, and appealed to the Irish patriotism over the Easter Rising of 1916 suggesting that:

> Had those few men not thrown down the gauntlet in Dublin, Ireland's position would be very different today... The spirit of Easter Week is the one thing which will bring us safely through this crisis.
>
> Please God, we shall be able to remain neutral to the end, but if we were to fight it would certainly not be for any so called ideal.
>
> We, knowing what lies behind them have had enough of those to make us sick. God preserve us from all such cant, for us Irish there is only one reality, our own life on our own soil free from the tyranny of money.
>
> I hope and believe that the end of this war will give us back our national unity and that the struggle which began in its latter phase on that Easter morning in Dublin will then be, at last, at an end.

The noise of falling bombs made Stuart's talk inaudible, but he was undeterred by danger. For he would reiterate in later broadcasts, ideas of "vision" and "energy", words which he used in his diary to plan changes to his own outlook.

Away from Laragh, he determined his life would take a new direction, and he would try to understand, through painful self- examination, his relationship with Madeleine. Whatever mistakes Stuart had made with Iseult and other women, he was strongly aware of his failure and for perhaps the first time, realised that a change of attitude and behaviour had to come from him.

Madeleine was impulsive and constantly demanded attention, and if Stuart failed to respond, he was accused of being lukewarm. It was a familiar charge from Nora, who like Madeleine, sulked if Stuart could not express on demand the tenderness expected of him. To worry about it was the wrong approach, for,"These things cannot be thought out. They must be 'felt' out. By 'thinking' I can never get inside her and see from her feelings..."

Stuart was convinced that if he was guided by a certain "inner" vision, he would avoid the mistakes of the past, both in his personal life and in his own writing. With a greater reliance on imagination and emotional experience, Stuart thought he would write a different kind of fiction, one where: "there must be no forcing. All must come from the central core which I have now found...". The broadcasts would simply be another means of expressing part of this truth. He did not doubt that whatever he felt deeply from within could be anything but the truth, and excited by this discovery, had to share it.

More mundanely, Stuart and Madeleine visited Frank Ryan whom they had not seen for over a year. He was glad to see them, and after a glass of vodka gave Stuart some Irish newspapers and extra food, for supplies were short. Madeleine went to visit her mother on 23 April, who demanded her back home. Stuart felt over anxious, probably remembering Iseult's constant visits to Madame MacBride. But Madeleine's mother had been appalled when her other unmarried daughter, Traute became pregnant, and treated her so unkindly, that she left home. Stuart had admired Madeleine's sister for being loyal to her boyfriend and praised her too much to Madeleine, who realizing the implication about herself, rushed off to comfort her mother. Two days later, Madeleine came back to Stuart saying she wanted to live with him and would stay until they found a flat together.

The turmoil of the week nervously exhausted Stuart, who was in no mood to write much about his fortieth birthday, which he celebrated with Frank Ryan, the Clissman's and Madeleine. "Forty yesterday." Stuart wrote in his diary on 30

April, " Youth gone. Do I regret it ? I do not much regret it. The part I regret is the pure physical part, the health and strength which cannot be so great. But I know that what is gained is worth the price of that..."

He was pleased when *Die Woche,* serialised *The Coloured Dome,* and although well paid, the money was useless to Stuart in Berlin, but could now be sent home to Iseult. Letters from Laragh were rare, and with censorship, there was little that they could say.

After a while Ryan formed an attachment to Madeleine's sister Gretel. This made Madeleine moody, who had a serious quarrel with Stuart ostensibly because he joked about her English. Realizing how much he had hurt Madeleine, he pondered the best course :

> To be gentle and understanding. But not to submit to this subtle form of bullying. All the same to remember always how deeply deeply true she is...no-one was ever so loving and devoted to me. Not even Iseult...For there was at first her mother whom not to hurt and whom she would deny me to. As I remember one night at Roebuck how she did not like that her mother knew she was in the room with me after she had thought she had gone to her own room. That was always from the first...I had failed her very much too. Not that *au fond* it is a question of failing but of a capacity for that passion of love, which Iseult never had and did not believe in. But S.(Madeleine) would never deny me to anyone. Though she is not married to me.

As far as the war was concerned, Stuart thought it would end by the following year, and when he read some Irish newspapers, he felt "a strong atmosphere of home..."

On 16 July Stuart considered an offer to broadcast on a regular basis to Ireland. There had been about four broadcasts since the first transmission on St Patrick's Day, but although he said nothing to advance the German cause, Hartmann considered he could be useful. Less sure than before, Stuart noted:

> Talking with Hartmann on telephone and asked to give a twice-weekly broadcast from the Irische Redaktion. Said I

would let him know in a day or two. It is difficult (though not impossible) to refuse. I do not feel any strong desire for this business. But might do so for a bit. I have not much illusion about its effectiveness, which in the mass of radio broadcasts would be very small...

As the University term was nearing the summer vacation, and would not resume until November, Stuart had plenty of time to think of what he might say in such talks. Eventually he agreed, fully aware of what he was doing. He recalled:

a nice old German in the Foreign Ministry advised me very much against broadcasting. He said that it would be guaranteed to stop publication of my books in English. But I somehow felt the necessity to broadcast. I could never be a writer in the bosom of society. Being in Germany was one thing, lecturing at Berlin University was bad enough - but going over to the other side of the street, slinking down a street, was something a writer could not do in peacetime...

However naive it might seem after the event, Stuart did not care about protecting himself, but deliberately wanted to expose himself to humiliation. In his self probing, he had now reached a disturbing personal crisis, which directly related to his decision to broadcast. The day after Stuart spoke to Hartmann on the telephone, he noted the main details of his life. "Looking back over my life," he wrote, "I see how little peace and quietness and security there has been. Beginning at ten, when, terrified, I was sent away to school, it has gone on ever since...". The lengthy passage in Stuart's diary is a sincere attempt to be honest with himself, for not only does he refer to Iseult "and all the upset and suffering, as well as joy, of that", but believed he only felt contented from 1924 to 1926. The diary entry summarises the un-fulfilled years, and perceptively analyses his own weakness and failures. Of the years when he began writing his novels, he felt that he had been:

working too much. Too isolated and the reaction of hectic plunging into the world. The mad vain search for fulfilment

through [various women]. Racing. Sunnymova and Galamac.
Trying to find fulfilment in the excitement of that and in the
mad hope of large winnings. Drink too. Then having finally
given up betting, drink and the rest, I came here and was
plunged into another kind of whirlpool out of which I am
only now perhaps emerging...

His obsessive years of turning "more and more to religion"
were partly motivated by his unhappy marriage, and the
hope of finding inner peace as an alternative. That approach
had been too intellectual. Now he was finding contentment
in Madeleine, he resolved to isolate himself with greater
determination from "the outer world", to try to find "The
secret, heavenly Jerusalem" (where) "...the only excitement
left is through God..."

This statement of beliefs, from one about to broadcast from
Germany, might seem at the least paradoxical and
incompatible. On a conscious level he understood the "moral"
question. But he wanted to publicize his understanding of
"inner truth", a way of thinking without which there could be
no new Europe of any value. He did not seek fame, and knew
he would find disgrace. The talks would concentrate on the
prevailing obsession with materialism, and the content
would evolve from Stuart's own personal quest. He had been
greatly impressed by *The Plumed Serpent* which he was
teaching at the University, and noted that Lawrence's
"Divine Eagle has the power to overcome the whole almost
endless edifice of falsity with which we have surrounded and
smothered the inner flame of life..."

CHAPTER 10

On the 5 August 1942, Madeleine announced, on the radio, "Next we would ask you to give your attention to Francis Stuart who every week at this time will take a topical subject or scene through Irish eyes." Sounding nervous, Stuart began:

> This talk is a kind of introduction to a series that I hope to broadcast to you at weekly intervals, it is certainly not that I have any desire to join the ranks of the propagandists but I believe that neither you nor I have the right to cut ourselves off from the storm that is raging around us no matter how much we may feel inclined to do so.
>
> Being neutral does not mean to remain unaffected by, or insensitive to events that are going to determine the sort of civilisation that is about to develop in Europe. In this series of talks I hope to comment on some of these events and tell you some of my ideas as they affect Ireland, but first I think it would be no harm if I were to explain very briefly my motive in doing so...

He continued that he had not come to Germany to be involved in the war, but of his own free will, and that his main reason "was the very same one that has driven millions of other Irishmen to leave their native land - the necessity of earning a living." He emphasized what would be a recurring theme, that he was:

> heartily sick and disgusted with the old order under which we've been existing and which had come to me from the great financial powers in whose shadows we lived.
>
> If there had to be a war then I wanted to be among these people who had also had enough of the old system and who moreover claimed that they had a new and better one... I had begun to see that no internal policy for Ireland could ever be completely successful unless joined to an external one that [would not(?)] shed our ancient links with Europe and European culture...

Since he arrived in Berlin his feelings and ideas once "vague", were now clearer, but he feared:

> this relationship between Ireland and Europe, above all between Ireland and Germany as a one sided case. I not only want to bring something of Germany and German ideas to you but I also try in the Berlin University and elsewhere, to make people here and especially young Germans conscious of Ireland and interested in her problems and outlook.

Aiming to show that Germany was interested in Irish culture, Stuart mentioned that both he and O'Flaherty had novels serialised in German newspapers, and then indulged in unashamed sentiment about Ireland of a kind he had never sincerely believed in.

> at times I get such a longing for home, for that peculiar atmosphere that is symbolized in different ways for each of us. I see again the Antrim boglands where I spent my boyhood, a small farmhouse and a row of trees around one side of it for shelter and a bicycle leaning up against a whitewashed wall. I feel now that the very mud on the tyres of that bike is sacred and at such times even to speak to you at home - some of you perhaps listening to me from that very bogland - is something.

Stuart wanted his talks to have a wide audience, and by evoking Aunt Janet's farmhouse, hoped to attract uncomplicated country people and not just the sophisticated or well educated. Rather than launch into his beliefs at once, lest he deterred any potential listeners, Stuart stressed that by distancing himself in Germany, he could perhaps appeal to people as individuals, rather than parties or movements.

> It is true that only a comparative few of us at home had a clear vision of Ireland as a nation; most of us have simply not that gift; most of us are too busy farming or shopkeeping or being politicians to have much conscious idea of our national destiny.

All that matters is that there are always a few with enough vision and energy to plan for the whole nation but it is not to this section or that that I want to address these talks.

It is to as many of you as will listen to me whether you have much interest or not in the problems of Europe, there is only one thing that I take for granted in you... and that is what you think strongly about Ireland even if it is only a few small fields or a line of hills. I want to speak to all of you who have that feeling of some corner of our country. As to those comparative few who not only love Ireland but who are ready to sacrifice all for the freedom of Irish soil, I do not flatter myself that I can teach you anything.

I will only say this that you may now feel isolated and alone but have patience - the past has belonged to the politicians and the financiers, the future is going to be yours.

What kind of future that was, Stuart did not say, but an announcement stated that he could be heard at the same time the following week, at 9.30 in the evening. For those who did not switch off, there was some Finnish folk music, followed by a propagandist play set in Ireland.

Stuart was dissatisfied with his talk, which he had altered at Frank Ryan's suggestion, and had not read it well. He hoped to improve, but his thoughts continued on Ireland when he received a letter from Samuel Beckett in Paris. "...He seems to be living there even more cut off from Ireland and isolated than am I. One of the small number of those from days of peace with whom I had something in common..." Stuart had written a novel called *Winter Song*, which he hoped to publish in Berlin. The manuscript had to be submitted to the Ministry of Propaganda, and on 20 August he heard permission for publication had been refused. He had few illusions about Nazi ideals now, and wrote bitterly in his diary that day, "The Propaganda Ministry has no interest in nor knowledge of truth, indeed Propaganda departments are in a deep way perhaps the very worst feature of modern war, or peace too..."

Bitter about Germany, he was outraged when he heard that six IRA members who were found in a Belfast house, were all sentenced to death for the murder of a policeman. As all men were present at the shooting, all had to hang for the one who had committed the crime. The case was well publicised, and Sean MacBride set up a reprieve committee to influence a repeal.

Commenting for the first time about Irish politics, in his broadcast for 30 August, Stuart complained about the presence of American troops in Ulster, but wanted to:

> send you the sympathy of the many Germans who have spoken to me of the fate of the six Irishmen condemned to be hung in Belfast. It is the first time that I have ever been asked to say something in these talks to you and I do it very gladly because I know the people who have asked me and I know that their feeling comes from their hearts.
>
> I am not going into the question of the trial. The accused men all denied the only charge which would have given their captors the slightest excuse on legality to do what they intend to do. Perhaps the facts are possibly simple. These Ulstermen, whose corner of Ireland is overrun with foreign troops, whatever views there may be about the diplomacy of their action...was a natural one.

The remainder of the talk was addressed to Churchill, asking him to use his influence to reprieve the six men, and to remind him that:

> for its size, Ireland has poured out more blood, tears and sweat than any other nation...we do not know whether having asked your own people for such endurance, you believe you can give a final recompense, that is not our affair. What is our affair is that Irish blood, sweat and tears should not have been spilt in vain. And we tell you now that the blood of those six Irishmen will be about the last that you and your fellow statesmen will have the opportunity to spill within the seclusion of prison walls.

If the British Prime Minister found the bombing in London difficult to endure, Stuart speculated how much longer seven hundred years of suffering at the hands of Britain had been to Ireland, and concluded:

You may think that the lives of six Irishmen are unimportant compared to the thousands being lost on the fronts which you yourself are directing, but to us it is not yet the matter of six more added to the thousands and millions of Irish lives lost directly or indirectly through the domination of our country by yourself. This river of Irish blood, tears and sweat is now, whether you like it or not, going to [be spilled?]

It was quite unlikely that Churchill heard his talk, but Irish Intelligence was carefully transcribing what was not indistinct, and probably passed a copy to the Dublin Government. For when Stuart applied to have his passport renewed, the Charge d'Affaires in Berlin told him the Irish Government refused to authorize it. The Charge d'Affaires explained he could reapply, but Stuart considered this a waste of time.

While the fate of the IRA men was being considered, Stuart went for a week to Vienna with Madeleine. It was a year since he was there alone, and began his ill-fated *Winter Song*. He was glad to have company, but realised he could not:

> continuously live in close contact with anyone, even S.(Initial of pet name for Madeleine). I must be a lot alone. I must be independent and this independence hurts S. all the more because like nearly all women (and perhaps all the more, the more they are capable of deep love) she expects me to be absorbed by her. But I can only be absorbed by her at times. But of all people she is the one closest and dearest to me. That I must not forget when, through irritation and more than that...I long to be alone again...

A few days before Stuart returned to Berlin, just one of the men in the IRA case was executed on 10 September, a fact Stuart was unaware of. His thoughts in any case were about Madeleine. Despite being:

> closer to her than ever before...nothing outward, even like being in Vienna with S. can give me happiness. Happiness

lasting longer than an hour or two can only come from being in communion with the supreme truth. Once having tasted that secret joy, all others of the earth are a bit spoilt... not that my love of S. is, at its highest, of the earth...

Nevertheless, when Madeleine went to stay with her mother for a while, Stuart missed her greatly, and thought positively about the good that she was doing him:

I can see that among the many essential things I have gained from her, the being cut off from unessential people, especially women has been a great thing. All that terrible social falsity! Though I was fairly free of it, not enough so. Now I am really quite free and see almost no-one unless I want...

Stuart had spoken to Frank Ryan, who had refused to broadcast himself, and tried to warn him about the nature of the Nazi regime. Determined "to do something about the Irish position" Stuart ignored Ryan's opinion. "As far as F. [Frank] goes, I see a tendency to... stagnate in 'conferences' talks and side issues. Not that I have not admiration for F. and all his activity of the past," Stuart wrote, "but he is obviously tired, isolated and a bit apt to attach undue importance to bureaucracy..."

Ryan's deafness made conversation difficult, and Stuart had to prepare a short memorandum of his ideas. At least something Ryan had said made Stuart consider, "for the most part, I see that all this is not my work, and I must not become too involved. But at the same time, it is right for me to do something..."

In September, Ryan, Stuart and another Irish broadcaster called John O'Reilly, or "Pat O'Brien" discussed what stance Stuart should take in his talks. Neither were of the slightest help, and Stuart came to regard Ryan as "an example of the tyranny" he wished to escape. His attitude to the Nazi regime was ambiguous, for with his aptness to "attach undue importance to bureaucracy," he made friends with "some very nasty people", including Dr. Edmund Veesenmayer, who was later promoted to a higher position in Czechoslovakia "and did away with a lot of people..." as Stuart recalled.

He never seriously considered what would happen if Germany won the war, beyond the thought that "if I had really asked myself in a sober mood in 1940 whether I wanted a German domination of all Europe, I don't think I would have desired that." "Who speculated very much on it was Ryan," Stuart remarked later. "I was never, to be quite frank, greatly taken with Ryan... I remember walking down to lecture at the University, and Ryan walked with me, and he was in one of his moods. And I had disagreed with him, or something, and he said 'You know, Frank,(ie. FS), when Germany wins the war, I will be a member of the Irish Government,' as though I had better keep in with him. That annoyed me, but I didn't say a word. I thought it somehow, very brash. He would have been, had Germany won the war."

In late September, Stuart realized that apart from talking with Ryan and O'Reilly, he had spoken no English, for Madeleine was still staying with her mother. Stuart had to speak German which he disliked, and could use only superficially. When he was with Madeleine they always spoke English, even in public places and once were accosted by someone when they were in a restaurant, who challenged them with the remark, "How can you be speaking the native language of the enemy?" Madeleine replied that Stuart was not an enemy, but an Irish neutral who had come to Germany at great risk to lecture there, and how dare the man say anything about it. Surprisingly, he apologized meekly, which Stuart thought would be difficult to imagine, if the German language had been overheard in London.

Meanwhile, Stuart had news of Nora O'Mara, when he called to see her Russian friends. She had been taken ill, and gone to Munich, and had apparently given up the idea of having an acting career.

Of more immediate concern was Madeleine, whose mother had taunted her to make the best of Stuart, because once the war was over, he would return to Ireland. Madeleine had written in despair about this, aware that she could not have the security of marriage in their relationship. Stuart vowed in his diary that whatever happened he would not leave her. "That may seem a rash thing to say, looking back. But I say

it solemnly and knowing all the difficulties..." It was a
promise that would be severely tested, but for the time being
Stuart could only look forward to Madeleine's return the
following week, when they drank wine saved from Vienna,
and read books together.

Stuart found it difficult to endure too much either of his
own company or that of Madeleine's. If they went anywhere,
she became jealous and wanted his undivided attention, and
if he spoke to friends, she created unpleasant scenes. At
times Stuart could not cope, for he was not "...a young man,
unformed, uncertain," and thought it pointless "being
uselessly tormented. There is no good being made to feel
guilty because of expectations that I can't fulfil."

In the midst of the confusion of trying to come to a rational
understanding of his life, Stuart wondered if he should live
with Madeleine at all. He could not become what she wanted
him to be, for, "I am what I am, I have gone through fire and
worlds of demons and the long struggle with my own
weaknesses and treacheries and have come out..."

Madeleine knew of Stuart's reputation with other women,
and to safeguard herself, wanted him to "live as a hermit,
going nowhere, meeting and speaking to practically no-one."
While he saw the value of a reclusive life, "for those who are
'called to it' as they say in pious books, that is not altogether
my way. I want some support in the times that are coming
and not another battle to wage as well as the outer one..."

Two days later, on 16 December, Stuart allowed his
personal anxieties to influence his sense of the rational. In
his broadcast that evening, he praised Hitler and what he
had done for Germany, a complete reversal of his distaste for
Nazis which he had already stated in his diary. Stuart does
not believe he was under any pressure to broadcast what he
did about Hitler, although he was unable to state the real
feelings of his diary. He may have still been fooled by Hitler,
but whatever the circumstances, his outburst was
inexcusably blinkered. Recalling the years in Ireland before
the war he said:

everywhere I heard...jeers at Hitler...jokes about the new
Germany. Like most Irishmen, I have no time for secondhand

opinions...I began to find out something about Hitler and the new Germany, and...was completely fired with enthusiasm, for here was someone who was freeing life from the money standards that dominated it... here was someone who had the vision and courage to deny financiers, politicians and bankers the right to rule...it seemed to me at least preferable to be ruled by one man whose sincerity for the welfare of his people could not be doubted, than by a gang whose only concern was the market price of various commodities in the world market. I was under no illusion as to our position in Ireland; we might have a certain political freedom but very very little social freedom, and life in Ireland was largely based on money standards just as in England and in America...

As a remedy, Stuart told his listeners that to build an Irish future, there had to be "...a break from partition, a break away from the system of life which is dominated by money and a turning towards Europe." By this he presumably meant some system of National Socialism, but after stating there were "difficulties in the way of this", had no time in the broadcast to explain how the turning towards Europe was to be achieved.

The talks were becoming monotonous and repetitive, and Stuart seemed unable to decide what he wanted to say, or how to vary the content of his message. A few days later, Stuart was given an old copy of the British magazine, *Picture Post,* for 11 April 1942, which mentioned the broadcasts in an article by the English literary critic Cyril Connolly:

The question which puts out all Irish conversation is "How do you think you would fare after a German victory?" One or two may believe in the freedom of prosperity promised to the Celtic races by Hitler and Ireland's Haw-Haw, Frances (sic) Stuart, but most, however anti-British, are left without a reply...

Stuart was not without a reply, in his diary for the nineteenth of December he commented that the *Picture Post* had:

said the Irish were not impressed by my promises. (What promises have I ever made?). A piece of cheap journalism that anyhow I have got, far, far, beyond. Anyhow I daresay there has been or will be worse than that. I don't see it myself...

Concluding the year with a talk called *"How I spent Christmas."* which was full of nostalgia for Ireland, Stuart would hardly publicize a difficult Christmas day he spent with Madeleine, who continued to be over possessive. They had their festive meal on Christmas Eve, cooked in an old biscuit tin on a much repaired cooker and, reconciled to Madeleine two days later, Stuart thought of Ireland on St Stephen's Day, wondering if he could return there when the war was over. "One thing is certain," he wrote, "it would take armies to stop me going back there to Laragh again, evenings in the glen, going in to the chapel at Donore and looking from O'Connell Bridge along the quays in the dusk."

There was no possibility of returning to Ireland, for his passport application had again been refused. The First Secretary at the Irish Legation was apparently responsible for this, for although friendly towards Stuart, did not approve of him broadcasting. Determined to complain in his next talk about the passport, Hartmann advised him to remove the reference, in case the British should hear of it.

"How I hate the whole petty Government lot and their offshoot here" Stuart wrote, and remembering the carefree days in London in the 1930s, continued, "All that fever is gone too. But I had to have it, it was part of the way towards the truth. It was delight, even intense delight though fleeting, the early days and nights in London."

In the new year of 1943, in addition to the heavy night raids, Berlin suffered an exceptionally severe winter, and to find any food at all, usually meant weary trails around the shops. Stuart spoke about hunger in Ireland in a January broadcast, and wrote a few days later:

From now on, I refuse to write anything that does not serve my truth, ... rather than the nauseating war propaganda. I was not keen on doing it, but all the same why not ? If they are ready to acquiesce in my truths well and good...

There was nothing in his last broadcast that gave any hint of propaganda, and the only controversial subject he had spoken about recently was his extraordinary conclusion about Hitler. Stuart now recognized that his own truth was of no interest to the broadcasting authorities. Germany was suffering heavy defeats on the Russian front, and was desperately looking for any support, however useless. In Stuart's determination to be concerned with the 'truth', his understanding of 'propaganda' when it was to him, falsely invoked in the name of religion by others, could not be ignored by him. Roosevelt was the subject of his second broadcast in January, for Stuart had heard that the President had stated in an address to Congress that the Axis countries had broken the Tenth Commandment. He pleaded with the Irish to "...keep to true and lasting values in the face of war hysteria and diversion of truth and hypocrisy all around us. I believe that is exactly what you are doing. May you go on doing so till the end."

If Eire had been involved in the war, Stuart's remarks would have had some point, but the Irish could do nothing even if they were aware of "war hysteria and diversion of truth".

Beyond publicizing his own position on capitalism and the hypocrisy of the Allies, the talks were useless as propaganda. That he was given broadcasting time at all, reflects a lack of understanding of Stuart's own purpose, by those who let him speak, and shows how desperately Germany was trying to gain support.

Stuart visited Frank Ryan in mid-January, and found that he had suffered a stroke which had affected the left side of his body. He was in bed, and Stuart arranged for him to be taken to hospital where he and Madeleine called a few days later. Although severely ill, he spoke to Stuart about Hugh McAteer, former Chief of Staff of the IRA, who had escaped from the Crumlin Road Jail, Belfast. Ryan heard that he wanted to flee to Germany, and Stuart promised to speak to Kurt Haller, of the Abwehr to have McAteer brought over if that was what he wanted. As he was shortly afterwards re-arrested, the situation did not arise.

After one of the worst nights of bombing in Berlin in

February, Stuart arranged for Madeleine to work longer hours at the Redaktion, afraid she might be transferred for other war work and become separated from him. Their safety was ensured for the time being, but when Ryan returned to his flat, his windows and door were shattered by a bomb blast, which seemed to symbolize the breakdown of his own health. He knew how unwell he was, and gave Stuart some soap and a shirt, which he would soon have no use for.

Madeleine and Stuart were exhausted after a month of anxiety. When travelling on the bus, Stuart noticed the white faces of the passengers who like him, had very little sleep. After walking to the Rundfunkhaus through bombed streets one evening, he had the worst quarrel ever with Madeleine over Nora O'Mara.

Madeleine had to work with Nora who was back in Berlin, and if Stuart met her, Madeleine expected him to behave in a way that was "...quite forced and unnatural for me as though I was guilty or she (Nora) was guilty of something - heaven knows what.." Madeleine's jealousy was provoked by love but he felt suffocated by this, and found it hard to make her understand his feelings.

Gradually Madeleine managed to control her feelings about Nora, for only a week later, she read with her and some others, a play Stuart had written called *I am Raftery,* based on the blind Gaelic poet which was to be broadcast to Ireland on St Patrick's Day.

When the University term ended, Stuart went for a holiday with Madeleine to Hamburg, and visited her father's grave in Silesia in Poland. They returned to Berlin in late April, just before the devastating air-raids in Hamburg. Madeleine's sister Gretel who had been working as a nurse there managed to escape to Berlin before the conflagration, but it was not long before that city suffered similar attacks.

Stuart resumed his broadcasts, and on 31 May urged Irish voters not to vote for Fine Gael led by William T. Cosgrove in the election set for 23 June, 1943. The Irish Government protested that Stuart had unjustifiably interfered in internal Irish affairs, and Warnock, the First Secretary was forced to dress formally, and complain to the German Foreign Office.

The rebuke from Dublin did not stop Stuart broadcasting,

but when pressure was put on him to criticize Russia, he refused. It was planned to move the Redaktion and the staff to Luxembourg because of the air raids, and Stuart saw this as a chance to remain in Berlin, and to finally cease broadcasting. Madeleine was officially transferred to Luxembourg, and once more afraid they would be parted, Stuart agreed to go with her. He hoped that once out of Berlin, pressure to speak out against Russia might stop. Granted leave of absence from the University, they left a smouldering Berlin on 12 August, 1943 for a Luxembourg hotel. This was owned by a Mr Petit, who was French, and hated the Germans. When he learned they were Irish and Polish, he was generous with food, and Stuart and Madeleine ate far better than they had done in Berlin.

One night in the hotel bar, Stuart announced "Heil Moscow" in a loud voice. As it was dangerous to make any anti-Nazi statement, especially as the Gestapo frequently drank in the hotel, Petit hurried over to Stuart, and told him to be quiet.

Less fortunate was a Scots sailor, whose ship had been sunk by the Germans. He was brought to Luxembourg, where he opted to work in the radio station, rather than be held as a prisoner. Often drunk, he made incautious remarks about the Nazis. Stuart opened his bedroom door one morning to admit two SS Officers, who explained the sailor wanted Stuart to know he was being taken away. He did return after some time, but his removal was a reminder to Stuart of the potential dangers.

Nevertheless there were advantages in Luxembourg, such as a good English library where Madeleine studied for her final exams, due the following March. Stuart swam, or played golf, and at times it was possible to forget the war.

The radio station was extremely inefficient. Not only was there no map of Ireland in the building, but the Irish news reports were not even transcribed. A woman responsible for this had stopped because she claimed no one read them. In such shambles, Stuart hoped there was a better chance than in Berlin, that his request to stop broadcasting would be granted, but it was not. The authorities were dissatisfied with what he wrote, but rather than let his audience suppose there was something wrong by taking him off the air, he had to substitute talks on literature. Stuart might as well have been giving a Third Network programme for the BBC for all the relevance his talks had now.

As Madeleine had to return to Berlin in November, about her University course, Stuart decided to go with her, and to discuss giving up his talks.

Before they left, a letter came from Ryan, mentioning that he had been in hospital having ulcers treated but was having difficulty in finding somewhere to stay where he could be looked after. Chiding Stuart for not having been in touch he wrote, "Are you dead ? If so, please let me know so I'll have a permanent address for you..."

Because Stuart's Berlin flat was on the ground floor, nobody took shelter when the raids began. Traute and her boyfriend Martin, arrived to celebrate Madeleine's 28th birthday, a day early, on 22 November. The evening meal was interrupted by a bomb which destroyed the next building and blasted out their windows. Martin and Stuart climbed on the roof, where the women passed up buckets of water, to stop the flames from spreading to their flat. After it was out Stuart hurried on foot through the burning streets to check that his own books and papers were safe in his old room in the Rankestrasse.

A few days later, he asked Professor Schirmer of the University to use his influence to claim him back for University work, and when this application was refused, Stuart returned to Luxembourg with Madeleine, glad at least to leave the raids.

After a pleasant Christmas Stuart prepared what would be his final broadcasts, and transmitted them in January 1944. In his talks now, Stuart did not even vaguely hint at Ireland's place in the New Europe, for it was obvious that Germany was losing the war. He even doubted the wisdom of a united Ireland:

> Until Dublin becomes a much better place for the average working family to live in than Belfast, we lose more than half the force of our claim to Belfast. This may not be a very palatable statement, but I think that to most of you it is quite obvious...

To achieve improved prosperity, Eire had to break away from Britain's 'financial and social conditions', the one point he had consistently emphasized through every broadcast. He was now tired of the situation in which he had become embroiled, and explained in one of his last talks, "If I don't speak any more it will be because I can no longer say what I want, what I think is the truth. I will be asked to say things I don't believe, so if I stop talking, you'll know why."

Stuart emphatically told Luxembourg that he refused under any circumstances to broadcast again, and asked if he could return to Berlin. This was granted on the condition he reported to the Rundfunkhaus, to which Stuart readily agreed. Privately, he had no intention of doing so. As Madeleine had to work for her exams, they were back in Berlin in late February. When their rooms were destroyed, Stuart and Madeleine took a couple of rooms in the Pension Neumann, where he had stayed in the early years of the war. The evenings were spent trying to find safe cover from the bombs. If there was enough time, Stuart and Madeleine went to the packed Bunker near Banhof Zoo until the all clear. After the exams were over on 8 March, Madeleine and Stuart visited Frank Ryan, who was now in an expensive sanatorium in Dresden. It was a depressing visit, for although Ryan was slowly dying, he pathetically remarked that he would be in Ireland the following spring. Stuart's refusal to report to the Rundfunkhaus, was punished by a visit from the police in May who removed his identity papers and passport. He was telephoned in the middle of the night and told if he did not continue with the talks, he would be arrested and sent to a camp. Referring to this, Stuart wrote that he had "some fairly well placed protectors". Pressure had come from the Nazi Propaganda Ministry, but Stuart's friends who could help were based in the Foreign Office, especially Weizsäcker.

The Irish Legation had been bombed by the RAF in the previous November, and all the files, including one on Stuart were destroyed. The First Secretary, Warnock, set up a temporary office outside Berlin, and Cornelius Cremin was appointed Charge d'Affaires in place. Stuart complained to him about the treatment he was receiving, and Cremin, more sympathetic than Warnock, intervened with the German Foreign Office. Meanwhile a letter Stuart had sent Kay was returned to him, supposedly because it had been censored, but was an indication that he was being carefully watched. Eventually the Foreign Office denied to Cremin that Stuart had ever been threatened and said he could collect his papers and passport from the Police.

On 10 May, a week after the new semester began, the English Seminar was destroyed in a daylight raid, and while Stuart waited for another room to be found, he had little to do. Frank Ryan had returned to Berlin and was now seriously ill, and Stuart and Madeleine called and found him in a pitiful state. They took it in turns to look after him when his landlady had to do war work in the night, and spoke vaguely of the future. There were hopes of travelling to neutral Switzerland, and Ryan suggested marrying Madeleine to give her the necessary papers to travel, after which he would later divorce her. They all knew the plan could come to nothing because of Ryan's health, and although he seemed to improve by 8 June, they had no sooner returned to their own rooms, when they heard he would have to return to the Dresden sanatorium.

Stuart helped Ryan to dress for the journey, and left him to travel with his landlady to Loschwitz in a whole train compartment, reserved by the government. The effort of the journey however was too much for Ryan, and the next day, Stuart had a telegram stating his friend had died suddenly on 10 June, shortly after reaching the sanatorium.

Stuart and Madeleine went to Dresden for the funeral, which was attended by about a dozen friends. Ryan and Stuart had never been particularly close, but shared a deep patriotic love of Ireland which they had often spoken of, in a Berlin which had become alien to them both. Stuart experienced:

> an intense sense of loneliness, leaving Frank's body there in this foreign place, down there far from everyone he liked. A terrible feeling of final and utter aloneness. And yet that is not the last word; I do not think it is the last word.

Geoffrey Elborn

It was not the last word, for Ryan's body was moved to Ireland, and given a second funeral on 22 June 1979, which Madeleine and Stuart also attended.

The University took little of Stuart's time, but he found it a burden, partly due to intense heat, but also because the daylight raids became increasingly disruptive. He surprised himself by being "drawn towards the war news", rather than his own inner life, and noted "If I was wholly and simply drawn towards my own life how quickly I should grow..."

It would have been difficult for one even as detached as Stuart to ignore the fact that Germany was suffering defeats on all fronts. Despite this, he did not want to leave Berlin, but was faced with the problem of what to do when the war ended. Deciding he and Madeleine would go to live with Iseult, his mother and the children, "...in a new way but better than before..." he did not think about the practicalities of such an arrangement, for neither of the women could have tolerated the other. Some of what he had seen in the last few months influenced a novel he was writing, called *The Kingdom of Polensky,* but by 14 July work on it was impossible, and Stuart thought of little but the war.

There is a tension, a waiting to see what is going to happen - because something decisive must happen there soon, within the next three or four weeks. Either the Russians will overrun German territory, or they will be held without the aid of weapons. Either event would again alter the war or at least this very important part of it...

The Russians had opened a full scale offensive on the central front in the previous month, and in Berlin the night time bombing drove Stuart and Madeleine into hiding in a cellar. An attempt had been made on Hitler's life which Stuart noted without opinion, beyond that fact that the incident belonged to "sensational days for Germany", and was more concerned that the University term was finishing on 2 August. He very much doubted if it would open again in November, and with that uncertainty, could make no plans for the future.

The most heartening news he had recently was the

resignation of the philosopher Benedetto Croce from the Italian Government, who refused to pay lip service any longer to Mussolini. He had been appointed a lifelong senator. A frequent critic of fascism, but never silenced because of his popularity, he was supposed to be the living proof of freedom of speech in Italy.

> It is something to know that there are still people left who will follow the truth as they see it and not submit to the policy of the herd or party to which they belong. Croce was critical of the Fascist regime and is now equally critical of the so-called 'liberators' and in both cases was not afraid to say so. That is the only liberation that is any use, freedom of the individual to stand above the power of politics...There is no real leader on the Allied side with the doubtful exception of Churchill, of any wisdom or stature...

Stuart imagined a Council to reshape Europe after the war, whose members were men who had shown freedom of spirit, such as Croce, Aldous Huxley, Knut Hamsun and possibly Thomas Mann. Although he doubted the latter because he had written well of Roosevelt, he could not remark on Hamsun's Nazi sympathies which he only learned of later.

Stuart himself had finished with all attempts to publicize his views, declining to write an essay on economics for a paper which expected to receive a contribution on the same subject from Ezra Pound. Important as the economic problem was, Stuart had realized it could not be taken in isolation. Neither would any reform of the social system, by itself, bring any real or new peace. He believed very strongly that he and those he knew best could not feel satisfied "unless we have not only the possibility of social security but also fulfilment for our inner needs...Without art and imagination the picture is bleak..."

With the liberation of Paris on 25 August a phase of his life was coming to an end. He and Madeleine had gone swimming that week, the hottest of the summer, for unable to leave Berlin, they could only wait as the war crisis deepened. Now Stuart worried Madeleine would be required for further war work, and he might be sent away if the University did not re-open.

To half-starved workers from the East who were ordered to clear the rubble, Stuart and Madeleine illegally gave bread when they could. Their plight represented the chaos and diminishing hope for survival, and Stuart applied to the Foreign Office in early September for a permit to travel to Munich, from where they hoped to go to Switzerland.

Through all the destruction, the linden trees in the square opposite the pension where Stuart and Madeleine lived, survived untouched by the bombs and falling masonry, and inspired Stuart to write one last poem in Berlin, *The Trees in the Square.*

The Foreign Office refused Stuart a travel permit, but he collected a temporary pass from the Police, by pretending he had to bring some belongings from Landsberg, some distance from Munich. Madeleine was given a pass as his secretary, and before they left, Stuart handed some of his books and manuscripts to his agent to look after. They said farewell to Traute, who decided to stay in Berlin to be with Martin who was in the Army. He had reserved two seats on the Landsberg train, which Stuart and Madeleine boarded at the Anhalter Bahnhof on 10 September 1944, for their last journey from Berlin.

They had no intention of going to Landsberg, and instead left the train at Munich. Near the station, refugees from the East queued for accommodation which Madeleine joined, and was given a ticket which gave them three nights in the tatty Hotel Schiller.

They were now homeless refugees, and began a seemingly endless pattern of having to move on after three nights in one place to somewhere else. Through September they travelled the outlying Munich area, finally returning to Munich at the end of the month, where they lived in a small *Pension* with the unlikely name of "Exquisite".

The weather was hot, and it seemed an irony that the sun continued to shine on a city which was gradually devastated by heavy bombing. Stuart and Madeleine often sat in the *Englische Garten,* and as the buildings collapsed nearby strengthened their own interior world by reading Rilke and

Eckhardt.

Winter arrived, and with it, unbearably cold conditions. Their rooms in the Pension were unheated, and the water pipes were frozen. After eating a dish of mashed potatoes and gravy, Stuart and Madeleine spent Christmas huddled in bed. It was five years since he had arrived in Germany, and as far as his 'inner' world was concerned, he had learnt much, "above all about God..." He needed all the reserve he had, for the new year of 1945 began with even colder weather. Since two raids on Munich on the first week of January, the "Exquisite" was without electric light, or lavatory, and there was only a little water for washing. As candles were restricted to one a week, Stuart and Madeleine went to bed after the evening meal, listening to the sirens.

Despite their discomfort, Stuart realised they were lucky to be under a roof: "that I must never forget. The simplest things, a leaf, a snowflake are blessed when one sees them in peace and truth..." How long the roof would last was uncertain, and Stuart and Madeleine speculated where they would move to next.

Stuart would have liked to have returned to Berlin to see the Russian troops, whom he knew would eventually arrive in the city. This was out of the question, for stories of pillaging and the advancing Red Army's treatment of women were widespread. They learnt later that Madeleine's own sister Traute, had hidden in rubble and dustbins for safety. The only option was to ask for help at the Irish Legation at Bregenz, and on 1 March Stuart and Madeleine boarded a train which would take them near it.

Madeleine was restricted to taking short journeys, and dared not risk going further than Kaufbeuren. At the station, Stuart threw his heavy suitcase in the luggage office with labels addressed to Lindau, hoping that it would be waiting for them if they ever reached the place themselves.

The train to Kaufbeuren had been cold and draughty, with cardboard windows instead of glass, but now they were faced with a walk of 40 kilometres in cold and sleet, and after trudging for about 10 kilometres, Madeleine was exhausted. They stopped near a wood to have some wine and a cutlet which a friend had given them, and later Stuart waved down a lorry and offered the driver one of their two bottles of wine for a lift. "The little express train has broken down," the driver remarked to Madeleine, and took them to Kempten.

Stuart and Madeleine were still some distance from their destination, but by now they did not care whether they were caught without the proper travel documents, and took a train for Bregenz. With all the chaos of the war, nothing was checked, and they could probably have taken a train for the entire journey.

Bregenz was a major disappointment, for although they met Cremin of the Irish Legation, he only offered a good meal. It seemed a certain Herr von Schenbeck would help, but he muddled Stuart with a former British Officer, Baily Stewart who had broadcast anti-British propaganda, and would do nothing for them.

The area near Lake Constance was packed with refugees hoping to reach Switzerland who had already taken any available accommodation. Stuart and Madeleine stayed in a hotel for a few nights, but as a foreigner he could not live within 15 kilometres of the Swiss border. Madeleine knew of a place called Tuttlingen beyond the limit, where a friend sometimes spent a holiday, and on 5 March, they caught a train which could only go part of the way, because of the threat of bombs from low flying aeroplanes. After a freezing night in a station waiting room, near Tuttlingen they left the suitcase and walked down bombed lanes, where houses still smouldered. There was no certainty that Madeleine's friend would be in Tuttlingen, and when they arrived at seven in the morning, they found she was in fact in Berlin. Nevertheless they were given a small room by a family who lived there. Extra ration cards that Stuart brought were helpful at the beginning, but after a few weeks of begging in the country, there was no food.

The family resented having Stuart and Madeleine, who left Tuttlingen and walked to Lindau Railway Station in early April. They had no idea what to do next, and during the days that followed, took a train anywhere to pass the time. At night they slept on the floor with many others in the filthy waiting room, and if questioned, Stuart always kept a valid ticket to show he had a right to be there. The whole process was exhausting, and when Stuart's ration cards ran out, they lived off scraps of bread because as a foreigner he was afraid to draw attention to himself by registering for more.

Stuart and Madeleine could only hope the war would soon end, and they felt miserable watching the tantalizing lights of Switzerland across the lake, unable to be there. Completely desolate and powerless to carry anything heavy because of weakness and hunger, they impulsively took a train to the small Austrian town of Dornbirn on 16 April, to waste yet more time. They had letters from no one, heard no news, and were unaware that on the same day, the Soviet Army began its final Berlin offensive. Within a few weeks the war would be over.

The following day, Madeleine was admitted to a refugee camp. Stuart was not allowed to be there, but was smuggled into an empty bunk. A week later, Stuart set out for Lindau, hoping to find out if they could go to Switzerland. On the way, at the shore of Lake Constance, Stuart met a company of German soldiers, who were stopping everybody on foot to examine their papers, and in most cases, turning them back. Stuart's own passport had expired, and made no sense to the German who called over his lieutenant to look at it. To Stuart's surprise, the officer asked him about Ernie O'Malley, for he had read his book, *On Another Man's Wound,* which had greatly impressed him. Stuart told him he had fought in the Civil War, and was imprisoned with O'Malley's younger brother Cecil. The connection saved Stuart, for he was waved on, and without it, would not have been able to return to Madeleine who was anxiously wondering what had happened to him.

Packing a few things, they left Dornbirn for the border town of Feldkirch on 23 April to join a long queue of refugees who were waiting at the border check point for Switzerland. Stuart and Madeleine were refused entry, and also the following day when they tried again. Stuart could have gone through, but was prevented the second time because he had written Madeleine's name in his passport as his wife. They could only return to Dornbirn, where Madeleine was given a small room by a couple who were caretakers for the local bank. Stuart went to a nearby camp until a room in the house became available.

It was now obvious that liberation was not far off. On 23 April, Himmler had offered to surrender to the Western Allies. News reached Dornbirn that the French were advancing towards the town, and food, clothing and boots were distributed in bulk, to prevent them being seized by the approaching army.

On 28 April, the day before Stuart's forty-third birthday, leaflets printed in German circulated in the town which read "The German Führer has fallen in the face of the enemy." In Berlin, Hitler's reign of terror was drawing to a close. On 30 April, he married Eva Braun and later in the day committed suicide. As the Russians finally took Berlin on 2 May, French troops entered Dornbirn, which was decked with the white flags and sheets of surrender.

Stuart and Madeleine, July, 1944

CHAPTER 11

The official announcement that the war was over, was made on 7 May, and on the following sunny evening, peace bells rang out. Stuart and Madeleine celebrated with tea and three slices of bread and cheese, and read together the Litany and the Salve Regina.

It was an extraordinary moment for them. It seemed another life away to Stuart since his son Ion had come into his room at Laragh to say that war had been declared, and for Madeleine who had given up her life with her mother and sisters. It hardly mattered that the amenities of civilization such as post, wireless and newspapers were unavailable, for Stuart and Madeleine read the Gospels to help make sense of their exile.

A typical day in Dornbirn was shaped by the lack of food, and their own religious observances. They attended early Mass and returned to Madeleine's room for a breakfast of tea and one slice of bread. Later in the morning Stuart would collect milk and anything else available from the local shop and read until lunchtime. They knew their meagre diet of maize and a few vegetables would be reduced, and tried to enjoy the food while they had it. To forget their hunger, they slept until the early evening, then collected the next day's provisions, generally leeks, which were plentiful, and a few slices of bread.

On 27 June, Stuart went to Lindau and spoke to an English Colonel about leaving Germany, but when he was given an unhelpful answer, he could not decide what to do next. His first impulse was to go to Ireland, and arrange to bring Madeleine over afterwards, but when he thought about this during the night, he realized this was selfish, and he must stay with her for the time being.

Stuart had constantly imagined himself at Glendalough, and the anticipation of the "indescribable relief and joy at leaving this chaos" had sustained him through what he had suffered. With that hope gone, he had to accept "...hunger, no settled room, the outward uncertainty and all the attendant

hardship and misery that completed the destroying for the
moment of the self centered part of me...". Yet, despite
Stuart's apparent acceptance of his predicament, which he
tried to convince himself of by writing about it in his diary,
he was still tormented by a longing to return to Ireland.

While sitting in the open air by a hen house, and shelling
wormy peas, Stuart felt a sense of anguish. He had passed
beyond the stage of rebellion into despair:

> I give up all, all: Ireland, my loved ones, my writing, my
> home all those things the hope of soon regaining which has
> been a light in the darkness of these days. So be it; I feel at
> this moment that physical death, if quiet and not too painful,
> would be preferable. My heart is sick, sick with the misery
> and disappointment of all these months...

Able to leave Dornbirn on his own, desperate homesickness temporarily swamped his love for Madeleine. A
return to Ireland would mean accepting all the problems of
his marriage. Madeleine had given up everything for Stuart,
and would not have considered abandoning him. Later
Stuart remarked he had not seriously ever considered
leaving Madeleine, despite what he wrote, and later, disliked
the 'homesick' poems he wrote about Ireland as not
representing his true beliefs. Trying to come to terms with
his emotions he concluded the diary entry for 28 June, "I
write this at the table in S's tiny room while she has gone up
to prepare our meagre supper of gruel... I have put out the
two cups and spread the two coloured rags that are our table
cloth..."

The following day, Stuart thought of his decision on
Ireland and remembered tranquil moments, none of which
included Iseult:

> Memories of Ireland: the hidden beauty of the days there is
> now so clear to me. Bridesbush, [home of Janet Montgomery
> in Duleek, Meath] the mornings there, the late breakfast, the
> fire in winter, the small room crowded with things each of
> which now has an almost endless preciousness. Or in
> summer walking not very far along those whitish thick

hedged roads, coming back down the lane by the railway bridge a little before lunch. Lunch at the dark mahogany table. Driving into Drogheda, waiting while Aunt Janet shopped, getting papers, looking around. And again more than these, the atmosphere of Laragh, the quiet days there full of infinite peace and richness. My room, the back room with its turf fire and the painted yellow walls, my mother gathering sticks, leisurely and happily on a still summer evening. The garden, the mountains...

Here, Stuart broke off, realizing the futility of self indulgence, and continued, "My God, there is no good trying to put these memories into words; they are endless. And all must be given up." Trying to put his own position on a broader perspective, he recalled some friends who had loved Ireland as he did, but who had died during the war years:

[F.R.] Higgins who loved and grasped a great deal of what Ireland is, as shown in his poetry. He has died and has left it. And Dan Leahy who loved it in another way, who enjoyed and grasped life greedily: the races, the Shelbourne, but the secret quietness was also not quite hidden from him. And Frank [Ryan] dead here after seven or eight years of exile, longing for Ireland, tormented by homesickness as he often told me...

By confronting his feelings, Stuart gradually accepted without bitterness that he could not return to Ireland. Had he not gained a certain 'inner' resistance from his period in Berlin he would have selfishly returned alone to Ireland. There was little else to write of except the small variations in their daily rations:

three slices of bread and butter, or bread and cheese, a teacupful of dried peas...half a cupful of a kind of porridge meal made into gruel or porridge. As well as this there is a little soup and sometimes a few vegetables...not all available at one time.

The lists of meagre rations appeared self-pitying, but

Stuart wrote them down to remind himself in the future of their constant hunger, and continued, " I note these things not to 'glory' in them because I have nothing to glory in, but to remember how it was when and should a time of plenty come..."

The miserable existence Stuart and Madeleine endured, was only bearable to them, by their study of the Gospels. This devotion was obsessional, but unlike the period Stuart spent at Laragh living his monastic life with equal fervour, he now groped towards a sense of truth which was revealed by deprivation. He recalled:

> the vision of those precious days at home, and I see myself walking back slowly up the hill past the Church to our gate, having been down to the village to post a letter and I feel again the peace that used to come to me at such moments. It was not the true peace, it was largely an earthly peace. I was blind then to the peace of God and so I lost all.

Stuart's diary was never intended to be a strict detailed record of daily facts, but rather an account of 'outer' events which provoked inner reflections. After reading a book about St Paul, he considered his own time:

> Hitler dead, Knut Hamsun taken from his home and arrested, Stalin lording it in the Kremlin, Gandhi still brooding and fasting in India as though there had been no war - and he alone really seems eternal! Joyce being tried in London, Marlene Dietrich in uniform in Paris or New York or somewhere... and I exiled and hungry in a village in Austria without a proper suit or soap or many other of the 'necessities' What a game it is, all this so-called living and even dying.

In some of the broadcasts, Stuart had praised Gandhi, and his opinion that Gandhi was now behaving "as though there had been no war...", is perhaps a comment on his own attitude to the war years. Until the bombs fell, Stuart had, on one level, lived "as though there had been no war..." and he may have felt a certain reasurrance that Gandhi, had also detached himself to further his own beliefs.

During most of July, Stuart and Madeleine lived between moods of hope and despair, as they tried to find out from various authorities if they could leave Austria. It was distressing for Madeleine to be told by a French Officer that she would be free to leave if she could marry Stuart. For his part, lack of food increased his awareness of others. During the war Stuart had taken for granted the ready supplies of food such as real coffee, and good meals in the Berlin Press Club. Now he was:

> grateful for what we have, all tastes marvellous. Our lunch of boiled potatoes with a few fried onions mixed through them and a thick barley soup... I have to learn to be grateful for the simplest things, for a roof, a bed a corner to read and sleep in. Being without all these things, I know what they are...It is a matter of having that pure inward eye in which creation is seen in its purity, simplicity and marvellousness. This 'pure eye' comes only when one has sufficient detachment from the world...

At various times in his life, Stuart had equally been drawn to the opposite extremes of Hedonism and asceticism. Neither was satisfying, or made him feel less troubled. It had not occurred to him that enlightenment was always possible through physical suffering, and only now because of his own plight, could he understand his experience in a camp, where, "People were half starving, their houses destroyed, with nothing on earth to hope for, as far as I could see..."

The summer heat was stifling, and as Stuart sat in his ragged suit, he had only the New Testament to read. Because no-one knew where he and Madeleine were, they had no letters for three or four months, and nothing from Laragh for over a year. With long days for reflection, Stuart tried to make sense of what he had experienced since he had arrived in Germany. Distanced from Berlin by poverty and hunger, he had achieved self awareness:

> Blind in chaos, escaping from my life at home of which I was making nothing. I came to Germany. For the first year or so

there it was only another chaos. But then through acute torment I began to be made receptive... In Munich the raids showed us the face of death and the *Englischgarten* the face of nature...great almost unbearable disappointments that brought about another step in self loss. Miracles by which we were kept from starving...

Madeleine's love was also breaking down Stuart's egocentricity, and through her, Stuart felt he was receiving some revelation of the love of Christ. If their circumstances changed, Stuart resolved to write a novel which would reflect their experiences:

all suffering in its simplicity, in its primitiveness. Death by bombs...And hunger... The humiliation of the outcast, the thing of having literally nowhere to lay one's head... All this must be in the ground work so that the book has a new taste, a new slant.

He had tentatively started a novel in the comparative peace of Berlin, and had convinced himself that it would be different from all his others. Now he wanted to combine his spiritual understanding with his experiences as a refugee.

In the meantime, they were constantly frustrated in finding help to leave Austria. Stuart made five visits in one week to the Centre of Repatriation, either to discover the place was locked up, despite an arranged appointment, or that he had to see some new official to whom their circumstances had to be explained again.

On 26 July, after such a visit, Stuart told Madeleine he imagined his mother spending her birthday that afternoon, enjoying a picnic with Iseult and the children. It all seemed remote, and when he heard that evening on the wireless that the Labour Party in Britain had come to power under Attlee, he realized that of the war leaders, only Stalin remained.

Stuart was at last told he could go in a convoy that left for Paris from Bregenz, at the beginning of August. He had to risk going, taking the chance of freedom, or separation, for Madeleine, who had to stay behind, might be moved in his absence. The transport for Paris took some time to arrange, and to be ready for it, Stuart had to leave Dornbirn for a Bregenz camp.

He enjoyed a meal with Madeleine on 3 August, and arrived at the camp that evening. Without her, Stuart was miserable, and almost returned to Dornbirn. When he learnt that transport for Paris only left in the evenings and the early mornings, he met Madeleine daily, either in Dornbirn, or at Bregenz railway station. Each farewell was tense, for it might be the final one, until over a week later, Madeleine arrived at the station as arranged, to find that Stuart was not there.

He had already been taken on the convoy of buses at 2 o'clock the previous morning, and had no opportunity to warn her. Picking up some of his belongings and a note which Stuart had left for her in an office, Madeleine returned to Bregenz. She could do nothing now but wait.

Stuart was as much surprised as Madeleine at his abrupt departure, but he had been included at the last moment, and having no time to adjust mentally to the change, found the journey in the coach nervously exhausting. He sat with a Jewish couple who had survived the camps, and stopped at Strasbourg for a large meal of macaroni cheese. Completing the last stage of the journey in a freight train, they arrived in Paris on 14 August. They were greeted by a welcoming committee at the station, which included a young man with red painted nails and make up. As Stuart had never seen such a thing before, he felt he "was suddenly back in the modern world...".

Stuart and some others were taken to the Villa Rothschild, off the Place Victor Hugo. Requisitioned by the Germans during the occupation, the French had reclaimed it, and Stuart saw impressive antique furniture amongst the filth left by the Germans.

He had little time to absorb liberated Paris. The only chance of bringing Madeleine over to Ireland was through the Irish Legation, which he contacted as soon as he arrived. He met the First Secretary, who told him his presence in Paris was an embarrassment, and explained that if he was picked up by the American Military Police it would be awkward for the Irish Government. Worse, "there was not

the foggiest chance" of his managing to get Madeleine to
Ireland.

While the First Secretary left the room to consult the
Ambassador for advice, Stuart managed to quickly remove
some embossed Legation paper, which he slipped in his
pocket. The Ambassador conveyed a message that Stuart
should return to where he came from, but before leaving the
building, Stuart was handed some money reserved for
repatriated Irish. He wandered round Paris, stopping for
coffee on the deserted terrace of the Cafe Dôme, the scene of
happier days in the thirties. He had written to Madeleine to
say he had arrived, but was plagued with anxiety for her
safety, and had doubts about having left Dornbirn.

Madeleine had little to distract her. Post was not reaching
Dornbirn, and had to be collected from an address in
Switzerland. To pass the time, she helped her landlady with
housekeeping, and as the autumn days arrived, worked with
her in the fields digging potatoes. At last a letter from
Stuart, confirmed that as long as he was in Paris, there was
the chance he could do something for her.

The money from the Embassy did not last, but Stuart was
contacted by an Irishman called Blair who gave English
lessons. He had more work than he could cope with, and
passed some of his students to Stuart who taught them in
the morning. When he was free in the afternoons, Stuart left
messages for Iseult at the Irish Legation, giving her a safe
address to write to. The Villa Rothschild was bug infested,
and Stuart moved to the nearby Hotel Copernic which was
primitive but inexpensive.

On one visit to the Irish Legation, Stuart was handed a
letter written by Nora O'Mara. He had heard nothing of her
since he had left Berlin, but she had half-expected he would
come to Paris at some point. She was living in lodgings near
the Seine, and hoped Stuart would visit her.

It was awkward for Stuart, who was worried about
Madeleine, but he felt that he should visit Nora for the sake
of their past relationship. When they met, Nora was
desperately unhappy. When she heard Stuart wanted to be
with Madeleine, she was tearful and emotional. Homesick for
Berlin to which she longed to return, she upset herself by

listening to German stations on the wireless. Stuart visited her once or twice, but by the end of August, he had already decided to return to Dornbirn, and left Paris without seeing Nora again.

Hopes of Dornbirn were shortlived. Stuart shared a truck with Tito-ist Yugoslavs he had met in a Repatriation Camp, who were trying to go home, via Germany. On 29 August on the way to Strasbourg, Stuart was told that he could not pass through the frontiers to Dornbirn, for some of his papers were not in order. He decided to continue nevertheless, strongly aware his only useful contacts were in Paris.

Stuart had not felt so miserable since he left Austria earlier in the month, for in Strasbourg he learned that letters he had written to Madeleine might not have reached her. He remained there for four days, and thought of his endless wandering since they left Berlin, "Munchen, Bregenz, Tuttlinger - Three weeks without a bed - Dornbirn, Paris, Strasbourg and what may come now..."

Madeleine read about the exodus of the Jews from Egypt. "How glad I would be" she wrote in her journal, "if I could wander with Tiger [Stuart] to the promised land." A week later, the promised land was no nearer, for Stuart was again in Paris on 14 September, making doubly sure that his documents were in order this time. From the Hotel Copernic, Stuart wrote to Iseult on 10 October, for some money. She replied a week later, and explained she had been trying to do this, but was hampered by the endless successions of government departments she had to deal with.

Stuart's correspondence to Iseult at this time does not survive, but he must have mentioned the difficult question of Madeleine to her, possibly describing her as his secretary. In any case, Iseult had tried to dispatch some parcels for Madeleine, but heard the Red Cross could not send any to Austria. The Department of Supplies stated that parcels could only go to near relatives, and the GPO told her nothing was reaching Austria at all.

It was a depressing tangle of yet more red tape, and Stuart in his anxiety felt his wife was not making much effort to help. There was the promise of a coat from Sean MacBride when safe delivery could be arranged, and when it eventually arrived, and did not fit, Stuart was convinced Iseult had deliberately sent the wrong size.

Iseult, who had been ill, and had an excuse for doing nothing, undoubtedly tried very hard to help. She sold an ivory tankard and a Jacobean cabinet, and also pressed Aunt Janet for money to send Stuart. Sean MacBride also contributed financially without grudge, and Iseult's efforts were particularly noble, because she only had money that Stuart's mother gave her. Stuart's salary had ceased when the war ended.

If Stuart misinterpreted Iseult, she was either unable or unwilling to grasp Stuart's position with Madeleine; that he would not leave her behind in Austria, or return to Ireland alone. Her letters show a deep concern for Stuart, but never mention Madeleine apart from the one reference to the food parcel.

It is not known how much Stuart told Iseult at this stage about Madeleine, but it is likely that Iseult was prejudiced by her knowledge of her husband's past affairs with women, and chose to believe that his relationship with Madeleine would end as the others had. Iseult who was no fool, was genuinely anxious about Stuart's circumstances, and was as Ion wrote, "wearing herself out with worry."

The marriage had failed, but Iseult may have found it difficult to look beyond her own hope that if her husband returned, it was preferable to the empty loneliness of her own life. Pathetically, she planted bulbs, believing Stuart would see them blooming in May.

Determined not to go back to Ireland without Madeleine, Stuart refused further money from his wife and family, and early in November set off for Austria, again in a train carrying Yugoslav partisans who had been imprisoned by the Nazis, and were on their way back to their own country. Stuart was questioned about travelling without a visa, and here he produced his trump card. The official writing paper from the Irish Legation, had been improved by his friend Blair, and in impeccable French, a typed order granted Stuart a free passage, convincingly concluding with an indecipherable signature by Stuart over a stamp. He left the train when it pulled into a junction, at Appenweiler the

German frontier, and looked for somewhere to spend the night. Hearing a Beethoven sonata coming from a shabby inn, he took a room there, exhilirated by the music. He was in Germany, and would soon be with Madeleine.

The following day, he took an express train to Dornbirn, worrying if Madeleine would still be there, but at the station he met by chance their landlady's daughter who told him Madeleine was safe.

During his days in Paris, Stuart had longed to hear the chime of a clock in a certain square in Dornbirn. Paris had its attractions but the mood and pace of exhilaration had palled. In Germany, where the streets lay in ruins and there was no rejoicing, Stuart felt more at ease, and as he walked through the market square in Dornbirn, the clock struck. He really was back with the defeated.

Madeleine was now living in one room of an otherwise deserted flat, and after a tearful reunion, they shared some Red Cross food parcels Stuart had brought and talked together until five in the morning.

The happiness of being together again in safety lasted less than a fortnight. Early in the evening of 21 November, shortly after Madeleine had returned from a French lesson, there was a knock at the door, and two plain clothed French Intelligence officers asked for a Gerda Meissner. They came in and searched the room, then said "Pack up for a night or two."

Francis and Madeleine were taken to a car that was waiting further up the street. The Intelligence officers only spoke French and Stuart told her in English that the situation was likely to be very bad. He knew the familiar euphemism a "night or two" could mean several years. They drove the short distance to Bregenz and at the Security Headquarters, interrogators examined papers Stuart was carrying. They were particularly interested in a cutting of William Joyce's trial, then in progress in London, which they took from Madeleine's handbag. An officer ostentatiously loaded a Weston revolver which he gave to a Sergeant who was instructed to take Madeleine and Stuart up to a cell in the dark. On the way Madeleine asked if she could remain with Stuart, and was told "Madame, this is not a hotel."

Stuart at first found himself with several French collaborators, and was afraid that he would be taken with them to some Paris Penitentiary. Never alone, he shared his cell at varying times with three to a dozen prisoners. One, the grandson of the Zeppelin inventor cut his wrists and was moved elsewhere. Another who was particularly unpleasant and nasty, was a German manufacturer who had employed forced labour, and protested his innocence above everyone else there. After interrogation he was badly beaten up, and taken to another cell where he later killed himself. The cell mates for three days concealed his death by propping up the body, so they could share his rations.

Madeleine was with women who either were involved in Black Market dealing, or had tried to escape across the border to Switzerland. As far as the authorities were concerned, she was regarded as *Gerda* Meissner, a spy they were interested in, and consequently, a prize female prisoner.

The food was disgusting, but worse were infestations of fleas and lice which brought the prisoners out in sores and boils, which had no chance of healing because of lack of nourishing food. A Belgian doctor tried to treat the outbreak with ointment, but this was merely cosmetic. After some months of ill health, Stuart thought he had come to the end of his endurance. When interviewed by Anthony Cronin in 1979 he spoke of this experience:

> in chaotic conditions... far too crowded, you know... several Belgians who belonged to... Degrelles, a Fascist group, who'd been repatriated to Belgium for trial. I was with all these people, as well as having all sorts of nasty skin diseases. You know, you were starving. I thought I had reached the lowest ebb. And what struck me was as a writer I shall never get a book published. I would write one, you know, I had begun to understand certain things. But I thought, who's going to publish? I'm here in a cell of traitors...

Madeleine was strengthened with the knowledge that Stuart was at least under the same roof. Having to mix with political prisoners and without his guidance, prison life changed her views, so that she "...became critical of the world and its ways around me..." Never had the Gospels a more enduring appeal for Madeleine, especially the relationship between Christ and Mary Magdalene, which influenced the evolution of her own name through "Magdalene' to Madeleine. Mary Magdalene was:

> the person who inspired me most and I would have loved to be like her, I could not imagine a life without love, no matter how imperfect that love is...she is called a sinner because of her various love affairs [but]...her nature was so deep and passionate that nothing could fulfil her until she met the Lord; and then she virtually fell head over heels in love with Him. At last she had found Him whom her soul had been seeking...

During her imprisonment, Madeleine believed that every human has something of the divine, and that her love of Stuart was also part of her love of Christ. Her personal interpretation of the Gospels, concerned with a redeeming love, had nothing to do with any Church dogma of morality. Unable to be together, Stuart and Madeleine exchanged notes with the help of a friendly warder who let them meet for a short while on Christmas Eve.

After Christmas, Madeleine was moved to a new cell which overlooked the exercise yard, where Stuart walked round each morning. In the New Year, the Belgian collaborators, were taken away in weekly lorries to their own country, generally to await the death sentence. No decision had been taken about Stuart, although he had been imprisoned for three months without charge. Reflecting on the past, Stuart wrote to his admirer Basil Liddell-Hart on 12 February 1946:

> since these terrible years since we saw each other, and you were good enough to say some encouraging words about my book *The Angel of Pity* I have several times wished that we could have met and talked together. What we have gone through since those days has, I think, fitted me to write a novel which will have the breadth and maturity which *The Angel of Pity* lacked. In planning this

book, I have strangely enough, thought of you and hope one day I may be able to accept the invitation you gave me so long ago and bring the book with me. At the moment I am in an Austrian Prison, but this time will pass like so many other bad (but perhaps fruitful) times in these past years...

It was a remarkably restrained letter and without self-pity, given the conditions Stuart was in, perhaps because the length of correspondence was officially limited. He may have hoped, that because his outgoing mail was read, the authorities would notice Liddell-Hart's rank as a Captain of the British Army, and this too might help him.

In the meantime, Madeleine had heard a confused report that Stuart would be travelling with the Belgian prisoners, and in a note of 12 March warned him he could be moved within a few days. It was little consolation they would be allowed to see each other for a moment if Stuart was taken away, and the tension of waiting was unbearable. Weeks passed and nothing happened.

Liddell-Hart wrote on 13 March that he was glad to hear from Stuart again, for he "...particularly remembered *The Angel of Pity*, at a time when I was conducting a campaign to arouse people to the danger to freedom and humanity threatened by the Nazis..." Liddel-Hart was interested to hear of Stuart's projected novel, and:

your experience in the years that have passed, under the Nazi rule of Europe - now happily broken...I am perplexed at your remark that you are at the moment in an Austrian prison, for I find it hard to imagine any cause for such a predicament. Do let me know more about this, and if there is anything I can do to help.

At last there was some hope from outside which Stuart gratefully acknowledged, explaining in a letter to Liddell-Hart in April, that as far as his arrest was concerned, he had:

never been told the reason, but only that my case had been sent to London 'for decision.' If this is actually so your help would be especially valuable. As you know that I was deeply opposed to Nazism and State tyranny, and my experiences during the war only deepened this opposition. It is not the hardship of detention here, but also the hold up in that work which I believe I could now do, is hard to bear with patience...

Liddell-Hart remained mystified, but assured Stuart on 14 May he had written to Noel Baker, the British Foreign Minister to discover if the case had been referred to his Office. The greatest anxiety for Stuart arose not from the physical aspects of the prison, but the distress caused by inaction.

On the whole, Madeleine was well treated, and had hardly been questioned at all. Once she said to one of the prison officer, "Why do you always refer to me as this Gerda Meissner. My name is not Gerda, but Gertrud." Madeleine knew there was a Gerda Meissner, because she was inadvertently given her ration card. After pointing this out, she was summoned for interview. Her interrogators were pleasant and friendly and explained she and Stuart would soon be released

On 24 May, six months after their arrest, Stuart and Madeleine were taken on a train and accompanied by two French Officers to Freiburg/Breisgau. The freedom offered was limited, for they were taken to a villa, in the charge of a German guard. He wanted to separate them, but after the intervention of a French guard, they were both given the same cellar. Although they were back in occupied Germany, under house arrest, it was in the French Zone. The worst of the ordeal was over, for they could now walk in the garden without supervision, but were not free to walk out on the streets.

Stuart was interrogated by either a French Officer, who deliberately intimidated him by picking up a whip from his desk, or an Officer from Alsace, who was intelligent and enjoyed Stuart's company. The Alsace Officer was interested in subversive movements, and asked Stuart for information about the IRA. Once when Stuart was talking to him, screams were heard from the French Interrogator's room above. A door closed, and the French officer came down, remarking in French " If we had known what we now know about Stuart, he wouldn't have come off so lightly", to which the Alsace replied " Well you don't have him now," and continued to be sympathetic.

What however, was there to know about Stuart that so infuriated the French interrogator?

The Goertz affair, and the broadcasts were the only possible areas which might have caused the Allies to view Stuart with suspicion. Goertz was not mentioned, and the broadcasts only in passing.

The French seem to have regarded Stuart and Madeleine as a problem, and indicated they would be moved to the British Zone. Stuart dreaded further interrogation, but they were only moved to an unlit cellar in the same building, where they were kept for three days in a state of nervous and physical exhaustion.

On the stairs down to the cellar, the French had placed photographs of the victims of Auschwitz, which were pointed out to Stuart by a French Officer, who said "You in your own way are responsible for this, and now you're looking at it, but you escaped retribution." When Stuart was shown the photographs and given details of the final solution, he could hardly absorb the horror of it due to his own circumstances. He had heard rumours of what was happening when in Berlin, but believed that it was part of the Allied propaganda he despised. No-one could avoid knowing of the gradual reduction of rights for the Jews, for these were published in Bills before the war. Stuart has said that had he known of the atrocities he would not have gone to Germany, and while he would not "go one hundred per cent with the French officer's comment, but up to a point. [It] ...was a certain suggestion that one couldn't quite refute... I had made great mistakes." He had gone:

> about things... in a way that was bound to be mistaken. Some sort of lack of judgement, and very easy for a writer, especially an isolated writer to get so...concerned in one's rather lonely way; one becomes nothing else - everything else is blurred except what one is doing, and trying to do.

Unexpectedly, a German warder told Stuart and Madeleine on 13 July to collect their things and leave, with the proviso that they must remain in the French Zone. They were given a room, and after settling in, amongst the first things Stuart did, appropriately on Bastille Day, was to write to Basil Liddell-Hart giving him their welcome news. Stuart believed his friend's agitation had speeded their release, and thanked him deeply for his kindness at a "time of great discouragement". The British Foreign Office may have acted on Liddell-Hart's communication to them in May, (their file is still unavailable for inspection for the unforseeable future) but Liddell-Hart was only able to pass a letter Stuart wrote to him on 8 July, to the Office of the British Foreign Minister on 24 July, in which he tried to find if "their enquiries had produced any result". By this time Stuart had already been released.

Madeleine and Stuart moved to a room elsewhere which was a mistake because the landlady quarrelled with her daughter, and tried to involve Madeleine in their scenes. Then towards the end of October, Stuart was arrested for the second time, and taken to prison in Freiburg, and put in a cellar. As Madeleine had not been detained, she visited him and brought what food she could manage. Beside herself with anxiety she wrote to Basil Liddell-Hart on 28 October 1946 pleading for his help. After apologising for bothering him, she continued:

> only I don't know what to do and from where to get help for Mr Francis Stuart who has been again arrested - although he had already been 9 months in prison, he has not yet overcome the first imprisonment and is in such a bad and undernourished state of health.
>
> Please, please dear sir, help him! Francis Stuart has such a fine and rare soul, the influence of which humanity has great need of..

This was intercepted and eventually sent to Liddell-Hart, but caused Madeleine to be detained for a night. Basil Liddell-Hart sympathetic as always, had not earned his nickname "Bless his little heart" for nothing, but as he explained in his reply on 11 November, his knowledge of Stuart was confined to an acquaintance with his work more than ten years previously.

> it is evident that the view of the authorities is based on much more recent matters, followed by his return to the Continent in 1940.
> But if he is innocent I feel that a proper investigation by the British authorities is the best thing that could happen in his own interests, and I imagine that the latest step is a prelude to such an enquiry...

By then Stuart had already been released, for on 1 November he hastened to explain to Liddell-Hart that his "difficulty" was now over.

Liddell-Hart in the meantime, had a letter from the United Kingdom Representative to Eire [the equivalent of the British Ambassador and a nomenclature created during the war], Sir John Maffey, written on 29 October, which seemed to indicate that the Stuart case was still open. Maffey, like Stuart was educated at Rugby, but the connection did not encourage any old school tie fondness. The correspondence is scant and guarded, but it seems at the request of the British Foreign Office, Maffey had been asked to read a file he already held on Stuart. His letter to Liddell-Hart notes he saw:

> from the papers...you have interested yourself in the case of Henry Francis Stuart. So far as I know there has been no final decision in regard to his case, and I should be very grateful if you would let me know what view you took and why. To us it seemed an extremely bad case. Stuart left Ireland on health grounds in January 1940 with a permit to go to Switzerland. Up to that time associations with Germans in Dublin was, I suppose, normal for an ill-disposed neutral. However the case became interesting when in May 1940, Goertz landed by parachute in Eire and was harboured by Francis Stuart's wife to whose house he made his way immediately on landing... I need not go into further details as you will understand that to us this case looks pretty bad.

If there is any other side to it which you could confidentially let me know I would be most grateful...

Maffey's letter brought the Goertz affair to Liddell-Hart's attention for the first time, but does not mention the broadcasts. The authorities had not waited for Liddell-Hart's reply to Maffey, written when Stuart had already been released, but his answer comes very near the truth in explaining Stuart's motivation and behaviour.

Liddell-Hart was "sorry to hear" what Maffey wrote, but he explained to the Representative that he had been "...impressed by some reflections in a book of his which expressed a humane and liberal viewpoint, and wrote to tell him so. After that he sent me a play he had written...I heard no more until I got a letter from him in April this year..." Summarising the correspondence he had with Stuart, Liddell-Hart continued:

> from the somewhat dim memory I have of the book I read, it expressed an attitude that was essentially different to that of Nazi Germany, and I cannot imagine that if he had had any Nazi or Fascist sympathies he would have corresponded with me at that time, when I was writing many public warnings about the growth of the Nazi danger, and also the way that the Germans were trying to exploit Franco's rising in Spain for their own purposes. It does not make sense.

Liddell-Hart had looked up Stuart in an old *Who's Who* and had noted that he was lecturing at Berlin University sometime before the war. He speculated to Maffey that possibly Stuart's interest in Berlin was to continue his relationship with Madeleine, conjecturing that it had begun at that time. Because Stuart had remarked in a letter that he hoped to marry Madeleine at some later stage, Liddell-Hart reasonably deduced that his marriage had ended, and it was therefore possible that what Iseult "had done in Eire, after he left there, may have had no connection with his own actions or attitude." Of course Stuart was not responsible for what happened to Goertz after their brief meeting. But as Liddell-Hart continued to Maffey, "As a student of history, I have often found that what seems on the surface to have some deep political significance may not infrequently be due to more romantic urges." Regretting that he could offer so little, Liddell-Hart's letter appropriately ended: "Romantics ought to keep out of politics."

CHAPTER 12

Although no longer prisoners, Stuart and Madeleine could not leave the French Zone, and had to report weekly to the French Securité. They still were given no explanation of why they were arrested and imprisoned. The French authorities seemed to be unaware of Stuart's existence until he went to Paris when his contact with the Irish Legation must have led to some initial investigation. The French authorities knew about his broadcasts, for they were referred to once in passing during his interrogation. Had he been guilty of anything, action could only have been taken by the Irish Government, and it is unlikely they would have sought the help of French or British Intelligence to question Stuart.

The British Commonwealth and Foreign Office does hold a file on Francis Stuart compiled in 1946, and presumably dates from the time Liddell-Hart wrote to the Foreign Office in that year. But the present British Prime Minister's obsession with secrecy over matters of state continues to ensure that the file will not be released, although many sensitive documents relating to the last war are available for public inspection under the thirty year rule. It is possible that British Intelligence at some point, interfered illegally in Stuart's case and examination of the file would reveal information which would prove this assumption. Whatever the reason, it is difficult to imagine that the publication of the facts could possibly "endanger the state."

It was only much later, Madeleine heard the details of the spy called Gerda Meissner, who had operated in Marseilles at the time when she was attending Berlin University. During one interrogation, a sympathetic French Officer said to Stuart "I hear you were a communist", information he had extracted from a man called Schobert, who had tried to persuade Stuart to broadcast anti-communist propaganda. Stuart also heard that his Irish friend Blair had spoken to a French General in Paris who had intervened to secure their release, but he knew no more than that.

Whatever the truth, the only thing that mattered now to

Stuart was that he was with Madeleine, and wanted to publish a novel which would reflect his experience, and the new understanding of himself. On a practical level, it was difficult to work, for the lodgings were uncomfortable and did not provide the much needed sanctuary. Fortunately while Stuart was detained after his second arrest, he had met a woman who introduced him to a Frau Piening who offered hospitality to displaced persons including Lithuanians and Roumanians. Known as "Mutti" she also welcomed Madeleine and Stuart, who were glad to leave their freezing lodgings, and sit near the stove in her kitchen with hot soup. Madeleine taught English to some of the Lithuanians, who skilfully supplemented their food from the black market.

It was at Mutti's that Stuart and Madeleine spent Christmas, considerably heartened by an encouraging letter from Victor Gollancz, who was looking forward to receiving Stuart's novel. Despite the bitter cold, Stuart finished and sent it off to him by mid January, 1947.

Stuart had begun the book in the previous June, and although work was interrupted by his arrest, he had worked quickly, believing *The Pillar of Fire,* the new novel, was a definite advance on his earlier books. Negatively, Ethel Mannin wrote to Stuart suggesting that he should divorce Iseult and marry Madeleine, and expressed her own fears that no-one would publish Stuart's novel because of his attitude during the war. She had thought as she heard the broadcasts, "He is killing Francis Stuart the writer."

In his diary, Stuart noted:

> I begin to see that the new difficulties that have arisen out of my attitude during the war have gone to help in my development as a writer. Not only were the war years in Germany necessary to me as a writer, but the worse years of the aftermath too and the time of imprisonment... I can never recall too often that in those quiet years at home I did not as a writer progress. I widened my scope, I tried this and that but did not really progress along my path towards truth...

Now Stuart and Madeleine spent days huddled in blankets

because of the sub-zero temperatures, and visited the cinema more for warmth than any desire to see the film. They often saw an American friend Gary Nellhaus, who was attached to the Quaker Centre where Stuart occasionally taught, and who tried to help out with food when he was able, but for most of January they had only been allowed bread and little meat, with no dairy produce, sugar or cereal. By February when, there was almost nothing to eat, a food parcel arrived, for Ethel Mannin had encouraged friends to send some parcels through the Red Cross, and others through Switzerland. Many never arrived, but the collection procedure made the claimants feel they were not entitled to what was rightly theirs.

The time had now come to sell the heavy gold ring Stuart had bought just before they left Berlin, but when it was mistakenly offered to two people, he had to return an advance from the person who made the first offer. The incident, although ostensibly small was later embellished and made significant in his new novel, *The Pillar of Cloud*.

Because of the difficulties with their landlady, Stuart and Madeleine tried to find a room in a cheap hotel, but the choice was limited. Stuart wrote:

> My God, how weary I am of this outer misery without end, semi-starvation, cold, no real corner that one can call one's own and the shadow of prison never completely lifted from us, living under the surveillance of the French Police as we do...

A visit to Titisee in the Black Forest was a waste of time. A small *pension* would take them, but they could not be given anything above the food allowance on the ration cards, and would be worse off. Stuart tried to begin a new book, but first there was no seat in the reading room of the local library, and then someone complained he had no ticket. Both he and Madeleine were defeated at every turn, and on 27 February were, "...entering a time of starvation such as we have not had for a long time since this time a year ago in Prison and for a bit of last summer in the Beethoven Strasse..." Only turnip was always available but they were nauseated by its taste and could not bear to cook it.

Relief came through the wife of a French Officer who invited Stuart and Madeleine for supper. Beginning with a sweet tapioca soup, Stuart, uncertain what would be served next, surreptitiously tried to eat as many slices of bread as possible, before two helpings of pork and cauliflower. When their host heard they were starving, she produced the remains of lunch for them. After a liberal supply of white wine, bread and cheese, and finally coffee with brandy in it, Stuart and Madeleine felt they had been at a banquet, and all these details Stuart recorded in his diary because he could not recall when they had last eaten so well.

Despite this, Stuart was now suffering from malnutrition, and had to lie in bed from weakness. He had a letter from Iseult, who was still upset by his absence. He could do nothing to alleviate this, and was also worried to hear that his mother had been seriously ill. She was now recovering, but Iseult in another letter in early April, suggested to Madeleine, that she should "pack Stuart off" and send him home. It was now pointless for Stuart to go into the endless arguments about why he could not return, for he felt Iseult would never understand him. She:

> would not in the past, put her whole heart into our marriage, that we might have a living relationship. Perhaps she became weary and disillusioned so that her good will dried up. I cannot judge her in this, but the state of our life, that I can, and must judge, and it was largely sterile and miserable. The beautiful and good hours at home were those when I was alone (when they came at all) or occasionally with the children. I speak of the latter years.

Stuart determined not to write to his wife, but nevertheless did, trying once again to explain that it was hopeless to resume their marriage. On 11 April Iseult wrote Stuart a letter which "showed a faint glimpse of understanding... All the others were full of a natural enough, refusal to see anything beyond my failure as a husband...". She also gave more news of Lily, who in the confused state of being half awake, talked to herself about Stuart, something he thought "...really frightful to hear of." He realised that despite her impassive mask, his mother really was fond of him, and he was pleased to have in May, "..some very touching letters from Lily, who thank God is better. Written in her simple, primitive way, which nevertheless reveals a great depth of love."

As far as Iseult was concerned, there was too much "mutual suspicion" for understanding, but Stuart did not want to deliberately hurt her, and to show her that he really was trying to be sincere, wrote simply and directly about the problems. He knew nothing of Iseult's sadness over Goertz. The war had ended, and no decision had been taken about the spy *manqué*, who was still in custody. Goertz was afraid he would be handed over to the British for interrogation, and wrote to Iseult, asking that if anything should happen to him, she would contact his wife and send his love. His letter was intercepted and never reached Laragh.

During the morning of 23 May, Goertz heard he was to be transferred to another prison, and following his country's military code of honour, swallowed a phial of cyanide. He died an hour later, and although first buried in Dublin, his body was later moved to the German cemetery near the Dublin-Laragh road.

On hearing that Goertz was dead, Iseult wrote in French in her diary, "what will be, will be." Stuart remembered him as "an idealist who was completely inefficient... if the Germans really needed someone for this job, they couldn't have chosen a worse man..."

Ethel Mannin who planned to visit Freiburg, had also been in touch with Gollancz, urging him to take Stuart's novel. It had reached England safely but he had heard nothing until Gollancz wrote to say they needed a second opinion on it. As time passed without any decision, Stuart prepared for the inevitable blow of refusal:

My novel is too different to the other novels to be quickly or easily accepted. It should not surprise me or disappoint me that Gollancz hesitates so long to find a decision on it. It should not even surprise me if he finally rejects it. But what is difficult is not to worry over its fate. Still, at moments I reach a place from where I can regard all this in peace.

There was only Ethel Mannin's visit to look forward to, but as the exact date of this was unknown, her arrival on 21 June was a surprise, and a local sensation, when she turned up in an army jeep that flew a Union Jack. When they met, Stuart was struck by the fact that Ethel was the first person from his past whom he had contact with since the war began. After lunch which Ethel brought, they went for a walk, and Madeleine made macaroni with a tomato soup sauce for the evening meal. In an account of the visit, Ethel Mannin remarked on the lack of vegetables and salad, and suggested Madeline should steal some turnips belonging to someone else. In fact Madeleine did steal some vegetables from outside a shop, and was rebuked by Ethel for doing so.

Part of the purpose of Ethel's visit was to take messages to friends and relations at home, but she also hoped to persuade Stuart to leave Freiburg with her, and to renew an old intimacy of the past. Naturally this is not mentioned in her published account of the visit, *German Journey,* but she could not write objectively of Madeleine. It was now clear Ethel had been probing on her own behalf when she suggested Stuart should divorce Iseult. The three day visit ended, with Ethel feeling that he was:

> the prisoner upon whom the gate would close. Yet only the evening before he had insisted, quietly, that he was not trapped in his life; life had shaped this way and he was submitted to it; in time the pattern would change; he and Lisa [Madeleine] would not live out the rest of their lives among the ruins waiting for food parcels to arrive, but for the time being, this was their life and they accepted it..

Stuart asked Ethel to explain their position to his family and friends, and after she had gone, he and Madeleine wept, and went to bed emotionally drained. Both were strongly aware that Ethel could simply drive out of Freiburg, while they could not.

Madeleine knew of Stuart's past affair with Ethel, and he was touched that her bursts of jealous temper did not surface to mar the visit, which "...far from separating us it brought us closer together than ever..."

Ethel returned to England, to find a letter from Gollancz, finally declining *The Pillar of Fire*. The company had received widely differing reports about it, but because of the post war slump in publishing, the book could only have a minute sale. This would not normally have worried Gollancz, but he was already committed to other titles. Stuart had not let his post war experiences settle enough to write objectively of them, but had believed intensity was enough to shape the book. The news was a bitter blow, but Stuart persevered with the second book, writing nine or ten pages a day. Given the circumstances in which *The Pillar of Fire* was written, rejection was not surprising, but feeling depressed Stuart became drunk for the first time for five years, and had an unpleasant scene with Madeleine. He wondered if he should after all continue work on his new book, for if Gollancz had rejected the first, they were unlikely to take the second. One reader's report had criticised the main character for being an Australian painter, which provoked Stuart's comment, "For me it is only the revelation of his inner being that is important. This is the test. Outwardly he can be anything. I am not interested..."

His reaction was over defensive. Iseult once complained that he always first blamed everyone else when something went wrong, and in this case, he was unable to accept his book had faults, determined that he alone was correct in his judgement of it. He had to have faith in his work, or he could not have continued, and decided that:

> ordinary people will not like my work, even people like Ethel will not care much for my work. This discovery is a shock, but it is also a clarifying of the position. It will be hard for my... novels to get themselves accepted. But if they are... they will mean a great deal to a few...

Nothing seemed to be going well. The food problem worsened through the summer, and Stuart and Madeleine gave English language lessons, for which they were well paid. Money would not buy food, but parcels arrived irregularly.

On 1 September, Stuart read a newspaper account of the

arrest of his friend Libertas Schulze-Boysen, and her husband in 1942. It was the first he knew of their death, and in his diary that day he wrote:

This news (already so old) affected me strangely. To think that this girl whom I had held in my arms that night at the Wittenberg U banhof was so soon afterward destined to suffer all that horror. Every detail of the few times we were together suddenly became important, although till now I had thought of her fleetingly. Now she suddenly seems to me to have had a peculiar quality, a nobility that at the time of course I did not grasp...

Through the autumn, he went swimming with Madeleine, only otherwise interrupting his work to be with a few friends. By sticking rigidly to a timetable he completed the first draft by 9 October after seven months' work. The book now had a title, *The Pillar of Cloud,* and while he was correcting the typescript, he heard from Ethel Mannin that her publisher Jarrolds, was bringing out a book with a long section about Stuart, Iseult and Goertz and which was wildly untruthful. Ethel Mannin proposed to have the book read by a libel lawyer, and if it was defamatory, Stuart would sue, "...gladly if it really turns out to be an attempt to label me as a traitor or a spy, if I can get the money and also if the case can be taken in my absence..." The book was libellous, but nothing could be done because of Stuart's residence in Freiburg.

When the anniversary of his second arrest came round, Stuart recalled how easily he could forget the anguish of those days. He now accepted *The Pillar of Fire* had faults, and was resigned to news from his New York agent in mid November that it would not be published in America. Some poems of his were to appear in an anthology, his first acceptance since the war, but some unpleasant remarks a priest had made about him rankled, because he knew that he was being misrepresented. Without the publication of his fiction, he could not hope to make his beliefs understood. He had suffered worse than when he was, "...accused of being a communist by the Germans - by Schobert (an official at the

Ministry of Propaganda) in particular, and of being a Nazi by the Allies..." He knew his work ought to be better now, because in the past he had:

> wanted money, and fame and another time it was power. All these false desires! And all quite a short time ago, traces of them remained up to six or seven years ago. But now I am free from the more coarsely false desires Deo Gratias...but...I am very far from casting my bread on the water.

Stuart's American agent complained that the great fault of *The Pillar of Fire,* lay in the fact that despite living in Germany during the war, the main character had little feeling about it, and was on the contrary "concerned with his own personal life." It was exactly the stance Stuart had taken himself, but if that was the main fault, then he was "glad of it." Stuart reflected on the war, now over for two years, in his diary, and only intended for himself:

> What I had to wait, so long to understand begins to be revealed to me. And that is my own place in the whole cataclysm, the war and its aftermath. I see why I and S. had to go through what we did, had to be persecuted, arrested and kept eight frightful months in prisons. I came under suspicion not because I was a Nazi, which God knows I never was, but because I was not on any side. Because I did not believe in one propaganda or the other. Because I had a more or less blind instinct against three quarters of the whole organized civilization, the machine monster with all its camouflage, of false idealism, under which I had lived. And if I spoke on the German Radio to my own people in Ireland it was primarily to say this. Perhaps I was wrong to speak, perhaps it was identifying myself too much with the horrors of Nazism and it was a later realization of this that made me refuse to speak further. Of course in one sense better I had kept clear of the whole business, but had I done so, had I not suffered I would not have come to my present knowledge.
> I had to experience the whole horror first hand,- a horror that was not merely the Nazi horror, but this horror of a world which the Nazi was but a part. Now the Nazi horror

has gone, but the great horror remains. And the same old mistake is being made all over again. The whole blame is being laid on the communists or the capitalists, or on anything but the real core of the matter which is the fundamental false basis of our civilization. No, I am glad that I suffered (and S with me) and I know what I suffered for, because in my blind way I was not on the side of the victors, because I know there was no real victory...

The material quality of their lives gradually improved and as Christmas approached, three food parcels arrived. Despite the setbacks, Stuart concluded that the year was a good one in which his "relationship developed and strengthened..." and a year in which he "...at last continued the struggle towards inner integrity and truth."

There seemed to be no prospect of leaving Freiburg in the new year of 1948, for Stuart and Madeleine were still under surveillance.

The most encouraging news they had since the war, came from Victor Gollancz in March, accepting *The Pillar of Cloud* without reservation. He had not yet read it, "but I have had a quite magnificent report on it from my reader, and am most anxious to publish it...I judge it from the report to be a novel of very great beauty and significance."

Stuart's reaction on reading this letter, and sharing it with Madeleine must have been emotional, but he did not even mention the acceptance in his diary. His faith in his own work at last confirmed that others shared his ideals.

Before Stuart left for Germany, he had published thirteen novels. *The Coloured Dome* and *Pigeon Irish* proved he could be an original and imaginative writer. If he had remained in Ireland, his books would have continued to be as poor as the last he wrote there. But Stuart had deliberately detached himself from the progress of the war, until the heavy bombing forced him to take notice. If he could have returned to Ireland after the war ended, his fiction would only have reflected his comparatively narrow existence in Berlin. It was the aftermath of the war, rather than the war itself, that provided Stuart with the material to write *The Pillar of Cloud*. The personal diary Stuart kept in Berlin and

Freiburg was a long preparation for the novel, and without it, he could not have adequately interpreted the theme he chose for *The Pillar of Cloud*.

He had always identified himself with the outcast for very personal reasons, but an outcast in isolation. After the war, by being with other outcasts, especially homeless refugees, his work had a breadth it had previously lacked.

The hero of *The Pillar of Cloud*, Dominic Malone is an Irishman who finds himself in Marnheim, a town in the desolated French-occupied zone of Germany in the aftermath of the war. He cannot find any meaning in life until he befriends Halka and Lisette, sisters who are Polish refugees. Malone hears of Halka's experiences in a concentration camp and an asylum, and realises that her suffering has not made her bitter, but given her the capacity to forgive, even those who tortured her. Malone only fully understands this after he had been imprisoned, and released:

> While I was in the cellar...I saw how good life could be if only we understood the secret of real communion - not just physical contact or even friendship, but fraternity, and especially fraternity with a woman...

In this spirit of fraternity, Malone deepens his relationship with the sisters. Although he loves Halka, Lisette has severe tuberculosis, and Malone marries her so that he can take her to Ireland to be cared for. Their attempt to leave Germany fails, and Lisette dies. Malone now understands the value of personal sacrifice, which also embraces compassion, and re-united with Halka, he sees the joy of simple things for the first time:

> They had come through fire and were tempered...They had not sought to save themselves in the world, to save their lives, and life was being given to them. They felt it poured into them...from a measure full and running over. It was something that they could not speak about. They each, in their own way, felt this fullness of life in them...

Malone had realised the worthlessness of political theorising, including the possibility of anarchy suggested by one of the characters:

> no words, no promises of a new era of peace on earth were any use in the face of the night that had descended. All this was part of the old temptation. To try to establish peace and equity on earth through organising, calculating, planning. And even the anarchist's plan to do away with all organising and all plans was a plan just the same... and...would prove in the end inadequate, powerless against the great power of darkness.

Stuart does not suggest any conventional interpretation of religion would dispel "the power of darkness", nor that belief in any prophet would offer:

> promise of peace on earth. Only something that is neither promise nor plan...If I love my brother or sister for the sake of ultimate peace and fraternity on earth, then it is really for my own sake and the love is already corrupt in its root. It is the old tale of the Devil offering Christ the kingdoms of the earth. But the peace and fraternity that Christ had to reveal could not be imposed like that, as reforms and revolutions are imposed.

When Malone is challenged by the anarchist, who asks if things would be worse without Christ, he replies:

> Yes. I can and do believe it. Not that the desolation would be worse, that there would be even more ruins, more hunger, more misery on earth, but that there would not be any possibility of understanding these things. And that would be the ultimate horror - if Christ had not suffered these things and foreseen them, then it would be the end. But He was the one prophet who did not promise peace on earth, but destruction and desolation...He did not preach revolution or any counter measures. He said.. above all "Love one another as I have loved you." That is, through all these things, even through passion and death. And that is our fraternity, and the only true fraternity.

When the novel was published in 1948, Olivia Manning, wrote that Stuart's pre-war fiction would be remembered "for their high literary quality and perhaps for their atmosphere of romantic unreality which debilitated the conflicts they described..." *The Pillar of Cloud* was however:

> written with a poetic force that comes out of the very core of suffering. Apart from its quality, the novel is unique in that no other English-speaking writer has been in a position to touch upon its subject except from the outside. Mr Stuart writes with convincing certainty of the reactions of a starving man from whom a promised food-parcel is witheld by the incompetence of officials, the simple acceptance of a morality, the spiritual triumph of these people who somehow surmount the desolation of their physical condition, the evolution of the Irishman who voluntarily chooses that condition...

The Swiss critic Serge Radine, who reviewed the novel in a Swiss journal in 1951 [two other titles of Stuart's were published by then], thought that much of contemporary writing reflected:

> an essentially comfortable world - a pre-war world...remote from the hopes and torments of the present age...Francis Stuart's novels, however are about the world we all know too well, the world created by the War...In the bitterest suffering, the cruellest disappointment, even in the worst humiliation there still springs up lasting hope ceaselessly, invincibly. The original and beneficial worth of Stuart's books flow from this fact. In contrast to their fellow men who only live in the bygone world of memories, incapable of grasping the terrible change which took place before their eyes...Francis Stuart's heroes realize the great task imposed on them by their appalling experiences. They seek peace in the middle of chaos; they know that there reality is patience, freedom from conceit, self-sacrifice, altruistic love...

Radine refuted the suggestion that Stuart's work was similar to that of Graham Greene's, whose literary world is disconsolate, "turns away from earthly life and human love" and offers humanity "eternal salvation as a way out of Creation when otherwise there is now way out". In Stuart:

> there persists in the deepest misery a mysterious hope rooted in our nature, and for him fleshly life is always related to the fate of the soul. That is why this writer, inspired with poetic fire, appears to us as a great prophet of Godly love. Stuart's whole work is inspired by the Russian idea - Dostoevsky's influence is visible here - of forgiveness of sins through suffering and love...The greatness of Stuart is his ability to embrace all the pain of men and still to preserve hope.

When a new edition of *The Pillar of Cloud* was published in 1974, Sean MacMahon wrote:

> If this novel had been re-issued at any time in the lush economic-miracle days of the sixties it would have seemed dated: a cosy, horripilatory glance at a word decently buried under...tourist roads. Now as we begin to remember fear it becomes very much a book for our own time.

CHAPTER 13

Iseult wrote from time to time, and sent new trousers and a pair of sandals. Stuart at last shed the suit he had brought from Ireland and worn almost daily for nearly ten years. His wife was now reconciled to the fact that he would not return to her, and suggested that he should surrender his share of Laragh Castle in favour of his children. As Stuart knew they were well provided for, and that Iseult herself would inherit her mother's house in St Stephen's Green, he hoped he might have a stake in one of the other properties. He had nothing apart from his half share of Laragh, he wanted to at least feel he had somewhere of his own in Ireland.

While he waited for an answer, Ethel Mannin came to stay again for a few days, and after she left, Stuart and Madeleine managed a day at the Baden-Baden races. He had lost none of his old skills, and after backing the winner, the three hour journey back was made with a sense of exhiliration they rarely felt.

Success on the race-track seemed to herald a change of fortune, for Madeleine was given the status of a displaced person and could now make positive steps to emigrate. Then a new barrier arose from currency revision, and the old mark became worthless. Each person was given forty new marks, and once again, Stuart and Madeleine were concerned about how to pay their monthly rent.

The currency reform created a surplus of food and other goods in the shops which no-one could afford. Stuart was considerably cheered when Gary Nellhaus and Betty Collins another American friend from the Quaker Centre, brought a proof copy of *The Pillar of Cloud* for correction. It had been sent to Nellhaus for safety, and he returned in the evening to collect the proof for posting. Stuart added the dedication "To Magdalena", setting a seal on his relationship with Madeleine. They both knew the significance of this first book for nine years, and what it had taken to write.

There was no word from Ethel by July, despite her promise to write from England, but she did not have Stuart far from

mind. In her novel called *Late Have I Loved Thee,* the main
character Francis Sable was loosely based on him. The book
was completed in 1946, and in some respects, her portrait of
Stuart was scarcely disguised. In the opening the narrator
speculates:

> what became of Francis Sable, I wonder? One never seems to
> hear of him nowadays... It was somewhere in the early
> thirties that Francis Sable 'faded out'...no-one seems to know
> if he is alive or dead, and the younger generation, never
> having read him, are indifferent...to all intents and purpose
> Francis Sable is forgotten...

Ethel Mannin had loosely written of Stuart's early life,
and his new approach to writing after the war, but the novel
showed how little she really understood him. Ironically it
was enjoyed by Madame MacBride, who wrote to Ethel that
it was "...the greatest of all your books". As she was furious
with Stuart, and considered he had abandoned his family,
she could not have identified him as the hero.

When the Allies sent Stalin an ultimatum about the Berlin
blockade, Stuart dreaded that what had been achieved since
1945 would come to an end. The danger passed, and now
there was the possibility they could move to Venezuela. Both
made vague plans with this in mind, but the process of
granting Madeleine her full status was extremely slow. Since
their imprisonment, Madeleine and Stuart dreaded any
knock at the door, and when a French policeman arrived
without warning in August, and asked Madeleine to go to the
Police Station, they were terrified of arrest or separation.
The visit was only a routine screening for the *Permit de
Séjour,* a document which confirmed Madeleine's Polish
birth, and allowed emigration, but when Madeleine went to
Rastatt to appear before a commission about Venezuela,
Stuart was apprehensive about leaving Freiburg, and
remembered the loneliness of Paris. He was tired from
concentrated work on a new novel, which he completed at the
end of September.

After sending it to Gollancz, Stuart could concentrate on
trying to leave Germany. Venezuela had come to nothing, and

three years had passed since he had hopelessly wandered around Paris in a bid for their freedom.

While waiting for answers to various enquiries, Gollancz sent an advertisement for *The Pillar of Cloud* which quoted Compton Mackenzie, "Wonderful: the most profound book about the aftermath of the war I have read in any language. I really am left without words to express my admiration." Gollancz added "I should like you to know how very proud indeed I am to have published the book..."

On 23 October 1948 the Security Police told Stuart he soon could leave Freiburg. He would have preferred to have gone to England, to hear his own language, and to be near Ireland to see Lily in her old age, but he had to move cautiously. It was enough in the meantime to be without the "continual shadow of some authority or another". When all obstacles that blocked his travel were cleared, Stuart was "exhausted with relief." But he added in his diary, "I must not forget that exactly two years ago I was sitting in a cold dungeon in dread and uncertainty..." Anxiety about the reception of the typescript, was dispelled when Gollancz, reassured Stuart that his reader found the new novel to be "an intensely moving experience. *Pillar of Cloud,* I am very glad to see, is receiving some splendid tributes, but this is, to my mind, a finer book."

Gollancz had paid £75.00 for *The Pillar of Cloud,* and increased the advance for the new book to £100.00. He suggested the proposed title, *Psalm above the Fish Shop* should be shortened, as advertising space was limited in the national press and Stuart changed it to *Redemption.* It was particularly annoying that his agent in Berlin, who had done nothing to help, insisted on keeping 25% of any translation rights for *The Pillar of Cloud.* The novel was making its mark in England, where Basil Liddell-Hart read it "with keenest interest and appreciation", and wrote to Stuart wondering what had become of him. In thanking Liddell-Hart, Stuart expected "...before long to go to Paris and from there hope to come to England, at least for a visit, before we finally find somewhere to settle down..." Liddell-Hart wrote again in a few days, anxious for a detailed account of Stuart's situation. In his long reply, Stuart mentioned in passing that he had heard from the French authorities that he had been detained "...on recommendations made by the English authorities...because of some broadcasts I had made to Ireland from Germany during the war..." He explained the problems of getting Madeleine out of Germany, and wondered if Liddell-Hart could find out if there was any barrier to his going to England, and if there was any chance of finding work for Madeleine.

Stuart suggested that their detention had "not much bearing on our present position," something with which Liddell-Hart disagreed. He had had a confidential telephone conversation with Maffey in Dublin, and presumably now knew the reasons for Stuart's arrest, for Maffey had asked him not to repeat what they had discussed.

Stuart and Madeleine enjoyed a quiet Christmas, which they hoped would be their last in Germany, but he was downhearted because he had not heard from Liddell-Hart. The new year of 1949 began badly. Not only was their money coming to an end, but Madeleine was afraid that she might be pregnant. They both suffered the worst anxiety since their imprisonment, and the only hope came from Liddell-Hart, who they heard from in January. He had taken several months to write, because his enquiries at the Home Office were hampered by the fact that he knew no-one in the Attlee Government. Nevertheless, he had gathered that:

> there is likely to be a difficulty there unless the matter of your broadcasts can be cleared up. Could you give me full details about these, and the circumstances? It should be needless to say that it would be important for any efforts that I can make that you should be completely frank - for my information - as otherwise the attempt may be wrecked on some uncharted rock...

Liddell-Hart had passed *Pillar of Cloud* to some people who had influence, hoping it would give them an insight into Stuart's "mind and fundamental attitude..." To help Liddell-Hart, Stuart sent what is the earliest statement on the subject of his conduct during the war:

I made these broadcasts on the so-called Irish programme weekly, and for a time twice weekly, from about August 1942 until January or May, 1944. These talks were never addressed to any public except the Irish. They never dealt with Military matters. My main theme was Irish neutrality which I endorsed and also the question of partition. They were certainly anti-British from an Irish Nationalist point of view but never pro-Nazi. I never dealt with any aspect of the war that had not at least an indirect Irish concern. But I said things which I have certainly no desire to defend. And this came, as I later saw, from the position I was in of being free to criticize the propaganda and intentions of English and American Statesmen and not the German. Needless to say I never dealt with the German occupation and oppression of other countries, though I claimed that the North Ireland nationalists formed a legitimate resistance movement.

There may be points now that I do not remember after five or six years but this gives as honestly as I can the outward drift of my broadcasts...

He explained that his own attitude during the war was pacifist, and that he had looked on most of what was said about the war on all sides as a lie. His original intention in agreeing to broadcast was to expose this. That position was weak because he had been "...only free to deal with the dishonesties (according to my view) of one or two of the belligerents." Stressing that he had never mentioned Russia, although urged to do so, Stuart:

saw that if I criticized Russia I was putting myself at the service of the German cause, as also if I had praised Nazism. This may seem a small distinction, but to me it was very real. I considered it possible to speak to Irish people as an Irishman about aspects of the war of concern to Ireland without identifying myself with the German aims.

Gradually I began to see the difficulties in which I had involved myself. I wished to stop broadcasting in the summmer of 1943, but allowed certain circumstances to influence me to continue. One of these was that it allowed me to take my friend [Madeleine] away from Berlin where

213

her position was bad, and which in any case was undesirable to remain in, not to mention the beginning of the bad air-attacks...

After showing Stuart's letter to a barrister who was also an MP, (possibly Harold Nicholson, whom Stuart had some contact with before the war) Liddell-Hart's answer in late January was disappointing:

while the Home Office attitude is likely to be that while they would have been willing to drop action against you over the broadcasts, it is more than can be expected that they should provide you with asylum here, and there can be no grounds for making special concessions in this matter...

Liddell-Hart intended talking to the MP when he was next in London, and explained he himself understood far better the difficulties Stuart had become involved in, and why. Liddell-Hart's contact at the Home Office, still left the question of their intervention with an Irish neutral unresolved, for the British Home Office could not "drop any action", for legally it had none to take. In the case of William Joyce, the prosecution for the Crown could not press the charge that he had broadcast for the enemy, because Joyce was an alien. He was convicted as a traitor because he nevertheless owed allegiance to the British Crown. Stuart had an Irish passport, and if his broadcasts had aided the enemy, he could only have been charged by the British Crown, under the Treachery Act of 1940. This covered acts to assist the enemy, by any person, not just British subjects, within the United Kingdom. It would have been difficult to interpret the sound of Stuart's radio voice as constituting such an action. His final statement on the subject is found in a Foreword he wrote to a book called *Le Reveur Casque* by Christian de la Maziere which he translated into English as *The Ashes of Honour*. De la Maziere who was from a distinguished French military family, became a member of the Waffen SS (the elite fighting troops of the German Army, as distinct from the SS used as extermination squads and in concentration camps) at the point when the Allies were winning the Second War. He was eventually captured by the Russians, and subsequently tried, found guilty and imprisoned as a collaborator. When the book was published in 1975, Stuart's comments on the author threw further light on his attitude to his own period in Germany, for he was writing as much of himself as de la Maziere.

Stuart notes that a certain time had to pass before such a book as De la Maziere's could be published. "The relief", he wrote, "at having overcome the evils of Nazi ideology and practices... ensured that for a long time war books would be accounts of heroism in a just cause." Singling out Primo Levi's *If This is a Man* about survival in a concentration camp, as "classic" because it had "the self revealing quality of art," however far apart Christian de La Maziere and Primo Levi were, both books were remarkable for the same reason: "the revelation of a human psyche under extremes of isolation and threat."

The author had not apologised for what he had done but attempted to convey certain states of mind, even if they had led to the wrong decision:

> What matters finally is not the mistake of a very young man in supposing his political and social beliefs were likely to be promoted by Hitler, but his abiding instinct (it was more than an idea) to follow his own deepest conscience no matter where it led. It is not an instinct that everyone will approve of in all circumstances, but in the growing lack of credible ideologies, governments and churches ever more evident, it is all that many of us have to cling to.

Gollancz had now read *Redemption* and could not remember when he was "so profoundly moved by a book". He accepted Stuart's position in Germany during the war, and also accepted Madeleine without moralizing, and sent her "blessings" in the same letter. Gollancz's views were shared by his editor, Sheila Hodges, who was trying to find an American publisher for both novels, and thought *Redemption* "in particular...too wonderful a novel to be handled by any publisher as 'just another book.'"

There was some reassurance in that others Stuart knew

were leaving Freiburg, but his exit visa for France was delayed by red-tape. Madeleine had accepted work as a maid for a French General and his family in Paris, and was to start in March, but heard that they did not want her after all.

In the same post as this news, Viking of New York, rejected *Redemption* because they thought it would not have wide acceptance in America. "I don't ask for it to be a success," Stuart wrote " but that it may have enough readers to give me a footing in the solid world so that I can subsist on it..."

Olivia Manning, in her review of *The Pillar of Cloud* had doubted "if even Mr Stuart could write another novel about these [wartime] experiences...he has beggared them of emotion." In this she was mistaken, for Stuart had found his theme, and enlarged it in *Redemption*. Critics were be divided about which was the finer novel. Stylistically not as well written as the earlier novel, *Redemption* is perhaps more powerful. Ezra Arigho returns to Ireland after witnessing the horrors of wartime Germany. Estranged from his wife Nancy, Arigho believes that his lover Margareta, whom he left behind in Germany, has been killed in a raid. He resents the complacency of the inhabitants of Altamount, where he now lives, who are contentedly indifferent to the war they were not involved in. Arigho is haunted by his past, and compelled to relate his experiences to various people who seem emotionally shallow, disturbs their attitude to life. These include Father Mellowes a colourless priest and Romilly Mellowes his sister, an innocent girl about to enter a comfortable marriage and Kavanagh, a coarse fishmonger. Arigho brings the war to Altamount in a sense, and unwittingly prepares the central characters for an act of violence which disrupts the town, and for which he is morally responsible. Kavanagh hates the attitudes of the conventional morality of Altamount, whose authorities force his mistress Annie to leave his employment. Partly stirred by what he has heard from Arigho, and the desire to strike back against respectability, his anger drives him to murder Annie after she has taunted him with accounts of her unfaithfulness to him.

The crime Kavanagh commits is shocking, but Stuart does not engage sympathy for Annie, but for the real victim, Kavanagh. Arigho at first doubts the power of goodness against the evil he has evoked, but reluctantly unites with the main characters, who form a small community and establish a bond of fraternity in the sanctuary of Kavanagh's house. The murder has redeemed the lives of those affected by it, including the priest whose attitudes are transformed from banality into saintliness. The shadow of death that Kavanagh lives under, is made tolerable by the understanding of the community, who transcend material values. Margareta who is alive but crippled, comes to Altamount to bring a healing love not only to Arigho, but to the others. Kavanagh is finally saved from ultimate despair by the spiritual love of Romilly, who marries him to comfort him in his last days before his execution.

In *Redemption,* Stuart challenges ideas of morality, the role of the Church, and stresses the importance of personal renewal in suffering. For each member of the community already possessed the capacity to love, which it only required a catalyst to awaken. However, despite the many allusions to the Crucifixion, and the recognition of evil and good, Stuart does not offer any answer to the question of divine purpose, that Ezra Arigho asks the priest at the end of the novel:

"All this destructive pain," Ezra said, "what can come of it? All the pain that cannot be borne, or submitted to. What condemned men go through and children and others. Can there be any point in it or isn't it the sign of chaos?"...
He saw Father Mellowes' smile...and knew that this was the nearest to an answer that they would ever get.

Outside the main structure of the novel, there is a relatively brief account of Arigho's wife, Nancy, who Stuart largely based on Iseult, portrayed to emphasize the falseness of their past to which Arigho will not return. Stuart reasonably factually relates the circumstances of his own life with Iseult. Arigho tells Nancy that while it is true on one level that he knows:

the story that you tell yourself, and perhaps others. 'I gave
my youth and my faithfulness to whom ? To a blind, egotistic
boy, who later turned into an adventurer and gambler,
leaving me to my loneliness and waiting.' But there are so
many levels, each with its own strange story, contradicting
all the others. If you could have shared with me in my
adventures and in all my stupid or worthless passions, then
we could have been close...

Nancy is proud, and:

living in a tower of idealism that she cannot escape from.
She is trapped behind the wall of her own judgements. She
has judged the world and most of its activity to be evil and
foolish and has been proved right, but what satisfaction is
there finally in being right? To prove oneself morally right
and to get no pleasure out of being so, is not that
bitter?...There's no use trying to begin all over again...If we
were to shut ourselves up together like all the couples, we'd
soon explode apart, and this time violently...There's only one
thing to do, and that is to renounce our marriage...and to
approach each other as two people might who have been shut
up in prison together, sharing the same cell, and are now
meeting again outside, in freedom...if we now make up our
minds to stand by each other, not out of some duty or rights,
not because we're married, but because we're neighbours....if
we now stand by each other, then we'll have begun
something better than we ever had before.

He appeals to Nancy to leave her home and to share her
life with him, Margareta and the others. She declines his
offer, but suggests that he should at least visit his aunt
Nuala who was fond of him in the past, and is dying of a
kidney disease.

Nuala, Stuart based on his Aunt Janet Montgomery, and it
is she, stubborn and difficult, who becomes a member of the
fraternity, nursed by Margareta. Crippled and humble,
Margareta is everything Nancy is not. She cannot speak
much English, and therefore unlike Nancy, cannot
"philosophize" or "intellectualize". Her communication with

Nuala is more on an animal level of tenderness because they cannot converse. Nuala gradually achieves a sense of contentedness which she has never experienced before, and this at least partly reconciles her to the prospect of her own death.

Nancy's appearance in *Redemption* is interesting for the way Stuart projects his view of his relationship with Iseult, and how he imagined her concept of him to be. Nevertheless, in an otherwise rounded study, Arigho's characterisation is flawed by his judging Nancy in a rather self-righteous manner. He accuses her of lacking in insight towards him, by insisting on judging him.

Stuart had written to Iseult asking if she would help him and Madeleine to go to Ireland. This would get them out of Freiburg, and satisfy Iseult's hopes that Stuart would return. Iseult however wanted Stuart back in Ireland, more for the sake of the children, rather than for herself, a point that is clear from some of the surviving letters. According to their daughter Kay, Iseult had endured a great deal, but the suggestion that she should share her life with Stuart and Madeleine was far more than she could bear. He knew of Iseult's reaction on this point, for it also features in *Redemption.*

Redemption was written at a desperate period of Stuart's life, but by the time the novel was published, he and Iseult understood each other better. She was therefore upset to read of herself through Nancy, with her "distaste for sex", and other charges to which she could not reply. It was obvious which details were autobiographical, but when Stuart heard of Iseult's reaction to *Redemption,* he wrote, "I did no more than touch on the whole business of Iseult and my family. My children and Lily I did not mention..." He had heard nothing from either Kay or Ion, feeling that they held:

> some disapproval of my having left Iseult and them to be with G. [Madeleine]. But how weary all this 'disapproval', this tacit abrogation of the right to 'judge' makes me! By what laws and concepts can we judge? For me only by the pure movements of the heart or soul. Only through that, through the inner passion, will one become integral and

honest enough to be able to judge and then one won't want to 'judge' anymore...

Commenting on this later, Stuart thought Iseult had a right to take up an attitude towards him, but not his aunt, whom he imagines in *Redemption* criticising him to Iseult. While he realised he had hurt Iseult, he never harmed Janet. Stuart has his aunt reconciled to him before she dies in his novel, in actuality, he doubted if she ever was. He could only see her as a cantankerous character, and had not forgotten the comment her maid had said to him before the war, "Miss Janet's in a very bad mood, like a wasp under a jar."

Whatever accusations Stuart made of Iseult, she made a point of never discussing her emotions about him, and hardly hinted what she felt even to her own children. Meanwhile Stuart received a bitter letter from Ethel Mannin, attacking the book, and saying that it should not circulate in Ireland, because the Irish would not stomach its blasphemy, and for other reasons which Stuart does not go into in his diary. These probably had something to do with Madame MacBride, whom Ethel was trying to ingratiate herself with, and the MacBride family. Madame MacBride was apparently fond of Ethel, nevertheless, Tiernan, Madame MacBride's son-in-law, disliked her intensely, and considered her a busybody. *Redemption* was not popular with Madame MacBride who waited for Ethel's novel about Nazi Germany *Every Man A Stranger,* as "something to take away the nastiness" of Stuart's book.

When the novel was published in America, a postcard from a crank forwarded to Gollancz read, "No. I'm sorry I bought it. It is a pornographic moronic effusion and I am surprised that you published it. I put it in the furnace. Money wasted." The crank's view was an isolated opinion. Compton MacKenzie considered *Redemption:*

a magnificent book, and if its beauty and terror do not win Francis Stuart the recognition he deserves I shall begin to despair of contemporary English criticism. *Redemption* has given me at sixty-six the kind of thrill Dostoevsky used to give me at sixteen.

The Russian influence was also noticed by Elizabeth Jenkins in *The Manchester Guardian* who said it was:

> understandable that Francis Stuart's work should invite a comparison with that of the great Russian novelists...because of the deep quality of his imagination and the direction he gives it: towards an understanding of man rather than of the mechanics of man's environment...The book presents the Irish scene with a serious realism which reveals its inimitable grace without a hint of artificiality; but no description can do justice to such a work.

Whatever accusations Stuart had from Iseult that he was neglecting his children, Kay and Ion had an opportunity for themselves to judge the situation, when they stayed for a week with Stuart and Madeleine in mid-June. Ion had already spent a few days there earlier in March, and in a letter to his father told him that he had spent some of the happiest days since his childhood. Kay was slightly overwhelmed when Madeleine welcomed her by dancing round the room because she was happy to see her. The visit was valuable, and for Stuart, " ...a real joy, a kind of reconciliation between us all, especially between us and Kay. With Ion it had already taken place. The harm and loss of all these years was largely undone and we have been given back to each other..."

Not unexpectedly, when Kay and Ion returned to Laragh, Iseult was curious to hear about life in Freiburg, but not from any sense of malice. Kay recalls that far from being bitter about Madeleine, she was only concerned that her husband should be happy.

A few days after the children left Freiburg, Stuart completed his new novel, *The Flowering Cross*, and the following day, 21 June 1949, his passport was ready, stamped with an exit visa. Stuart could now make positive plans to go to Paris.

Coincidentally, Gary Nellhaus, the young American who did voluntary work at the Quaker Centre was going there to stay with friends, and he called on Stuart and Madeleine several times between the 20 and 23 June, to discuss ways in

221

which he could help Stuart, whom he hoped to meet in Paris. He took the typescript of *The Flowering Cross* to post, and although Stuart was not happy with the final chapter, it was more urgent to arrange a job for Madeleine in Paris than rewrite it.

At the end of the month Stuart and Madeleine met friends from America in Basle, who showered them with presents, Stuart and Madeleine missed their train, and their long walk back to the next station, was the last they would take together in Germany.

Uncertain of the length of time he would be away, Stuart was reluctant to leave Madeleine with the difficult landlady, and they found a smaller room elsewhere. The gloom of the Schwarzwaldstrs. no 2. was now only a memory, and although the days ahead were anxious, they were hopeful.

CHAPTER 14

Stuart left for Paris on 2 July, and as soon as he arrived, called on Nellhaus, who was staying in the Avenue de Breteuil. The apartment belonged to a Hungarian writer, Lodzi Dormandi, known to his family as Laci, and who lived there with his wife Olga and their daughter Judith. Olga suggested Stuart should have an attic room when it was available, and in the meantime, he took a cheap hotel near the Cite Universitaire. A few days later Nellhaus:

> Met Francis - we sit at cafe, talk of many things, his feelings that the old art - viz. Botticelli - has nothing to give today. His serenity, gladness to be out of Germany ... He dines with us (Dormandi's) Tuesday evening 5th, then we go to a Beethoven concert. After concert Francis, Judith and I sit and talk a while...

During the conversation in the Avenue de Breteuil, Dormandi immediately offered to sponsor Madeleine for a job on condition that Stuart organized all the paper work. Stuart gratefully trudged around Paris doing this, and when he chanced to see a display in a bookshop of *Redemption*, was struck by the wrapper, printed as *Francis Stuart's Redemption*.

Towards the end of July, he heard nothing from Madeleine, except one angry letter. Distraught at being alone, she imagined Stuart has abandoned her, and instead of writing directly to him, told another friend in Paris in a letter that she had been accepted for Australia. Madeleine could not understand the delay in bringing her to France. Stuart had already sent off reams of official papers about her job as the Dormandi's maid, and worried about Madeleine until he had a reasurring letter from her on 28 July.

Gollancz had sent Stuart the reader's report on *The Flowering Cross,* part of which read:

> Stuart's talent is erractic and his vision is a confused one. The first novels, marked a "steady advance towards, order,

clarity and coherence ... [when] Stuart ... seemed to be recovering from the profound emotional shock of his wartime experiences, and gradually to be coming to terms again with life. But for me, the present novel is a retrogression towards the peculiarly enclosed world of the first of those ... the unpublished and unpublishable *The Pillar of Fire...*

The reader suggested that Redemption was as far as he could go with that particular theme, believing the real trouble was that:

Stuart is not really a novelist at all, but a poet philosopher. He is incapable of approaching a novel as a piece of craftsmanship, to be undertaken for the pleasure of the craft (or to pay the rent): he must be conveying his vision.

Gollancz himself read *The Flowering Cross,* and although he thought it was "an easy book to guy" (sic) wrote on 2 August, "I very definitely want to publish it... there are insights in it very rare indeed nowadays - in fact perhaps unique..." and concluded "... The trouble of course is that real Christianity - Blake's sort of Christianity - is quite out of fashion today..."

Acceptance of *The Flowering Cross* at least guaranteed money needed to set up in Paris, but on the long term, Stuart could not afford to slip back into his pre-war tendency of writing quickly for financial security. Profound as his message was, he was in danger of repeating his own war experiences, and characters to the point of obsession. Having found new readers, he had to hold them by offering nothing new.

Stuart could not think beyond Madeleine's struggle to leave Germany. At last, on 8 August, he had a telegram from Madeleine confirming her contract for the job had arrived, that she was leaving at once for a camp at Rastatt, and would arrive in Paris in a few days. Stuart could hardly grasp that Madeleine would be with him soon, and found it difficult to accept that their long torment of captivity was almost over.

Due to various formalities, Madeleine did not reach Paris until 19 August, when she telephoned the Dormandis to say that she would be at the Gard de L'Est at 2.30 in the afternoon. Stuart met her there with a bunch of white carnations, and for a moment, Madeleine thought she had "stepped into paradise". Stuart knew they would never forget their reunion.

with the day of our release [from prison] it was the greatest joy we have had - together or alone. And now these days of fulfillment - out of that shadow that was always over us in Germany.

The Dormandis welcomed Madeleine before taking a holiday in Brittany, leaving Nellhaus to look after the apartment and their attractive but bad tempered Siamese cat, Kira. Nellhaus noted on 20 August:

Kitten Sophie on my lap. Gertrude Meissner here after Dormandi's gave contract, it worked out in short, five weeks. Marvellous. Francis very happy, not shy before me anymore as he will even tenderly stroke her hair in front of me, almost as if I weren't there...

Sophie had taken to Francis at once, and the Dormandi's gave her to Stuart as a present for Madeleine. She was the first of many cats, and the most loved, representing the start of the couple's new life.

The attic room was bare apart from a couch, which Stuart wrote from, but there was the promise of a second room, where Stuart could work. He could not earn enough to live by writing, but Madeleine had a cleaning job with friends of the Dormandis.

Iseult had passed on Stuart's address to Florrie, Cecil Salkeld's wife, who wrote that various people in Ireland had considered *Redemption* a "great book", an opinion which proved contrary to Ethel Mannin's. Nothing detracted from Madeleine and Stuart's happiness, as Nellhaus observed in his diary entry for 27 August: "Francis and Gertrude - in some ways anti-intellectual. Francis has sharp sights for writing. Gertrude can be a bit silly" something which Nellhaus then recognized Stuart disapproved of:

> Noticed it several times ... Gertrud has almost Eastern way of dramatizing her likes, exhibiting affections. Still, no matter, both are wonderfully honest - perhaps best about them. In some ways both need taking care of, are as "undzundtaendig" [incompetent] as they come... Francis considers sex central passion of life. (I think it becomes central because of our social emphasis on it.) But Francis and I agree on need for tenderness.

Judith was surprised that her father who could not be "difficult" had taken to Stuart so quickly, but Dormandi had noticed there was something remarkable about Stuart which he liked. She remembered:

> they would come down for a bath, and were extremely discreet when they came through the apartment. One didn't know they were through. When they were invited to come down we had very nice evenings. He was very spirited and good humored, and seemed more Irish than the real world. In his way of speaking he took so much care not to disturb us, and had very intelligent feelings.

Before Madeleine took up her cleaning job, she and Stuart spent a week's holiday in mid-September in Versailles, in a house lent to them by Stuart's publisher, Paul-Andre Lesort, who had taken the French edition of *The Pillar of Cloud*. The holiday was interrupted to lunch with Victor Gollancz and his wife and daughter in Paris. Madeleine was nervous, for she knew no-one, but Gollancz went out of his way to be friendly, insisting she sat next to him, and kissing her hand when they parted.

By the end of the month, Stuart and Madeleine had the promised second garret room which they converted into a study. It was farther down the corridor from the one they lived in, but once whitewashed and furnished with a desk from Dormandi, Stuart had somewhere to work for the first time in ten years without the threat of being uprooted.

The Pillar of Cloud, ironically translated as *La Colonne de feu,* was published on 23 November, Madeleine's thirty-third birthday, and later that evening, Lesort gave a party. Stuart found it an ordeal, but Madeleine enjoyed the recognition that was given to him. In his diary that evening Stuart wrote:

> Francois Mauriac tall, grey, nervous, came up and praised the book, which I was told was a rare honour. When I spoke admiringly of his work, he said rather strangely and charmingly 'Touche, touche'...

A problem arose over the French edition of *Redemption.* Gallimard had the legal right to publish it, and as a more influential publisher than Editions du Temps Present, could afford to pay more. Despite constant money worries, Stuart hoped Lesort would take it, for he did not care for Gallimard's impersonal approach. From England, the financial horizon looked brighter. Gollancz had placed *Redemption* with an American publisher with the promise of an advance of £300. Christmas was spent in modest comfort, only marred by the news on Christmas Eve, that Gallimard had stood on their legal rights and would publish *Redemption.*

As was his habit at the end of a year, Stuart reflected in his diary for 31 December, on what had been "..the most fruitful and eventful of all years." He had gained "a certain, if hesitant growth in wisdom and perhaps in peace," and in his relationship with Madeleine, "a deepening of understanding, a growth in patience and humility." He remembered the reconciliation with his children, the new friends they had made, and the pleasure of Sophie. With editions of his novels appearing in France, Britain and America, there was a chance he could at last live off his writing.

Stuart made no entry in his diary for 1950 until he recorded on 25 February that Madeleine was in hospital for appendicitis. She was out on 5 March, and after Stuart received the American advance for *Redemption* he had the strange sensation of writing his first cheque for over ten years. Buying much needed clothes, and visiting art galleries were small signs that Stuart and Madeleine were once more participating in 'normal' life, but Stuart still preferred to be reclusive. He re-read Joyce's *Portrait of the Artist as a Young Man* in March, and thought it "a small work of genius in the great desert of shoddy work. A few passages of really great art."

With Ireland on his mind, he was glad to introduce Liam O'Flaherty and his companion Kitty to Madeleine when they met in April. It was ten years since Stuart had seen his old friend, and over a meal in the Cafe Dôme, Stuart heard of the death of Ankaret Howard Jackson, and Enid Raffael. Both had been close to the two men in the thirties and both had died tragically. After O'Flaherty and Kitty left, Stuart brooded on other recent deaths including Aunt Janet who had died of Parkinson's disease. Often difficult and abrupt, she had been significant in his life, and he was in no mood to continue a comic novel he had begun some months earlier. By May Stuart had written eight chapters of *Danny Boy,* hoping that this book would 'pay the rent.'

If critics thought Stuart was obsessed with his war experiences, he was surprised that instead of these "fading and decreasing, the effect has grown...", and he was conscious of "the moral isolation with the revelations of Nazi atrocities after the end of the war, all suspects like ourselves were looked upon as at least tacit participators in these crimes..."

His days had now settled into a pattern, beginning at eight o'clock, and ending before ten o'clock, with only rare excursions in Paris. Stuart was happy to prepare lunch for Madeleine when she returned from her cleaning job, and often the evening meal as well, for he did not have any inclination to become involved in the Bohemian aspects of Paris.

O'Flaherty called again in June, and for Madeleine, his visits were particularly memorable because of his conversation. "It was as if he had opened a magic suitcase full of wondrous tales, credible or incredible, they were sheer magic." Madeleine wrote in her Memoirs. "I was spellbound. Stories when he had won one or two pounds, would end up with suitcases full of pound notes so that he couldn't even carry the lot and had to take a taxi and then put the whole lot on a hack and lose it all."

They went to a race meeting at St Cloud, where O'Flaherty arrived late with a hangover, and spent the rest of his money in the buffet. Often argumentative and difficult, he was now friendly and kind, but Stuart "saw the distress in him...I perhaps understand his fears, hopes, despairs better than many..."

The only really cheerful incident was when Madeleine found:

> a thousand franc note on the ground. There were so many Arabs there shuffling about in tennis shoes with loads of money. We were delighted and instead of water drank wine. On the way home, Liam who was in front next to the driver while we sat at the back, entertained the whole bus by shouting, amongst other things, a joke in French and then in English.

O'Flaherty stayed in a hotel in Montmartre where he spent an evening with Stuart in a bar, frittering away money. When Stuart tried to meet him the next day, his friend had already left for Ireland without a word of farewell.

Shortly before O'Flaherty's visit, Stuart heard from Florrie Salkeld in July, that Iseult was in hospital with angina. Knowing no more than that, he waited in vain for Lily to write. When a letter did come from Dublin, it was from Peadar O'Donnell, the editor of a literary periodical, *The Bell*, who pressed him to write about Frank Ryan. *Danny Boy* was just completed, and although Stuart wanted a rest from writing, he sent a long piece which was published over two issues.

When *The Flowering Cross* was published in July, the Dormandis invited Stuart and Madeleine for a celebration dinner, but the family made "quite a violent little attack" on the book, mainly led by Lodzi. By chance, the first review Stuart read in *The Observer* was unfavourable, and although better ones followed elsewhere, he was despondent. As far as 'outer' events were concerned, Stuart and Madeleine worried that if the Korean war accelerated, they might be separated. Paris was a haven after Germany, but they did not feel comfortable nor accepted there, and it was a relief to go in September to Denneville, a coastal town near Caen. As the weather was chilly, Stuart and Madeleine cut the holiday short, returning to Paris via Lisieux, where they spent an afternoon visiting the home, and Convent of St. Thérèse. The Saint was untarnished by what Madeleine considered the "cult of complacency and sugary piety" and for Stuart, St. Thérèse encompassed very human qualities and those of the divine to attain a spirituality which could only come from one who "suffered most and was most happy." She was not a justification for the apparent contradictory attractions that had pulled Stuart in opposite directions, but rather, illuminated them, as he realized in Lisieux.

> Feel my life has been linked to this extraordinary being's, poles apart as it is from hers! There, in that ugly little town, was aware of the secret difficult wisdom which she served and which in my own fallible way I try, and shall ever try, to serve through art...

When they returned to Paris, a letter from Gollancz advised Stuart not to publish *Danny Boy* for "...the good critics who are at the moment intensely interested in every new book by you, will lose their keeness - and once that begins to happen it is almost impossible to make them take an interest again." His colleague Sheila Hodges reassured Stuart that they had a high opinion of his work, but they were:

> desperately anxious, in an age when people tend more and more to read worthless novels to the exclusion of the good and thoughtful ones, to establish your work in the place which it deserves...it would be quite fatal to your future as a writer to publish a novel which the critics might be tempted to regard as a minor work...

The verdict was not unexpected by Stuart, who later thought "the book was bad, though there were some good isolated passages. A peculiar blindness I had towards it, though in my heart of hearts I suppose I felt uneasy about it..." He was more optimistic about another novel, *Good Friday's Daughter,* which he felt was better written, but beyond that, he was uncertain, and found it hard not to feel he was stagnating. Reconciled to Dormandi, Stuart and Madeleine spent Christmas with him and his family, and were joined by Ethel Mannin. She raised the possibility of the couple coming to live in England, at some point in 1951. Tentative plans had to be abandoned, when Stuart heard in March from Iseult that Lily had a stroke and was dangerously ill. He flew over to Dublin at once, on 7 March to spend some of the "strangest days of my life - this return to Ireland after eleven years." He was met by Kay who drove him on to Laragh, and the anxiety over Lily partially distracted Stuart from the awkwardness of seeing Iseult again, whom he noticed was unhappy and lonely.

They had not met for eleven years, but hardly spoke of the past because their meeting was painful to them both. Kay remembered that her father's voice was much thinner, and how he nervously hurried about doing odd jobs, such as cutting wood. Stuart read to his mother as she recovered, but felt increasingly that he did not belong at Laragh, and was glad to leave. After he had gone, little was said about his visit, but Iseult told Kay that at least Stuart could still make her laugh as few could.

Before returning to Paris, Stuart stayed in Ethel Mannin's comfortable house in Wimbledon, and contacted Gollancz who accepted *Good Friday's Daughter,* subject to some revision. After shopping with Ethel to buy some presents for Madeleine, Stuart flew to Paris on 21 March.

Ethel Mannin suggested employing Madeleine as a domestic servant to bring her over to England. Stuart would have preferred Ireland to be near Lily, but as Madeleine was refused entry there when she applied for a visa, they decided to take up Ethel's offer.

With only the advance from *Good Friday's Daughter,* Stuart and Madeleine prepared for London. Unable to carry the bulk of Stuart's manuscripts, books and papers, including many letters from the war years, they were left in the care of the Dormandis. Madeleine's visa arrived in June, and before finalizing the travel arrangements, she and Stuart attended a party at Gallimard. After an emotional farewell from the Dormandis, on 16 June 1951, Stuart and Madeleine took the train for Dieppe, with Sophie in a basket. She was taken away at Newhaven, to be put in quarantine while Stuart passed quickly through immigration, Madeleine was delayed by medical screening, reviving all the old anxieties of separation and detention. Once safely on the train, they experienced "...one of those rare, intense impressions of joy... that are milestones in our life..."

Ethel Mannin met Stuart and Madeleine at Victoria Station London, and they stayed with her until they found their own accommodation. While Sophie was in quarantine, space did not matter, and Stuart and Madeleine took one pokey room after another. They visited Hackbridge where Sophie was kenneled, and as the world of nature and especially of animals became increasingly important to Stuart, observations of their habits appeared in his novels. In his Diary Stuart recalled that Sophie was:

> hissing at the girl who was trying to lift her. I went round and she let me take her. She climbed on my shoulder and was soon purring as she was for most of the time we stayed with her. Then when we left I had a very vivid impression of her fear or sadness. Her quick jumping down to the door, her eye looking up anxiously, her crying and jumping up to the shelf at the bars. As I said to Madeleine I couldn't conceive of the expression of more affection than she showed at our visit. How strange this emotion of a small beast!

Stuart had written to Iseult in August, to ask her if Lily could apply to the Executors of a Trust, which she benefitted from, to release some capital on his behalf. Lily wanted to help, but she had made a similar request to her Trustees when overdrawn at the bank, and was refused. Iseult's own health was poor, and she was exhausted looking after Lily. Ion was shortly to be married, and Iseult speculated that if she survived to see them having children, "incredibly battered and decrepit though I have become, I still will never feel like being Granny..." Iseult accepted Stuart's relationship, in so far as she felt that Madeleine should have a child. Feelings of mistrust remained however, partly fomented by Stuart's recurring hopes of having a share in his house. "Yet," Stuart wrote in his Diary "I shouldn't in any way harden my heart against those at home, and not against Iseult in whom this suspicion and hostility is, I think a kind of perverted love..."

Madeleine had a cleaning job which paid £3.00 per week, but even with the occasional translating job which Stuart took, London was extremely expensive. Stuart was taken to Bavaria to look at the castles of Ludwig II by Brian Hurt, who wanted Stuart to write a script about the 'dream king'. The vist was a waste of time for the film came to nothing, and for three months Stuart struggled to live off Madeleine's small income. He lost ten pounds in a desperate effort to win money at Ascot. Earlier in the year he was ashamed of losing money at dog racing, and gave up smoking to economize. Now he took a job as a night security officer, in the Geological Museum for £8.00 a week. The work had its interest, but Stuart could not sleep during the day, and after some months, gave it up in August.

By November, 1952 Stuart counted they had made about nine moves of accommodation, the final one they hoped, to Shepherd's Bush, not far from the BBC Television Centre. It was shabby, but an improvement on the damp basement which was their previous address. Stuart had nearly finished *The Chariot,* his fifth novel since the war, and was struck that it was "less extraordinary" than the others, and that in one way "very little happens in it; not a murder or suicide, not even a death. No adultery, hardly ever any sensual scenes, no violence, nothing..." The novel to some extent, reflected his own life, which was unremarkable. Christmas promised to be cheerless, as royalties from the German translation of *The Pillar of Cloud* had not arrived by Christmas Eve.

Madeleine had a Christmas bonus of £2.20 from someone she cleaned for, which they spent on a chicken, wine and a few oddments, but she had to work until three o'clock on Christmas Eve. While she out was, Stuart heard the long awaited advance from Germany was waiting for him at the bank. Then:

> at the very last minute I could hurry about, buying a bracelet for M. which I had noticed some weeks before, getting back my pawned watch and so when M. returned from her work, and lit the tree, she found the bracelet, which I had wrapped up and hung round a bottle. When I told her the money had come it was too much for her and she burst into tears. Before knowing about it she had given me ten shillings of her meagre money.

The unexpected windfall bought Stuart time to complete *The Chariot* and the intense atmosphere of that Christmas, provided the ending of the novel. To celebrate the delivery of the typescript to his agent at the end of January, 1953, Stuart and Madeleine dined out, the first time they had been out alone together since 1950, when Stuart had finished *Danny Boy*. While Gollancz read the novel, Stuart read O'Flaherty's short stories which he admired, and Graham Greene's *The End of the Affair* which he did not. "Not a good book," he wrote; " there is a part towards the middle where there is a possibility of it blossoming, but it wilts as though nipped in the bud. And all the last part is a weary improbable dragging out of inventiveness. A surge from below never swells up and submerges the too exposed plot..."

Stuart had expressed the quiet intensities of an unremarkable existence in *The Chariot*, without the forced drama which sometimes marred his earliest work. He had, for the time being, left behind the experiences of the war, and perhaps to his surprise, Sheila Hodges wrote that she was "delighted" with the book. Stuart read some French reviews of his books, and always believed that the French were more perceptive in understanding his books than the English critics whom he considered "time servers." "The very fact," he confided in his diary in mid-February "that a 'critic' goes into the 'story' of my books in detail shows that he fails from the first to grasp what I am doing," and he concluded " I am only journeying safely toward my goal when I walk in the shelter of comparative obscurity..."

It was a judgement which anticipated remarks Victor Gollancz wrote of *The Chariot*. He liked it "better than anything you have written.... However you must not expect sales...The English are becoming almost as bad as the Americans in their failure to understand your basic attitude to life, which is the only one that corresponds to reality..."

In February, Stuart had a letter from a young man, called Ron Hall, praising *The Flowering Cross*. In his reply Stuart wrote that it "is always an encouragement to know that someone has been touched by what I try to express..." Shortly afterwards, Hall called for supper, and Stuart learned he lived with his wife and daughter in a Devonshire cottage in near penury. Hesitant and shy, Hall appealed to Stuart and Madeleine because he did not chatter simply for something to say, and had "none of the horrible false 'friendliness' one gets so easily involved in", as Stuart wrote, thanking Hall for his visit and some primroses he sent. At Easter they visited friends in the country, and the serenity they found out of London in pleasant company:

fascinated us, and especially M. and now her dream is that we should once settle in the country too. Surely we have learnt the lesson of the value of poverty sufficiently. A lot of money dulls experience, takes away the small joys and the privations without which sensibility is deadened. I know all this, but surely we might now get enough money to find ourselves a modest corner and settle into...

Ron Hall's visit had come at a crucial time to Stuart, offering him support, and helped him to accept the neglect and misunderstanding, that at times made him feel bitter. At the best, he knew that he could only write for a few who were also in search of what Gollancz had described his "basic attitude to life". He told Hall that for writers like himself it was enough to " live in a close communion, a small, new world, with a few people. Then all is fulfilled and he needs nothing more. Except, of course some money,- not much, though..."

Despite what he wrote, Stuart needed money desperately, and the subject was particularly bitter. Madame MacBride had died on 27 April, and Stuart knew that while his family had "...three houses... we have to live in a single rented room at a rent we can't afford. And I can't but still believe that anyone with two coats should give one to he who has none..." Madeleine had gone into hospital on 26 April for a minor operation, and was still there on Stuart's fifty first birthday, the day Madame MacBride was buried in Glasnevin Cemetery in Dublin. Concerned about Madeleine's health, Stuart felt little grief over his mother in law's death. He could not pretend he had ever liked her, nor had he ever tried to. She had done her best to understand him, but by acting as a safety net for Iseult, had been partly to blame for Stuart's and Iseult's inability to confront their marriage problems.

Iseult was bitterly hurt at hearing nothing from Stuart, and on 2 May, wrote "That you did not write to me a few words of sympathy has made me feel very sad..." Writing partly to invite Stuart over for a few days in late May, she described her mother's death:

one of those really beautiful things one reads of in holy books and doesn't quite believe in. She had gone through a lot of pain and misery the last two or three months. She was saying to me only a few weeks ago how disgusting and despairing it was, that all that, instead of spiritualizing her, only made her selfish and materialistic. As it is also my experience with this rotten heart illness, I could only wretchedly agree.

Then the day before her death, after she got the last sacraments, she had some kind of mystical experience and looked radiantly happy and young. One of the last words she spoke was: 'I feel now an ineffable joy.' Then she went to sleep breathing lightly like a child and died...The next day I drove up with Ion and accompanied the coffin to the church. I can't say I really prayed. I just kept seeing inwardly that picture of Our Lady of Perpetual Succour we have at home and feeling extraordinarily well and cheerful, and strangely enough, going out, in a deserted corner of the church near a big crucifix, I saw the picture, the same print as we have, and I lit a candle to it and thought of you...

Stuart was moved by Iseult's letter. Madame MacBride's:

> death must have been such pain for her, and in this pain and hope she thought of me. How glad I should be if all the estrangement of the last years should be overcome between us. But of course it cannot. It is hard not to harbour at least some resentment...

That Iseult had written to her husband, knowing perfectly well his feelings about her mother, indicates how she tried to bring some reconciliation. At her moment of unhappiness, she had turned to Stuart who did reply. His answer "...was not the best one..." and he "...should have shown more understanding" but Iseult wrote by return of post to thank him for his "...very nice letter. I liked it so much..." She was particularly disappointed to hear that due to his financial state, Stuart would not be able to visit her and his family until the autumn, and obviously wondered if she would live until then. She had:

> already lived much longer than I thought could be possible with such pain and decrepitude, but unless things took a miraculous turn this coming winter may well see the end of it. I am not saying this to make myself pathetic...

Iseult wanted her husband to come over to see Kay, for:

> more than ever that it has been a bad thing for her your going away and losing all interest in her. Very shocking (and not really like you) what you wrote to me a long time ago about having to live your own life and the children theirs and that they would quite understand etc. But you have often talked smug rubbish just to annoy me. What I suspect is that anyhow you don't think that way anymore but have got into that kind of groove...

Iseult had intended to write about Stuart's books, but from the few remarks she makes, she never would agree with Stuart's philosophy, which was essential to his understanding. To Iseult, *The Angel of Pity* written in 1935, was " ...all wrong, it nearly broke my heart that you had dedicated it to me." In some ways a thematic preparation for the first three post war novels, which Iseult considered "...far worse in the same key." Afraid of arguments she concluded, "No, perhaps we won't talk about all that when we meet, it's something I feel too strongly about, and life has taught me (or has it?) that talk is no good..."

Iseult read Stuart's letter quickly, for she asked about a job at the Geographical Magazine. In fact Stuart had taken a temporary job returning as an attendant at the Geological Museum in mid-May. There he spent the time, "strolling around the fossils". Iseult was still pressing Stuart to visit her in Ireland, and inevitably their correspondence included the question of finance. Iseult wrote "I would very much like to see you and get away if we can from this cotton wool fog barrage of tact and unreality that seems to be getting more and more impenetrable...". She felt now that even if she had any money, there was little reason why she should give it to him. Stuart wrote sympathetically, and in a second letter, a few weeks later Iseult tried to balance her judgement, by considering both their financial positions. She was feeling extremely low, and doped with drugs for her heart complaint, was in:

> a kind of limbo, wherein I don't write at all, or else stuff that in more sober moments appears to be rubbish...Above all, there is as you say (I was very touched by that passage in your letter) that question of trust between us. I often feel that I can't trust you, and therefore I am apt to think you don't trust me either. If there isn't trust between us it is no good at all to write. But I promise you never to lie or quibble in any way to you and if you promise me the same I will believe you... if you are at any time seriously stuck for money for your health for instance, let me know at once and let that be part of the trust we have in each other. I don't say for sure I'd be able to do much about it but I could have a good try...

Iseult remarked that she would like to read *The Chariot* and with better feeling between them, Stuart considered visiting her in October. Largely hostile reviews of the novel put a stop to any Irish visit, and Stuart and Madeleine hardly left their flat. They cut costs by heating their small room with a paraffin stove instead of the gas fire, and through the winter, read an anthology compiled by Gollancz, which contained an excerpt from *Redemption*.

As Christmas approached, Stuart sorted mail in the Post Office. The eleven hour shift made it impossible for him to work on his new novel, and contemplating the numbers of books that were published, wondered if it was worth going on as a writer. He did not accept that his particular method of writing fiction which used incidents from his own life had its hazards. He had done nothing of the slightest interest in London, and without the framework of something significant to report, novels like *The Chariot* reflected this. In his diary, often used to assess the year that was passing, he simply wrote, "I am in the happy position of not being likely to be forgotten never having been known."

Wedding photograph, Hammersmith, 1954

CHAPTER 15

Early on 22 March 1954, Stuart received a telegram from Ion telling him that Iseult had died in her sleep. He packed at once for the Dublin boat and arrived the day before the funeral. It was his second visit to Ireland since he had left for Germany in 1940, and his immediate thought was that he had only gone to the funeral as a matter of convention. He no longer belonged to Laragh, and the only comfort was that Iseult's end was peaceful, as she herself had hoped.

Stuart could now marry Madeleine, but as he stood with his children that evening in St Kevin's Church at Glendalough, where the coffin lay with his wife's name misspelt, and noticed a few daffodils left by friends, his senses were numbed into feeling almost nothing at all, "an acute and peculiar misery...that had nothing directly to do with Iseult's death but came from a sense of absolute isolation and a longing to be back with M."

In his novel *Faillandia,* written thirty years later, he analyzed his feelings about Iseult's death:

> What had been the very heart and intensity of his life lay inside, cold and still, beyond his reach, and now he found that he could recapture none of the joy and pain of those years. It wasn't, he surmised, that time and later intensities of emotions had annulled these memories, but rather that thick clouds had descended, a layer of insulation that cut him off from his earlier life. He had a foreboding that at a future date a memory of how it had been with her at its best would return to him in all its vividness, but for the moment he didn't dwell on the thought...

Stuart had come close to a reconciliation with Iseult, but he would think of his wife in her last years as lonely, with her closest companion a Siamese cat, who died two weeks after her.

Stuart spent an uncomfortable night in his old room, and the following morning, after Mass at 10 o'clock, Iseult was buried near the gate of the small cemetery at Glendalough. Because she was as interested in Eastern religion as Catholicism, Iseult would have preferred to have been cremated, which was not permitted then. She asked that there should be no headstone and that a silver birch should be planted instead, a request which Ion carried out.

Stuart felt an overwhelming sense of hostility from the curious who came back to the house after the funeral, and could only think of returning to Madeleine, whom he left for the same evening.

Amongst the first to hear the news that Stuart and Madeleine would now marry, was Ron Hall:

Gertrude and I are getting married in the Catholic Church here on April 28th. It doesn't really make any difference (except for Gertrude's papers) but it has a kind of solemnity. Only two or three people will be there...How I hate throngs, most of whom turn up out of curiosity as was the case at my wife's funeral! It was an ordeal for many reasons, those few days in Ireland, and it was only after I had been back here a couple of days that my inner balance came gently back again...

On the day before Stuart's fifty-second birthday, after finishing his night shift at the Science Museum, he and Madeleine married quietly in the Church of the Holy Trinity, Brook Green, Hammersmith. Madeleine had revamped a hat with white flowers and a black veil, and wore a black watered silk dress. With Stuart in his best suit, the ceremony was as quiet as his first marriage had been, but the whole day was a celebration and a declaration of their love of fourteen years.

Stuart had to work again that night, but they went to Newmarket for the 2,000 Guineas, where he had no luck, but Madeleine won on a filly she had only chosen because it was called 'Bride Elect.' They returned home exhausted, and Stuart had to change and set off for the Museum.

He was writing what would be called *The Pilgrimage,* and worked on it during the nightshift, or caught up with his correspondence. The Museum work was not unpleasant, and

Stuart would often elaborate amusing if not entirely accurate answers about some of the exhibits to parties of school children when he was there during the day.

Pilgrimage was finished by early July, and Stuart felt that the Museum work on its own was almost like a holiday. Meanwhile Gollancz had read it:

> with great emotion and admiration. I think it is, by and large a superb work, in fact I like it best of all your post war novels... God knows whether we shall at last be able to "sell you": I am bound to say that in the present state of criticism I have grave doubts. But one of these days you will certainly come into your own...

The book was favourably reviewed but Stuart, who perhaps disagreed with Gollancz's view of his novel, was tempted by his agent to look for another publisher who would promote his work to create greater sales. Yet he liked Gollancz, who had loyally supported him from the first, and had not particularly cared if the books paid their way or not. Madeleine now had a part time office job, but it made little difference to their financial position. Stuart eventually received half the value of Laragh, which meant they could try to find better accommodation.

In mid August, Stuart viewed a flat near the Albert Dock, in the Canning Town area of London, which they took, although there were only "two and a half rooms and kitchen" as Madeleine wrote. From the windows they could see the cranes of the nearby docks, but before they could live there, they had to re-decorate. With only a mattress they moved to the new address of 63 Barking Road, on 1 October.

For several months, they could not unpack, until they had furniture to put their possessions in. Madeleine enjoyed furnishing the house, and visits to Portobello Road, an open air market in the Notting Hill area, produced most of what they needed. Each purchase was celebrated with a bottle of red wine, and within a year, they added carpets and curtains which Madeleine bought at a reduced price from Courtalds where she now worked.

Stuart found a temporary job at Harrod's, as a Christmas

packer and in the new year, went back to the Museum.
Shortly afterwards, when Winston, the Museum cat died
suddenly, Stuart decided it was time to move on, and found
full time work in January 1955 in a Regent Street Finance
Company, at a salary of £6.50 per week. He despised "the
cut-throat money-making and incessant dealing! How brittle
too. For though sometimes it seems so solid, I know that at
the first breath the cracks will come and the toppling down
begin..."

It was a relief to take a long planned holiday in Ireland at
the end of July. For Madeleine it was strange to set foot in a
country which first of all seemed even greener than England,
after the scrubby vegetation of Germany and France, but
more importantly, she was in the strange mysterious country
Stuart had lectured to her about when she was a student.

Unavoidably, the Irish holiday was a pilgrimage to
Stuart's past. They visited Dolores' grave, overgrown and
unkempt, lunched in the Royal Hotel in Glendalough, before
going to Iseult's grave and on to Laragh Castle to see Lily,
now confined to a wheelchair. Madeleine who was
apprehensive about meeting her, thought she was a "lovely
gentle, old lady."

The peaceful atmosphere of Glendalough could not have
been further from congested London to which they returned,
and, recalling the holiday, Stuart wrote, "There were the long
days of endless sun, bathing and sunbathing...And in the
end, it dawning on us that - once - perhaps soon - we should
go and settle there..." The new year of 1956 was largely
uneventful. Stuart went to Beckett's *Waiting for Godot* which
he did not like, and lost heavily on the 2,000 guineas at
Newmarket in May. Such "reverses" to use his own word
gave him a:

> moment of 'exquisite' disappointment when, as the horses
> passed the post, I remember coming down from the stand
> and throwing away the racecard, the packet of sandwiches
> that Gertrude had provided me with, and some other odds
> and ends. I think the true gambler, which I am far from
> being - can sometimes get a queer piercing satisfaction out of
> losing; in fact, if this wasn't so, there wouldn't be any
> gamblers in the real sense.

A good win would have made all the difference to the Stuarts's comfort, and after a week or so spent with friends in the country they were looking forward to staying indoors as winter approached, re-reading books such as Tolstoy and Doestoevsky, which spurred Stuart to work on a new novel. He turned once again to Germany for his theme, but covered the period of 1939 to 1945 rather than the aftermath of the war. It needed careful planning, and the only interruptions were visits from his family. Kay called in September, and Stuart found her "reserved and welcoming all things with the same readiness." But at the Tate Gallery and at other moments, he was pleased to notice "...that she has her mode of assimilating new things." When Ion stayed with his young daughter, Stuart remembered the "magic and yet strangely precise world of young children." There was talk of Iseult's last days with understanding, of how she had:

> suffered towards the end and of how it had seemed to change her nature for the worse. But then he went on to say what to me was very illuminating: that towards the very end her intellectual pride, as he called it, was at last broken down. In the end, he said she was completely abandoned, and he blamed himself for his impatience towards her. She would have reached out her hand towards the first sign of comfort from anyone. This makes clearer what has been a mystery...

For Madeleine too, childhood memories returned when a telegram arrived on 20 January 1957, giving news of her mother's death in Poland. It was a terrible shock, worsened because they had parted on difficult terms before Frau Meissner moved to Poland. After the war the new frontiers made visits impossible but Madeleine was partly consoled by a letter from her sister Gretel, who told her that to her mother, Madeleine was her "all and only one", and that "everything was forgiven and forgotten."

There was happier news from Kay, who brought a friend in April, called Patrick Bridgwater whom she had met at Oxford, and would marry at Christmas.

The prospect of living indefinitely in hostile London preyed on the Stuarts' mind. They briefly considered the idea of living in a community made up of friends such as the Halls, and their sculptor friend Ted Lacy, but thought more positively of moving to Ireland. Nothing could be done until Stuart completed *Victors and Vanquished*. "I have to face the fact that it isn't really a good novel; none have been since *Redemption*," Stuart reflected. Before it was sent to Gollancz, he met Madeleine at Greenwich, and celebrated with a bottle of wine at the Cutty Sark Tavern.

It was the first free period of leisure Stuart had for over three years. Since Easter 1954, he had written every novel before or after a day's work, and this had shown in their quality. *Victors and Vanquished* was the most directly autobiographical novel he had yet written, with friends such as Frank Ryan clearly identifiable, as well as Iseult and Kay. With a less intense theme than his best work, Gollancz accepted it, and hoped for a commercial success.

The Stuarts spent two weeks in Dublin in July and were met by an old friend Peter Marron. After a day at the Dundalk Races, Stuart bought a local newspaper, where Madeleine spotted an advertisement for a cottage, "The Reask" which was to be auctioned near Meath on 23 September, 1957, and described as a:

tiled roof house containing kitchen and two rooms, E.S.B.light installed. There is also a cattle shed with tiled roof, the property stands on about half Statute Acre. Rateable value £2.10/-.[£2.50] It is situated about 2 miles from Ratoath and Dunshaughlin...

The Stuarts looked at the "The Reask", which had no lavatory or proper plumbing, but nevertheless, they decided to bid for it. After a few days at Laragh with Lily, they returned to Dublin for the last evening of their holiday. After a drink with Peter Marron, the Stuarts took him to a party at Brendan Behan's flat in Herbert Place. Flann O'Brien was also there pouring whiskey into a glass of Guinness, while a black fiddler played Irish folk music. Behan, was particularly friendly to Madeleine, and dressed in a once white but now Guinness stained shirt, with his trousers nearer his knees than his waist, sang and told stories until the party crossed the street to a nearby pub on Baggot Street Bridge. A little later, O'Brien fell down in the pub drunk, and when Peter Marron tried to help him up, shouted, "How dare you! Do you think I'm incapable of getting up of my own volition?" When the pub closed, Madeleine danced with Behan before she hurried with Stuart to catch the boat for Holyhead.

Stuart left Marron with a cheque, and instructions to bid on his behalf, and back in London, worried until they found an unnoticed telegram which read "Winner alright. Peter."

The move was planned for April, and Stuart took what he termed "well paid drudgery" in a job as a storekeeper in a shed near the docks, looking after ships' electrical appliances. Meanwhile Madeleine continued at the bank, and they saved £6 a week out of the £15 they earned jointly. It was not much to move with, but on their fourth wedding anniversary on 28 April and just before Stuart's fifty-sixth birthday, they arrived in Dublin, and took a bus to the cottage, arriving as the removal van was pulling up. *Victors and Vanquished* was published that day, and after opening some wine for a celebration, they began to make the place habitable. The rooms had to be plastered and decorated, and water drawn from a well in the garden. Stuart planned to grow vegetables to keep costs down, and although their new house was a paradise for the cats, Sophie, and Lulu, found on a bomb site, the first few months were a desperate physical and financial struggle. Indifferent reviews of *Victors and Vanquished* destroyed hopes of lucrative sales, and Stuart felt he was returning to a time of misery, so familiar from the past. Trying not to be defeatist, he realised after visiting Lily, who was in hospital for a hip operation, that he was:

far from being humble enough. There I was walking those streets again, having - as it were - been 'given another chance' and I was ready to expect and 'demand' all the same old things (almost) as before. Many of those I knew hadn't been given this second 'life' and I who had, was not nearly humble enough, did not see myself as I had been and am still.

A cheque for £48.00 for the French edition of *The Chariot*

247

was a short term help, but it was useless for the Stuarts to pretend that "The Reask" was the longed for haven. Wherever they went, they were tormented by money worries. "I have", Stuart wrote "to come to the point where I can honestly let all else go and have no urgent or gnawing desires of material ease or extra possessions...", in an effort to tolerate their circumstances. Even a modest level of financial security was impossible, and the Stuarts tried to find tranquility in their garden and the view of the Mourne mountains. Various short stories Stuart had sent to magazines were returned, until *Good Housekeeping* offered thirty guineas for a story called "Minou" which was written round Sophie in the guise of a wild cat.

By October, "The Reask" was transformed, and in between all the repair work, Gollancz accepted Stuart's latest novel, *The Angels of Providence*. Through lack of money, the Stuarts stayed for two weeks with Peter Marron in Bray in January 1959. Before they left for "The Reask", Ethel Mannin felt she had been snubbed because Stuart had not replied to a letter of hers, but:

> deep down in my heart I never believed, in spite of your silence, that our friendship, so old, with so many associations, was really finished. And instinctively in time of great trouble one reaches out to one's friends...

The main point of her letter was to let the Stuarts know that her husband had died, and to offer some of his clothes to Stuart. Both Stuarts wrote consolatory letters, but Ethel's success as a popular novelist had always rankled. Madeleine wrote:

> She had never liked F's world and his writings. She seemed to know better, apparently because she made plenty of money. I think that there is a kind of jealousy, she gets the money, but no reviews, while F. gets little money, but in general good reviews...yet...there is a very good side to her. But she does not mind putting a few little daggers into your back. Perhaps that is only human.

Yet it was Madeleine who was a little jealous of Ethel's financial success. Ethel had written nothing in her letter to hurt, and had gone out of her way to be helpful. She made it quite clear that her view of Stuart's work had nothing to do with their friendship. Admitting frankly that she had been excited by *The Pillar of Cloud* Ethel felt that with *The Angels of Providence* "repetition had set in. Well, to be sure, we do all repeat our themes...you have a ''thing', about curious marriages; a curious marriage occurs in all your novels, I think. I still hope one day to write a novel you'll like..." It was difficult for Madeleine to be objective about Stuart's work, and her apparent smugness in considering he was the only writer was irritating to Ethel, but forgivable. Ironically, since *The Angels of Providence* was about greed for money, the novel was unremarkable because it was written quickly for the advance.

Visits to Dublin were rare, and in a letter to Ron Hall, Stuart recalled his days in Freiburg.

> The peace and the circumstances were ideal: a smallish, beautiful old town swarming with people from all over Europe. We made many friends, we were thrown together by being apatriates, by deprivation, by hope and love. There were gatherings, parties, long summer nights by open windows talking, talking. And then the exhibition organized by the French, the French books all that we had been cut off from for so long. We found again with a new, pure joy and understanding...

Hall shared with Stuart an anti-materialist outlook, but did not deny the importance of fiction which promoted an understanding of social or racial injustice. At times Stuart found it difficult to concede that certain novels which were different in purpose from his own, had any merit even when it was generally agreed they had. He found *Cry, the Beloved Country,* "a bore":

> it is the way in which new patterns of relationship... are explored. As Lawrence said, about something else, it is one tip of man's consciousness unfolding. Therefore to use it, as

Paton does... for going over the same old ground (white versus black) without a single new inspired thought about the whole business becomes - to me - a bore. A great writer might take a white and a black and in exploring the depths of a single relationship illuminate all. But it would have to be subtle and new, not the old sentiments stirred over again.

It was partly this failure of Stuart to extend his imagination beyond his own world which marred his own fiction. His attacks on writers whose views he disagreed with, seem at times to be only motivated by jealousy, as his support of writers he agreed with, such as Montherland and Genet seem too consciously an effort to promote his own work. Stuart knew this, but could only project what he believed, and when he sent off another quickly written novel called *A Trip Down the River,* early in 1960, he was not confident of its acceptance. It reflected the atmosphere of the Stuart's life in London, where little had happened, and his books of any value, were generally inspired by the turbulent events of his own life as Stuart knew too well. "I am one of those writers who identify themselves closely with their fiction...it has been at the start of a creative phase that I have written at my best...out of a pressure of stored living and experiencing."

Madeleine prepared to go to Germany, for her sister Traute, whose husband Martin had died during the previous summer, had sent the fare. Stuart wrote to Ron Hall that he would, "...fortify myself in here, put a padlock on the gate and set the two cats as look-outs, after stocking up with drink and provisions." When Madeleine left in late January, he took the cats and stayed with Marron in Bray. Dormandi wrote to him there explaining that as they were moving from the Avenue de Breuteil, they could no longer store his manuscripts and books. Stuart could not afford to have them sent to Ireland, and asked his publisher, Paul-Andre Lesort to look after them, a decision which had unfortunate consequences in the future.

Madeleine's visit was a revelation, for Traute explained her marriage had been unhappy, and she had tried to commit suicide in 1956. She owned a small business in Berlin, and suggested the Stuarts should help her to run it. Madeleine did not seriously consider the proposal at first but when she returned to Ireland in late February, Victor Gollancz had declined *A Trip Down the River*. He explained that while "book after book" of Stuart's had not been a commercial proposition, this was unimportant. He had published them because he had liked them, but *A Trip Down the River* was "...a book I cannot bring myself to like." Stuart had anticipated rejection, and said so in a letter, but knowing of his poverty, Gollancz added in a postscript, "... My pain at having written the letter is now a little bit assuaged by the feeling you express in yours. With all good wishes, V.G." Gollancz wrote to Ethel Mannin later in the year," I am terribly sorry about Francis Stuart as it has of course been obvious for some time that no-one would publish him except myself."

The association with Gollancz, which began in 1932 with *Pigeon Irish*, ended with *The Angel of Providence*. Now without a publisher, the Stuarts decided they must live in Germany. Just as Madeleine was writing in her diary that she was "crushed" about leaving Ireland, a letter arrived from Laragh, asking if she and Stuart would look after Lily. Ion had won an art scholarship, and he and his wife, Imogen were going on a protracted tour of Germany.

They agreed, and at first Lily's arrival seemed a blessing, for while she needed constant looking after, her contribution to household expenses meant that Stuart and Madeleine could stay in Ireland. Later, Stuart resented his mother for hoarding her money for her grandchildren, and for refusing to accept that he and Madeleine were so badly off. Lily promised at one point to send £2.00 per week after she returned to Laragh, and then withdrew the offer, and Madeleine who had liked Lily the first time they met, became bitter about her meanness. On one occasion she told Lily that she should stop reading the light fiction she enjoyed, and read the Bible instead.

It was upsetting for Lily, used to a routine, and set in her ways, and unfortunate that Madeleine overheard her confiding in an old servant who came to see her from Laragh, how much she would like to be back there. After a quarrel with Stuart, Madeleine threatened to go to Germany on her own, and ironically, Lily gave her the fare. The strain of looking after his mother, made Stuart impatient, and he shouted at her, unable to understand she could not change her basically simple nature. Lily had never been close to him, but he must have seemed unapproachable to her.

Driven by financial despair Stuart was direct with his mother for the first and only time of his life. He told her that while he knew she was not particularly rich, it was his father's money she was using. He asked Lily if she ever considered if Henry would have wished his son to be struggling in harassing poverty. It took Stuart a great deal of resolution to say this, and she did not reply. The subject was not referred to again, but Stuart was glad he had set the record straight with her.

By July, the Stuarts agreed that one of them would have to go to London to take a job, after Lily returned to Laragh. As it happened Ion's German visit lasted longer than expected, and it was unlikely she could return before the end of August. Her health weakened, for her hip operation had not been successful, and Stuart's doctor told him his mother could not live for much longer. Lily was told she would have to go into hospital for a few days to have her hip dressed, and on the morning of 26 August, while they were drinking coffee at home, Lily suddenly remarked "tomorrow you won't be having coffee with me. You will be relieved." Stuart told his mother that he would be relieved only in that she would be receiving proper care.

In the afternoon, Lily was taken to Navan Hospital and when Stuart told her he did not know when Ion was returning, she replied "Nor do I", the last words she said to him. Two days later, on 28 August Lily died peacefully, just as the Stuarts were about to visit her.

Shortly before her death, Lily had recalled her son's conversation about his father and unexpectedly gave Madeleine a cheque which she had signed, and told her to make it out for whatever sum she needed. This Madeleine did, for about one hundred pounds. Lily was buried in a small cemetery not far from "The Reask", in the middle of a meadow, and her death, haunted him as "...an extraordinary, upsetting experiencing."

Despite the security of a legacy Stuart was due to inherit from Lily the bank would not alleviate their financial troubles in November, and Macmillan rejected a new novel. A dispirited Stuart wrote:

Hard work, dedication, faith, prayer, all is no use. Instead of the serenity that I felt here at times, for a long period now I have got up, moved, worked, eaten and slept in a kind of numbness. The acute joyous gleams never break through at unexpected moments...

After putting Lulu in a kennel, the Stuarts took Sophie and spent a week over Christmas with Lord Glenavy and his family at Rockbrook House which revived their spirits. It was unaccustomed luxury for Madeleine, and for her and Stuart, reluctant participation in charades and croquet. Nevertheless, it was a "strange, unexpected enjoyable time," after a year of misery, which brought the Stuarts closer together. There was still no sign of Stuart's legacy, and he mortgaged "The Reask". When it did arrive in April they bought a Ford Popular, but after struggling for six months, Madeleine's plan to work in London, was only thwarted by an unexpected cheque from Lily's estate in October.

Constantly poor, Stuart did not consider finding a job. He was a writer, and had decided in June to risk everything on a long novel which would take time to complete. He had told Hall:

(with some luck, or - to put it more truly - if it is my destiny, I shall manage it. As to the fate of such a big book, I don't even think of that. As long as we have a basic existence I am glad for a time to be free of publishers and agents, to be out of reach of the literary racket.

He did not say that if this book failed, he knew he was finished as a writer. By the summer of 1961 he had planned the chapters of what he first called *We the Condemned,* but later changed to *Black List, Section H.* and went on a camping holiday with Madeleine, which was abandoned when it rained. Both were glad to be home, and when Madeleine accepted a reasonably paid job teaching German in the vocational school, Stuart could at last, write without financial harrassment. He thought the novel would take nearly a year to complete, and the cold winter of 1961 was only an encouragement to keep him in isolation.

Of the friends Stuart valued, he heard that Beckett was depressed and that O'Flaherty had a block and was unable to write. Confident about the progress of his own book, he stopped work on it to go to London in March 1962 for a performance of a play he had written called *Flynn's Last Dive*. He and Madeleine stayed in Ethel Mannin's house in Wimbledon for a month, while she was in the Middle East, and looked after her cat.

The Stuarts attended the rehearsals for the play, and the following day, dined with Michael Campbell and his friend Bill Holden, before driving to Croydon for the first night on 6 March. When they arrived at the Pembroke Theatre, it was half empty, and everyone was relieved when the performance was over. There was little chance the play would be a success, despite fine performances, for the reviews were poor, but the Stuarts made up their minds to enjoy London regardless.

Before returning to Croydon for the last night on 17 March, the Stuarts re-lived some of the old London days, shopping in Soho, and walking round the Geological Museum, where Madeleine remembered the rain drops in some fossilized sand. They looked at their old flat in Canning Road, and were glad to be back in Ireland a few days later.

In April, Stuart celebrated his sixtieth birthday. Apart from enjoying some wine with Madeleine, which they drank in a tent in the garden because of a heat wave, the event went publicly unnoticed. By June he thought he had half completed his book, but was still preparing drafts in July the following year, when he took a break to watch racing. He bumped into Lord Glenavy who was looking ill, and who died the following fortnight. He had always been friendly to Stuart, but distanced himself from people if he felt that the companionship was becoming too close. Others found his conversation sarcastic and unkind, and he told Stuart at the end of his life, "I never read anything in which a detective inspector does not appear by the third page." Before he died, Glenavy wrote Stuart a letter from hospital, in which he reflected on his life, questioning whether it had "yielded any harvest at all." He was depressed about the state of the world, and felt compelled to confide in, "..one of the few friends whose intelligence and perception he respected." as his son Patrick Campbell wrote in his autobiography.

The past was very much on Stuart's mind, for he had written half a new draft of *Black List, Section H,* and as he told Hall in a letter of July 1966 :

> It didn't give me any shocks, though at times I feel there was less communication than I'd thought I was achieving. There is still the large second part to complete which now cannot be before early spring. But I look forward to the winter's work, without, let's hope, setbacks or interruptions of a serious nature.

He urged Hall to "... read Anthony Cronin's *A Question of Modernity*. Not because one can agree with his outlook totally, but because the questions raised are, for a change, the vital ones." Stuart had become friendly with amongst others, the novelists, John McGahern and Anthony Cronin. They represented a kind of writing that was breaking away from the tradition of Elizabeth Bowen and jaded "Anglo-Irish writing", with its apparently unlimited variations on "the Catholic problem," and the "Big House". For Stuart it was a hopeful sign that the renaissance he had despaired of in the 1920s was happening at last. Between writing, Stuart carried out much needed repairs to the house, but in August 1967, their domestic peace was shattered by the death of their cat Sophie, at over eighteen years old. She had been the constant sign of reassurance, through all the years of anxiety from Paris to Ireland. As Madeleine wrote:

> Her life was one of love and being loved. She shared the good and bad times when we had quarreled and could not come together again; she would quietly settle between us - and that was it - all was well again - no more arguing - we were

touched by her ways. Her innocence increased my joy in living, she opened the gate to the animal world for me...

Later, they went to a quarry near Glencree, and took a piece of oblong granite which they placed on Sophie's grave. When they left "The Reask", they took the stone to their Dublin garden, where it eventually provided the illustration and title for Stuart's novel, *Memorial*.

After an otherwise quiet summer, Stuart finally completed his *Black List, Section H*, which had then the provisional title of *The Legend of H*. Stuart explained to Hall it was "...in the nature of a fictional memoir. I don't think it is one of my previous books in a different guise, though I remember remarking once that that is what one always writes..." A friend was not encouraging about the chance of finding any sympathetic publishers, and Stuart suspected he would have to "expose it, and my self to their cold and probably hostile eyes..."

By the end of the year when the manuscript was returned by innumerable publishers, Stuart was not depressed, as in the past. He accepted the situation philosophically, for he knew he could not have written a better work. After keeping *Black List, Section H* for nearly a year and a quarter, the London publisher McGibbon and Kee, returned it with a dismissive and awkwardly worded report which included the comment:

> There's a flavour that isn't entirely convincing nor even very pleasant. The self stated literary ideals and excerpts cut little ice and are... embarrassing...Have we here in H the description of the kind of mind that makes for the cold, sometimes sentimental-romantic fascist mentality?...

Stuart declined the same publishers' suggestion of reissuing *The Angel of Pity*. for he had no interest in the book any more. His life at nearly 66 had now a certain stability, and as he told Hall:

> it is not a time of far-reaching decision or events with us, compared to certain periods of the past. My life is quiet and

orderly, one as befits somebody of my age; what dangers there were of my own making, such as becoming a gambler or heavy drinker are by now passed, and those that remain are, I think of a more ambiguous and spiritual nature.

Hall, to whom Stuart made these comments, after nearly ten years of repeated effort and determination had a novel of his own accepted, and Stuart was the first to offer him his whole hearted congratulations and his pleasure that "...the tide had turned at last."

The first sign that the tide was turning for Stuart came in a letter from a young American writer, Jerry Natterstad, who was working on a doctoral thesis on Stuart's work, and wrote to him in September for some information. By October Stuart lent him letters as well as copies of his own books, promising to let him see *Black List, Section H.* The novel had undergone many changes, some at the suggestion of Tom McIntyre, the Irish playwright, who had borrowed the typescript and had repeatedly telephoned Stuart to express his admiration of it. McIntyre suggested that the earliest part of the novel which dealt with a fictional account of Stuart's childhood, should be completely cut. As many of the characters as possible should be given their real names. Yeats (originally called Yardley) Iseult and her mother for example would be immediately identifiable.

Natterstad was supervised by Professor Harry T. Moore, the Lawrence authority, and after he read the novel early in April 1969, Moore wrote to Stuart, offering to have it published by The Southern Illinois University Press, Carbondale.

When Stuart heard the news, he was in bed with a virus, and it took both him and Madeleine some time to absorb the news. Madeleine wrote in her diary that they were "...like two little frightened mice - and didn't even have a drink on it.." They drank to the book on 10 June when Madeleine began her summer holiday, pleased that she would be able to give up one of the two schools she taught in when they resumed in the autumn.

Stuart signed the contract for *Black List, Section H,* in the following August, and Madeleine had her own success with talks on the radio for "Thought For the Day." The quiet life Stuart had settled down to ended in October when the Directors of The Abbey Theatre stopped in rehearsal a play, *Who Fears to Speak,* which Stuart had written to commemorate the fiftieth anniversary of Terence MacSwiney's death. MacSwiney who had died after seventy-three days of fasting in Brixton Prison was one of Stuart's heroes since 1920, and in September, he had written to Hall that the play, *Who Fears to Speak* would be, "... a lively, not to say controversial, little piece - I hope it will get past whatever watchdogs are guarding this particular place of entertainment."

Stuart told the *Irish Press* that the producer, Thomas MacAnna, liked the play, and began the rehearsals. The directors of the Abbey Theatre then summoned MacAnna, and forbade the production. MacAnna wrote to Stuart "I did my best to fight the matter, but it was the content of the script that they objected to...in a word, they felt that the script was using the MacSwiney motif to put forward what they regarded as a propagandist outlook on modern Ireland..."

The title of the play took on an appropriate irony, as Stuart explained in a press statement that "MacSwiney was deeply religious and deeply spiritual. He cared very deeply about Ireland, and would never have accepted our modern materialism." The play was an attempt to recreate MacSwiney's ideas imaginatively. In Stuart's opinion, "...they were so revolutionary, and so damming when one is confronted with present day Ireland that it is not necessary to add to them..." Seeing little difference between institutions such as the Bank of Ireland, the Dail and the Catholic Cathedral in Dublin, one of the characters says "I'm afraid I'm apt to recognize public buildings by what goes on inside them and, from that angle, its often hard to distinguish. The statements of profit and loss, sermons and Dail debates are largely interchangeable. The same old tune is sung in all of them." Dail Eireann, was described as "...the biggest, most elegant sacred cattle shed in the country", a line which seemed to cause the Abbey Directors to tremble.

Stuart was only stating how little Ireland had changed

since 1920, and how MacSwiney's life and thought was a measure against which to judge the bastions of the establishment. The Church was attacked because of its pressure to ban books that attempted to express the truth, because of its refusal to accurately interpret the truth of the Gospels; the political system for producing a Government and Opposition which were indistinguishable in appearance, and which had failed to preserve the "best and highest in the spirit of the community", and finally, a society at large, obsessed with materialism and commercialization.

In essence, Stuart had been repeating all these ideals through his novels, and even his wartime broadcasts, and was saying nothing new. The banning of the play gave more publicity than if it had been presented, and Stuart reported gleefully to Ron Hall, "it has been a mini bombshell in Dublin, talked of in all pubs, and, short of the flags being at half-mast, the news greeted with universal disgust! A lot of radio news devoted to it. Am determined - more so than before - to have this extremist piece produced." Efforts to silence the play did not succeed, for a shortened version of the play was read at Liberty Hall on 1 December 1970.

After years of comparative obscurity, Stuart was suddenly thrust into unexpected prominence. Roger McHugh, to Stuart's surprise, cancelled lectures he was due to give in The Abbey as a protest, and when Stuart gave some talks at University College Dublin, he himself he was both booed and cheered.

In December Stuart was visited by a Librarian from Carbondale, Illinois, who spent some days looking over the manuscripts and papers Stuart had preserved. He had already written to Natterstad, that because of the disruption of the war years but "...also because of a somewhat chaotic way of life, I have failed to keep copies of letters I wrote...", and to Hall he was dubious that anything would come of the "generous offer" which the librarian had made before he left. Nevertheless he was well paid, with the promise of an additional payment if he recovered the papers he had left behind in Paris in 1951, which included the manuscript of *Redemption*.

The course of lectures Stuart gave to post graduate

students at University College Dublin ended, but he was retained on a consultative basis to do a few hours per week after the Easter term. For the first time since Germany, he was earning a reasonable salary doing work he was suited to. It also gave him a platform for his views, and the opportunity to read Beckett. After studying his trilogy *Molloy* he considered it offered "...an experience unique in contemporary literature."

Amongst the papers in Paris was a long letter Beckett, wrote Stuart in 1942, but when he went to Paris, Lesort, had no recollection of having been given the box of letters and manuscripts. The office was searched, but he returned to Ireland empty handed, and repeated efforts since have failed to recover Stuart's archive of the war years.

While he was away, Madeleine looked after the latest arrival to their house, a Belgian hare, although it was really a member of the rabbit family. With the cats and now the hare, the Stuarts found country life suited them all very well, now that they had a better income. By chance when they were having a drink in a Dublin pub, Madeleine heard there was a vacancy in the German Vocational School, in Clonskeagh in Dublin which she applied for. When offered the full-time post Madeleine was in a quandry. Permanent financial security was guaranteed, and unlike previous posts, she would be paid during the long school holidays. It was possible to travel daily from Meath to Dublin, but more convenient to be in Dublin where Stuart was also lecturing part-time. It was obvious Madeleine should take the job, and move to Dublin.

After all the years of unsettled accommodation, Madeleine and Stuart had created their own refuge in "The Reask". However a dispute with a neighbour had recently soured their feelings for the place, and practically speaking, the upkeep of the land was time consuming and tiring.

Some of these considerations made the Stuarts reluctantly agree it was time for a change, but they were faced with finding somewhere to live in Dublin. This was solved through a young student, Neil Hickey, from Dublin who was writing a thesis on Stuart's work. During a visit with his mother to "The Reask" she remarked she was looking for a cottage in the country, and on 29 July it was sold to her. When the Stuarts packed to leave in mid-August, Madeleine felt depressed about the move. For her, it was "The Ark" which had sheltered her, Stuart, and the animals. She thought of:

> The view from the windows, especially the back ones, with their corn-field is unique, you could sit and watch it for hours. It is so peaceful. From the front window we could overlook our vegetable garden, the lawn, the giant sunflowers and then there is the little rockery which is especially colourful in Spring with its loboelias...

Mrs Hickey who rented out a house conveniently near the German School offered to lend it to the Stuarts until they found something more permanent. Twenty minutes by bus from the centre of Dublin, the house in Highfield Park near Dundrum, had a small garden at the front, and at the back was a large one bordered by trees on a slope which led down to a stream at the side of the house. There was also a large sun parlour, and after staying there for a few weeks, the Stuarts bought the house outright.

Highfield Park would not replace "The Reask", but it was bigger, and the garden was not backbreaking to maintain. Eventually Stuart divided the sun parlour in two to create a large space for the hare.

"The Reask" in Meath

Stuart and Madeleine

CHAPTER 16

In January 1972, *Black List, Section H* was published in America with a well meaning, if inaccurate afterword by Professor Harry T. Moore. The novel had still to find a publisher in either Ireland or the UK but that was not of prime importance to Stuart. He had begun the novel in May 1961, when he had written in his diary:

> how all else - concerning my work matters less to me. I no longer wait anxiously for news about novels or plays already done. Indeed when no news comes I am happy, for I have glimpsed the peculiar richness and intensity that lies far removed from the receiving of such news.

Two weeks later he had continued:

> Here I am, nearly sixty, and all my ambitions come to nothing. I have not even a publisher now! What an unexpected series of setbacks in this last year and a half, and humiliation! Yet, painful, terribly painful as this is, obscurely I can at times be glad and rejoice...

Stuart had found peace of mind, and an objectivity about the quality of his own work. He had come to terms with some of the weaknesses which had plagued him for many years, and in this understanding, was able to write *Black List, Section H*. By the summer of 1961 what he had been through was:

> almost insupportable. Yet what the pain has largely consisted of is the crumbling of illusion. This illusion extended to my work and covered it in a haze of pride and optimism; to prayer and religion, and gave me a false spiritual security. In other ways too, I lived in an unreal world. How disagreeable it is to be driven out of these refuges! Yet how salutary! For I was going along in the rut of producing sensitive, fairly well written novels at regular

intervals which Gollancz was ready to publish, none of which
in the past ten years had been really remarkable, and so it
might have continued.

Stuart's rejection by Gollancz seemed at the time a
disaster, but it was the impetus that he needed to rethink his
position as a writer, when he realised he could not go on in
the same way as before. As important, was Madeleine's
secure income and her own ungrudging attitude to working
at a tiring job, because she had faith in his work.

Lawrence Durrell raised a key question about the form of
Black List, Section H :

> when one confronts this extremely distinguished book...Is it
> straight autobiography or not? In tone and temper and style
> it presents itself as a novel- yet throughout we come upon
> "real" people like Yeats, Maud Gonne's daughter, Iseult,
> Liam O'Flaherty... Is what Stuart recounts about them true
> or has he invented their actions and sayings for the purposes
> of this fiction?

Durrell had gone straight to the problem of Stuart's
motivation as a writer, which hinges on his own definition of
"imaginative writer" as opposed to "inventive writer."
Anthony Cronin suggesting to Stuart that "the truths of
which you can be certain are merely the truths of your
personal experience," proposed there was:

> a move in your work from the creation of purely imaginative
> fictions, which in some way revealed these truths, to a kind
> of novel which is actually closer to the day-to-day
> experience...*Black List, Section H,* is nearer to the truth of
> actual experience...it's only rarely that the hero or the writer
> permits himself any imaginative extension beyond that...

Stuart replied that:

> What it comes to is everyday experience, but one's own and
> the imagination or the imaginary creation is drawing closer
> and closer...the run of the mill writers can't write like

Dostoevsky...but they invent..I would say imagination is something different. It's not inventing...it's boundless what forms it could take, this non-inventive, you might even say egocentric, writing. I wouldn't personally be at all afraid of the word.

Many thought the novel was straight autobiography, and while it is constructed to emphasize certain aspects of Stuart's life through the main character 'H' the "events" were not depicted strictly chronologically. In order to alienate H, Stuart deliberately exagerrated his delinquency, such as the sexual adventures. He shows H in the worst possible light so that the revelation at the end of the novel confirms and explains H's isolation, which is emphasized from the first page. Iseult especially, was presented with a directness that was more callous than her appearance in *Redemption,* and taking her "imaginative" characterization literally, some relations and friends considered Stuart had betrayed her memory. Others were disappointed to find they were not in the novel, and some falsely believed they were misrepresented under another name.

De Vere White ridiculed the book in *The Irish Times,* jibed at Compton Mackenzie's past support, and "suspected" that the "spiritual value" of the novel was "inconsiderable". He managed to admire Stuart for his frankness, but admits that "Failure to get Mr Stuart's message may invalidate my criticism. And what he sees as the justification of all his proceedings may be apparent to brighter eyes than mine."

"Brighter eyes" belonged to the critic Victoria Glendinning, (De Vere White later married her), who astutely wrote of Stuart, "Although it is hard to believe it, he is genuinely unpolitical. He, and his writings are profoundly self-centred...He is, by temperament a resolute outsider." She also understood, as few others did, part of the reason why Stuart went to Germany, "because personal disaster did not seem enough to extend the imagination as he wished," and prophesized that Stuart was "...one of those uncomfortable, inconvenient voices which, in the end, are generally heard."

Durrell's understanding of Stuart's stance as a writer was equally perceptive:

One feels the ebb and flow of loneliness which comes to all who cut themselves off from their land to get stuck in countries whose language they never master. Their self imposed exile is the bitter bread of the solitary artist and perhaps his greatest drive towards self-expression. One remembers Joyce's recipe 'Silence, exile, cunning'. Stuart has not been unresponsive to the invocation, and the result has been a book of the finest imaginative distinction.

When Stuart became known only as the author of *Black List, Section H,* he came to resent this, believing that it was liked because of the "tittle-tattle about Yeats and others." Publication of the tittle- tattle encouraged Stuart to work on *Memorial,* his twenty-first novel, as he approached his seventieth birthday, "... a rather awesome milestone to catch sight of at the dusty roadside." He continued in his letter to Hall, "We are spending it, and weekend, in Derry with some friends, who, though, I'm not really supposed to know it, are bringing out a small book to commemorate the event..."

The "small book" was *A Festschrift For Francis Stuart On His Seventieth Birthday* published by The Dolmen Press of Dublin. Edited by W.J.McCormack, nine contributors covered varying aspects of Stuart's life and work in the first collection of essays to appear on his work under one cover.

The Stuarts had now settled comfortably into Dublin, with Madeleine preferring life there to Meath. As a naturally gifted teacher, she was devoted to the children, but not some of the German staff there, whose formal attitudes and various intrigues she disliked.

As the school began early in the morning, Stuart drove her there, and wrote until it was time to collect her for lunch at home. Their hare had produced several leverets for which homes were found, and Stuart told Hall that the leverets were "beautiful creatures when you have time to watch and get to know them." They would play a significant part in the new novel, which Stuart put to one side to travel to Germany where he spent three weeks in Berlin and Freiburg making a television programme for the RTE series *Pilgrimage.* Stuart had been several times to Berlin since the war, but Freiburg was particularly memorable, for he had last seen it in 1949.

Memorial concerned the love of an old man for a young girl in a town resembling Derry, where she is killed in what the British Government euphemistically refer to as "the Troubles." Her essential tenderness centres around the old man, and a hare and her leverets. Written in a looser style than his previous novels, and despite the serious theme, humour is more developed in *Memorial* and Stuart introduces the first names of some dissident friends, "Bill (W.J.) McCormack who also wrote as "Hugh Maxton", and "Hayden" (Murphy).

The narrator resembles Stuart, who states:

> All my life I'd been obsessed with my fictions, getting little in the way of response. And now when I'd come to see myself as the constructor of, and dweller in, a very private ghetto...where only a few stray animals came, a group of militant young people, or perhaps that section of them who had rejected even militancy, wanted me to share it with them...

When it was proposed to pass an Amendment to the Offences against the State Bill, Stuart declared that if it became law in the form suggested, he would pledge himself to "...apply for membership of an illegal organization." It was the only way open to him as a writer "Without political or industrial power to express the whole hearted opposition to the curtailing of safeguards of individual liberty without which societies lose their human dignity..."

To Dormandi's daughter Judith Dupont, he wrote, "If this new Bill is passed we are well on the way to a police state, not unlike Greece except that in that country the dictatorship is open while here there is a democratic pretence..."

Stuart was gaining the support of younger dissidents for whom he often was a spokesman. He encouraged Hayden Murphy to start an 'underground' Broadsheet, perhaps thinking of *Tomorrow,* and took every opportunity to use his influence to disturb the complacency he thought was swamping the Republic.

On the personal level, Stuart was concerned about Ron

Hall, who had fallen in love with a young woman called Ruth, and had separated from his wife. Stuart told him in a letter that "...the pain for Iseult...has always been present to me, as I have tried to show in my fiction...". Hall and Ruth came to spend a few days with them in Dublin. After they returned to England, Stuart wrote to Hall of a visit he was making to London, to celebrate the publication in February in the UK of *Black List, Section H* by Martin, Brian and O'Keefe who had published *Memorial.*

The novel was praised in a half page feature on Stuart in *The Guardian,* in February 1975, and with acclaim from Robert Nye and Frank Kermode, Stuart was at last re-establishing his position as a writer beyond Ireland, and in danger of being promoted into the Grand Old Man of Irish Letters. He felt confident to begin a more daring experimental form of fiction which centred around the dark and lonely world of Emily Bronte, but as a living person in the imagination of a contemporary writer. He realised that for the time being he had exhausted his own experiences to transmute into fiction, and had to try something else.

As Stuart had projected MacSwiney imaginatively as a real person in contemporary Ireland, so too does Emily Bronte "exist" in the mind of the narrator. Hall heard Stuart was:

> preoccupied with the world of the Brontes, one of the strangest and most intense in all literary history. I entered it to begin to explore areas that I try to report on in the novel I'm writing, but later was completely absorbed there in the company of Branwell, to a lesser extent Charlotte and Ann, but above all Emily...

A Hole in the Head, was set in Belfast, but disguised as Belbury, because Stuart wanted the centre of violence to be anywhere. During visits to the North, he "...had convivial contacts with some semi-outlawed friends in the UDA. Huge energies up there ready let's hope, to be released into imaginative constructive channels when the time is ripe..."

When he returned, he and Madeleine were glad to take what chance they could to live quietly in Highfield Park, for there were increasing demands for Stuart to give talks, and broadcasts. When Longship Press of America wanted to publish his books, he prepared to travel to America and Canada with some reluctance, as he told Judith Dupont:

> I have a new novel coming out in London in April and in America in the autumn, and more unusual and less welcome, I am going there (USA) early next month to lecture...I shall be in about fifteen cities in America and Canada, a rather daunting prospect for me, but the pay in dollars makes it impossible to refuse...

Stuart found America anything but difficult to assess. "All the 'sights' they insist one must see, and the quantities of food!", Stuart remarked in a letter to Hall in April, and continued "Of all the 'sights' the most dismal, though memorable was the bridge over the Mississippi in Minneapolis from which John Berryman threw himself. I met a close friend of his there, a psychiatrist, Charles Macofferty, whose brother has a pub, which I know well, in Derry City..."

When he returned to Ireland "...with rather quickly diminishing dollars," he had forged a friendship with his new American publisher Bill Vorm and his sister, Sheila Taylor, who were promoting *A Hole in the Head*. The novel was well received, less obviously "egocentric" than some of Stuart's other novels because of the fantasy he creates with Emily Bronte. Once more, "H" is present, and it is to Emily that he confides "...the novels I was writing were ingeniously concocted instead of being wrung from the heart."

Significantly, friends who were allies or part of an understanding community that had come to know Stuart, figure in his novels in a much broader sense than the intense treatment of the characters he wrote of, for example, immediately after the war. This was at least partly due to the improvement in Stuart's own circumstances, where the stress of poverty no longer compelled him to turn to himself so introspectively.

For Victoria Glendinning, Stuart was:
  a powerful and interesting writer, not because he writes

particularly well but because he writes passionately. He can be funny...when...a literary lecture...develops into a surrealist evocation of a Garsington like party attended by Yeats, Edith Sitwell, Lady Dorothy Wellesley, Gandhi and a goat. But even here he writes like a man driven.

In comparison with the wilderness of the past, the last two years were "extraordinary". He felt less need to write his Diary, which in any case, he had put aside for two years, but at the end of August 1977 wrote, "A growing if limited response to my work at this late stage. M. and I, the haven of this place,[Highfield Park] and lately Paris, Gstaad [where he and Madeleine went for holidays to stay with Sheila Taylor] and all that went with these." And as he correctly predicted, "I'll probably write here less and less."

His Diary, never a journal of famous names, did not include an account of his memorable meeting in Dublin with Robert Lowell, and his Irish wife Caroline Blackwood, whom Lowell had come to visit. They "... drank a solemn toast to dead comrades, including those as far back as the one's buried in the old Quaker graveyard on Nantucket Island.", which would have its own poignancy for Stuart. Lowell died the following week in a New York taxi returning from the airport, after his Dublin visit. Neither would Lowell or the visit to America and Canada be forgotten, for the poet formed the basis for a character called Robert Banin in Stuart's work in progress, set in places he had visited.

Stuart's own health as he approached 76 was excellent, as his doctor confirmed when he applied for "a certificate of fitness" necessary for his driving licence. He drove to various schools under a scheme sponsored by the Irish Arts Council, and encouraged patients in the Mental Asylum which happened to be near where Stuart lived. Such activity ended when early in January 1979 Stuart slipped and broke his leg on an icy pavement. While it healed satisfactorily, as he wrote to Judith Dupont, at least there was "...the advantage that I have to sit all day beside a table and there is not much to do but write my long novel which progresses by leaps and bounds." The "long novel" would occupy him for four years. Before setting off for a holiday in France with Madeleine at the end of July, Stuart heard that he was to receive £9,000 from the Irish Arts Council, spread over three years. With the prospect of the first instalment in August, the Stuarts returned to Paris in very different circumstances than when they had left it in 1951.

Madeleine had not been back to France since then, and the holiday was nostalgic and evocative. Especially memorable when driving near Paris, was a chance visit to Auvers-sur-Oise, where Van Gogh had died, which they happened to recognize from a Church familiar from a Van Gogh painting.

The High Consistory was not published until 1981, but the idea for the novel may have struck Stuart in November 1977 when re-reading Evelyn Waugh, whom he told Hall in a letter was "probably the only English novelist of any significance since Henry James." He also mentioned a "wonderful passage in *Brideshead Revisited*" where Waugh "speaks of memories, comparing them to the pigeons in Venice, and seeing them as his most treasured possession..."

As Stuart grew older, the thought of death may have been on his mind, and that there were fragments of his life he had not used in his novels. He wanted his next book to be, "... a large collage made up of old notebooks, copy books, scraps of memory, longer documents, even short new clippings, against a background sombre in tone, with comic highlights..."

In *The High Consistory* some of the same real names, including Iseult occur again, and are even listed in a page of *Dramatis Personae*. Stuart allots his own date of birth to the narrator Simeon Grimes and to Grimes' father, his own father's first names. Simeon Grimes who is a painter, presents "events" in a kaleidoscopic pattern, taking sequences that had some basis in Stuart's own life, and reshaping them from the "actual" event into imaginative fantasy, so he, as William Trevor wrote "...plays at the same time the part of himself and that of his hero...". In March 1981 Madeleine had a hip replacement operation, which kept her away from school until the following September. While she was in hospital, Stuart heard that certain writers, artists and musicians, numbering not more than 150 in total would be invited to be members of a body called the Aosdana, which *The Sunday Tribune* referred to as "the elite group." When the list of the first members was published in December, Stuart's name was amongst them, and he later received the *Cnuas,* an income of £5,000 per annum for a term of five years. He was free to write with a guaranteed income, and as his eightieth birthday approached in April, plans were in hand for a celebration, mainly organized by a young writer and publisher, Dermot Bolger.

Bolger left his work in the library to found his own publishing company, The Raven Arts Press, and re-issued with additions, Stuart's only volume of poems *We Have Kept The Faith* first published in 1923. Bolger also commissioned Paul Durcan to write a long poem, *The Ark of the North,* in honour of the birthday.

A few days before Stuart was eighty, there was a celebration on 25 April in a Dublin hotel, when Stuart recalled how Liam O'Flaherty on his eightieth birthday was shocked to receive a telegram of congratulations from President Hillery. Had Stuart received a telegram from the President he would have been equally horrified, and preferred the evening in his honour when in the Peacock Theatre, Durcan read his poem, and Stuart selections from *We Have Kept The Faith.* Richard Ryan, the writer and diplomat wrote the sleeve note for a record Stuart made called *Alternative Government* which took its title from a phrase he used in an autobiographical passage on one side of the disc. All the tributes were appropriate for an elderly writer who had reached a milestone in his life, but Stuart refused to slip into a gentle decline of old age.

In 1982 the centennial celebration for James Joyce, twenty years Stuart's senior, gave him the chance to publish his *Minority Report,* a considered rejection of Joyce in a collection of otherwise laudatory essays. Admitting that he found *Ulysses* "about the funniest book" he had read, it was "something of a cul-de-sac, a fact of which its author was probably aware and which certainly would not have worried him."

Stuart was tired of the generally unqualified adulation for Joyce, and the frequently cited view that he was "the greatest writer of the century, made without reference to...the claims of Proust, Mann or Kafka." In support of his view that Joyce was not "the greatest writer of the century", Stuart quoted Edwin Muir, who had written *"Au fond,* a very meretricious writer, a getter of effects, and quite incapable of attaining the simplicity which is the condition of great art." Occasionally Stuart's protests seemed to be made simply for the controversy they provoked, rather than for an entirely rational and well reasoned argument. In cases such as the Joyce, like any Parliamentarian he quoted what he needed to support his argument, and omitted what was inconvenient.

Ironically it was through the celebrations for Joyce that Stuart spent a morning with Jorge Luis Borges, whom he had admired for many years. Various writers including Borges attended a State Reception for the Joyce Centenary in Dublin Castle, an event organized by Anthony Cronin, who also arranged for Stuart to talk to the Argentinian writer the following morning in the Shelbourne Hotel where he was staying.

Stuart told Borges that he was one of "a certain imaginative tribe of writers scattered all over the world" to which Borges replied that he hoped he belonged "to that secret brotherhood."

Throughout the long conversation, which was recorded, Stuart obviously pleased Borges by the understanding and knowledge he showed of his poetry. Despite Stuart's liking for Borges, he chose to be true to his own ideals, and would not comment on Borges' assertion that a certain line of Blake's could have been written "At least by William Butler Yeats. A very fine writer." Feeling that he had spoken too long, Stuart offered the writer his thanks but Borges told him that "No, I should thank you, for the fine morning you're giving me."

Before leaving, Stuart gave Borges a translation of *Redemption* which had been published in Buenos Aires, and Borges read aloud Robert Louis Stevenson's *"Epitaph",* which he assured Cronin and Stuart, that as he was "...saying it all the time, you can hardly stop me from saying it."

It was one of the most memorable meetings of Stuart's life, and one which must have been moving to witness. Old men of widely different backgrounds, sharing their love of poetry, and for Stuart, a re-affirmation of the values he had been

273

faithful to through great difficulty, from one who was deeply respected. Borges' presence was, "full of peace and wisdom, also...humility. Is it not reassuring to think of such people on this earth, for which reason, if no other, it may be spared as Nineveh would have been had it contained one just soul," Stuart told Hall later.

Due to the *Cnuas*, Madeleine gave up teaching in 1982, and Stuart spent some of the summer near Cannes with Sheila Taylor. They returned there for two weeks in the following May, establishing a pattern of holidays either on the Riviera or in Switzerland. In Dublin there was more leisure for quiet afternoons with friends or excitement at the race-course.

Stuart now heard less frequently from Ron Hall, who was in poor health, but who wrote a congratulatory letter on a collection of prose extracts called *States of Mind* which The Raven Arts Press published in 1984. He replied to Hall at the end of April, giving him news of the progress of the long novel he was working on called *Faillandia* which "...having resisted an earlier temptation to abandon...has now taken a turn for the better."

Dublin was then preparing for President Reagan's visit to Ireland, and the city was swamped with foreign press, and endless tedious publicity. As a protest, The Raven Arts Press published a book of poems, edited by Bolger, and dedicated to Reagan called *After the War is Over* subtitled *Irish Writers mark the visit of Ronald Reagan.* Sixteen writers, made a "humanitarian protest about the erosion of human values, the deprivation of human rights in South America...and the threat of destruction hanging over the earth." This was introduced by Stuart, who amongst other points stated that:

> to the official welcome that will be given to President Reagan there will be many of us to pronounce in our deepest selves an unofficial but resounding NO!...those of us who deplore the visit will dissociate ourselves from what goes on as best we can...we can take heart from the conviction that we are aligning ourselves with the millions who at this moment suffer pain and grief in Central America and Asia because of the direct intervention of his administration.

But Stuart was most concerned with the nuclear threat. Part of civilisation and culture had survived because man had preserved a "calm faith in the future," but now he was confronted "with threats that his spirit has not found a way of dealing with. Whole communities are affected by a sense that nothing matters if absolute evil is to have the last word."

The Raven Arts Press intended to reissue *Memorial* in 1984, and when Dermot Bolger called to see Stuart about this, Madeleine was absorbed in reading her diaries and papers. A more constant daily recorder than Stuart, she had written detailed accounts of their life together, and especially of their turbulent years as refugees.

Bolger suggested Madeleine should write her memoirs, and working together with Bolger through the summer of 1984, the result was *Manna in the Morning* published in November on the same day as *Memorial*. For Madeleine it was "one of the most wonderful moments of my life" for after spending over forty years with a writer, she enjoyed acclaim for herself, all the more appreciated because it publicly expressed her devotion to Stuart.

With the advance, she bought a garden hut, and a female Siamese kitten which she appropriately called Manna, and to whom she quickly became devoted. Instead of making a speech at the launch of the books, Madeleine sang "Lili Marlene", a song which brought memories of Liam O'Flaherty, who had died in September. When Madeleine visited him, his mind clouded by old age, she sang "Lili Marlene" which evoked a response from him. She knew that he had abandoned religion, and although she herself had her own strong faith, she did not believe when she heard at his funeral, that his alleged return to the Church, could have happened with his conscious knowledge.

After the funeral, Stuart, Madeleine and other friends, met O'Flaherty's companion, Kitty, at The Shelbourne Hotel, and Madeleine told her she strongly disapproved of her allowing O'Flaherty to be persuaded into the Church.

For Stuart, O'Flaherty had been his oldest friend, and the fact that he had not admired much of his writing was unimportant. "The thing about O'Flaherty was his fine

untamed spirit that never really got into his writing." Stuart
wrote to Hall, adding that he had too, "a welcome word from
Sam Beckett the other day, and I may say that our divergent
ways have not disrupted our friendship."

Beckett conveyed to Stuart an inscribed copy of his trilogy
Malone Dies, which pleased Stuart, who had wrongly
assumed that he had lost Beckett's friendship.

Shortly after writing, Hall died. For over thirty years he
had been Stuart's most constant supporter, sharing many of
the same values. He found in Stuart a teacher who re-
inforced his determination to publish a work of fiction which
embraced his ideals. Neglected and impoverished when they
first met, Stuart was sustained by Hall's support in times of
despair.

Madeleine began work on a sequel to *Manna in the
Morning,* when in July 1985, she had a masectomy operation
for a malignant tumour. Before she went to hospital she was
painting outside walls, and making light of her ordeal to her
next door neighbour, Peggy Doyle. She came home in early
August, and although she apparently made a full recovery,
did not feel strong enough to travel with Stuart to London,
where he attended a party given by Richard Ryan of the
Irish Embassy to celebrate Raven's publication of *Faillandia*.
While he was in London, she was overwrought, and lonely,
and Stuart determined that he would not travel in future
without her.

Publication of the novel coincided with a Channel 4 film
Two Lives on Stuart's life, by Carlo Gebler, of which the
Times wrote that "The viewer was left with a picture of
genius flawed by internal confusion."

Faillandia, even more than his previous novels, stressed
with an almost desperate urgency the importance of like
minds supporting each other with love and faith against
mediocrity and corruption. He quoted Dostoevsky and others
with whom he felt a strong affinity, and paralleled their
example with the struggle of the editor, Gideon Spokane,
whose imagination and vision in a revolutionary magazine
manages for a short while to displace a corrupt government.
He is forced, with his lover Pieta, to continue their efforts in
the sanctuary of an island where they are safe from hostile

intervention.

Stuart returned to the problem of reconciling spiritual and physical desire, which Sean Dunne in an enthusiastic review noted as, "...the difference between the love that is appeased by desire and the love that is free of desire, the patience that is both a mark of suffering and a condition of wisdom."

Stuart had first explored the paradox in *Women and God* published over fifty years previously, and as Dunne observed "Once again he takes us on this journey from eroticism to charity...Each time...it becomes more apocalyptic, the discovery of final freedom is more than ever dependent upon a repudiation of the existing world..."

Stuart had too, finally come to an understanding of his relationship with Iseult and in *Faillandia* through the character of Lydia, expressed a new tenderness for her. Stuart changed Madame MacBride to Lydia's father, and as Gideon explains to his daughter, the marriage:

> was hopelessly wrong from the start. The gulf was too great...Two different kinds of being, that's what we were. Your mother with much of the child in her, a not-at-all complicated nature, but unsocial and full of reserve, who loved and looked up to her father with that single heartedness of hers...
>
> Then I came along, somebody utterly different from both of them, complex, outgoing and at times excessive, sceptical of much of what your mother treasured including her father... But the fatal thing was that she loved these two people, her father and me, and we dragged her apart...
>
> Naturally she parted company with me...the worst of it was that she at least, never believed it was inevitable, supposing quite sincerely that it came from my perversity...
>
> I was aware of the pain, hers and mine, and was therefore more guilty than her father who was aware of nothing but the ups and downs of his [her] own career. I may have been as corrupt, though in a quite different and far more complex way.

Gideon is told by his lover Pieta that Lydia should not be forgotten. And when he suggests that "there are others to remember her," he recalls, "how little he had done to delight her, but on the contrary, sometimes used his intimate knowledge of her to irritate and even hurt."

Pieta insists Gideon confronts Lydia's memory, for "if you banish her from your thoughts, it's because you want to forget a period of your life, years and years that, good or bad, the good with the bad, you can't be indifferent to."

Old age had helped to bring an acceptance of Iseult's place in Stuart's life, for he could say that she was "a fine person." If *Faillandia,* was Stuart's valediction to fiction, for he was 83 when it was published, he ensured that what was possibly his last public statement on Iseult was unselfish, and an attempt at objectivity. The paradox in Stuart's attitude to Iseult, whether she had appeared as part portraits of "Nancy", "Julie", "Lydia", "Leonore" or in her own name in many of Stuart's novels, was, that he had always loved her, and was perpetually trying to exorcize their past in his fiction.

Correspondence about "The Nature of Reality" in *The Irish Times* stimulated Stuart into writing a short philosophical work, similar in its enquiry to the essay, *The Only Happiness* he had begun but abandoned in the 1920s. He read widely around the subject, and began work on an early draft, before travelling to Canada to take part in "Irish week" celebrations sponsored by the University of Nova Scotia in March 1986.

As promised, he took Madeleine with him where they stayed in the Lord Nelson Hotel, familiar to her through *The High Consistory*. While Stuart was driven through Nova Scotia to lecture and give readings, Madeleine happily stayed in the hotel, and although the visit was exhausting they both returned to Dublin, exhilarated by the experience of a different country under freezing snow bound conditions. The following day, with a disregard for jet lag, Stuart lectured to the students of Maynooth College.

In April, he read a tribute he had written for Samuel Beckett's eightieth birthday. This took place during a ceremony where Beckett's niece accepted on her uncle's behalf, the award of the *Saoid* from the Taoiseach, Garrett Fitzgerald, a gold torc voted as the highest distinction from Ireland by the *Aosdana*. Stuart had published his essay on

Beckett in the Aer Lingus in flight magazine. Seen by the London *Evening Standard,* their gossip column noted sharply that Beckett was no friend of Stuart. They were determined to credit Stuart with nothing, for they had already attacked him when he appeared on the Channel 4 programme. Alleging that Beckett had no interest in Stuart, they said he was unlikely to even glance at the essay.

Beckett's niece sent her uncle a copy of it, and Beckett responded by sending Stuart a friendly note, confirming he would like to meet Stuart and Madeleine if they were ever in Paris.

They hoped to do this, for several friends still lived there, but when they went to France in July that year, it was on holiday in Nice. During the time there, Madeleine noticed she was suffering from a gradual loss of appetite, but said nothing, not wishing to worry Stuart.

When she returned to Dublin, she fell in the garden, but hospital examination showed no trace of the cancer which had returned. By early August, however, Stuart was told cancer had spread to the liver and this time no treatment was possible.

The Stuarts agreed that if either had a terminal illness, there would be no secrets or deception however hard such knowledge would be to endure. Their love had been strengthened and tested by deprivation and hardship, and Madeleine heard the news with patient acceptance. After they left "The Reask", she wrote their Dublin home had:

> become... the new Ark, where Francis and I and our animals have found shelter from the world. It will become a refuge for us until the flood waters recede and we will enter another world, where, "The wolf and the lamb shall feed together, and the Lion shall eat straw like the bullock: and dust shall be the serpent's meat They shall not hurt nor destroy in all my holy mountain, saith the Lord."

It was to their "Ark" that Madeleine asked to return, assured that she could be nursed there, rather than in the clinical atmosphere of a Hospice. Conleth O'Connor, the Irish writer who lived nearby, and with whom Madeleine was especially close, came to help the Stuarts, and he and others, were moved by her complete lack of self pity in her last weeks, and her constant concern not to be a burden to others. With the sun streaming past her favourite sunflowers into the bedroom, Manna nearby, the rabbit in the sun parlour, and especially Stuart comforting and caring, Madeleine gradually slipped into a coma. Early in the morning of 18 August, she died peacefully.

Only a few days earlier, she noticed the disappearance of a stray black cat which for several years she had fed on the outside windowsill. Recognising the strange knowledge of animals, Madeleine remarked that she knew it would never return, with the words "he's a goner."

Remembering O'Flaherty's funeral, Madeleine asked that there should be no religious observance at her own, which took place the following day at Glasnevin Crematorium, Dublin. She did not want the hypocrisies of a Church she knew misrepresented her own beliefs, and as her coffin slipped from sight, the *cavatina* of Beethoven's late quartet in E flat which she had loved was played.

During Madeleine's last illness, Stuart re-read the memoirs of the Russian writer Osip Mandelstam by his widow, Nadezha *Hope against Hope* and *Hope Abandoned*. He had prepared for his wife's death with great stoicism, but as the winter approached, he remarked that if it was not for Manna and the rabbit, he would not trouble to get up in the morning. He completed his essay on the nature of reality, *The Abandoned Snail Shell*, dedicated "For Madeleine, whose death this essay is an attempt to commemorate", but his own existence seemed pointless.

If Stuart's life was unpredictable, even he could not have anticipated that what began as deeply needed and healing companionship from an old friend of his and Madeleine's, would develop into love.

Finola Graham, an artist who taught for a while with Madeleine in the German school, wrote to Stuart, sensing the despair he was suffering. They had first met after she had read and liked his books, and occasionaly afterwards in Dublin. Finola had her own private tragedies, including the

loss of twins which helped in her understanding of Stuart.
Early in January 1987, after leaving her small son Daniel in
the care of friends, she went with Stuart for a week to Paris
which confirmed their feelings for each other.

Stuart arranged to see Samuel Beckett, whom he had not
met for over fifty years. When he returned to Dublin, he told
the Press that:

> At first the meeting was chilly. Then it became very moving
> indeed. These two old men, dedicated to their writing, whose
> careers could not have gone more differently.
> In the end none of this mattered, none of it meant anything.
> There was a feeling of deep, very deep affection between us,
> and on my part, a very deep admiration.

A few days before Stuart's eighty fifth birthday, the event
was celebrated with a party by the Raven Arts Press in the
Winding Stair bookshop in Dublin, to launch Stuart's *The
Abandoned Snail Shell*, and followed with a reading by him,
Paul Durcan and Anthony Cronin in an over-filled theatre in
Trinity College. On the day itself, Mattie O'Neill, a friend
who shared racing and other interests with Stuart took him
and Finola for lunch in the Shelbourne Hotel, so often
Stuart's meeting place in the past. None of this meant Stuart
felt accepted, nor did he want to be. When he opened the
Yeats' summer school in Sligo that year he was no nearer to
the accepted establishment or received opinion about the
poet, and preferred opening an art exhibition which included
some of Finola's work.

When he heard he had to have a long planned hip
replacement operation, early in January 1988, he married
Finola on 29 December 1987 in the church of St. Francis
Xavier at Gardiner Street, Dublin. After Madeleine's death,
he probably would not have bothered with the operation, but
with something to live for, he made a quick recovery,
unafraid to enter a new relationship, with all the happiness
and pain which that entails.

Interviewed on the radio for his eighty-fifth birthday, he
told his questioner that he did not regard his age as any
achievement, simply chance or destiny. Old age took greater

resolution, but that the "main thing is never to sink into some sort of complacency."

With a new novel, *A Compendium of Lovers,* Stuart still lives his own intense fiction. Through all the paradoxes of his nature he has never abandoned his wayward search for truth and serenity, which remains a lifelong quest.

Stuart and his wife Finola

ACKNOWLEDGEMENTS

My thanks to Francis Stuart should be obvious, but I would like to acknowledge with gratitude, his patient co-operation. I am also grateful to F.C Molloy for following up certain clues in Australia, and especially for his help in discovering the details of Henry Stuart's death. Of studies on Francis Stuart, the best is John Wheale's *Redemption in the work of Francis Stuart*, which guided my way through Stuart's books. In Dublin, I received much kindness and hospitality which made each visit memorable. Dermot Bolger and Aidan Murphy have been patient editors, and I thank them for helping me to avoid many pitfalls. Others who assisted in diverse ways are, Eugene Ankeny, the late Samuel Beckett, Kay Bridgwater, Eduardo Canissimo, Humphrey Carpenter, Conn Daly, Peggy Doyle, Sean Dunne, John Fitzgerald, Finola Graham, Ruth Hall, Conleth O'Connor, Mattie O'Neill, Judith Dupont, Carlo Gebler, John Kelly, Paul-Andre Lesort, Adrian Liddell-Hart, Gary Nellhaus, John de Paor, Peter Parker, Princess Mary de Rachelwitz, Olga Rudge, Desmond Sollis, Kelvin Sollis, Ronald Stevenson, Bill Swainson, Tim Teeling, Mervyn Wall, Bill Walsh, Ian Watson, John Wheale, Anne Yeats, Michael Yeats. Thanks are also due for permission to reproduce copyright material: Francis Stuart for letters and Diaries, Dublin Castle State Papers No:S1369/10. and No:S1369/3. The Morris Library, Southern Illinois University at Carbondale, for letters from Victor Gollancz, Maud Gonne MacBride, Compton Mackenzie, Ethel Mannin, Liam O'Flaherty and Iseult Stuart. The National Library of Ireland for letters to Joseph O'Neill (Ms10864) Public Record Office Northern Ireland Cabinet Secretariat BBC Monitoring Reports PRONI CAB 9CD/207BBCMR. The Harry Ranson Humanities Research Center, University of Texas, at Austin for letters to Sir Compton Mackenzie, The University of London, King's College, London, Centre for Military Archives, for letters of Sir Basil Liddell Hart (LH1/665), Judith Dupont for letters to herself and Lodzi Dormandi. Mrs Ruth Hall for letters to Ron Hall, Dr.G.Nellhaus for letters and diary extracts. Letters of W.B.Yeats to Francis and Iseult Stuart courtesy of John Kelly and Michael and Ann Yeats.

BIBLIOGRAPHY

FRANCIS STUART BOOKS

We Have Kept The Faith Oak Press (Dublin) 1923
Nationality and Culture (Baile Atha Cliath:Sinn Fein Ardchomhairle) 1924
Mystics and Mysticism (Catholic Truth Society) Dublin 1929
Women and God (Cape) London 1931
Pigeon Irish (Gollancz) London 1932
The Coloured Dome (Gollancz) London 1932
Try the Sky (Gollancz) London 1933
Glory (Gollancz) London 1933
Things to Live For (Cape) London 1934
In Search of Love (Collins) London 1935
The Angel of Pity (Grayson & Grayson) London 1935
The White Hare (Collins) 1936
Racing For Pleasure and Profit (Talbot Press) Dublin 1937
The Bridge (Collins) London 1937
Julie (Collins) London 1938
The Great Squire (Collins) London 1939
Der Fall Casement: Das Leben Sir Roger Casements und der Verleumdungsfeldzug Des Secret Service trs. Ruth Weiland (Hanseatiche) Hamburg 1940
The Pillar of Cloud (Gollancz) London 1948
Redemption (Gollancz) London 1949
The Flowering Cross (Gollancz) London 1950
Good Friday's Daughter (Gollancz) London 1952
The Chariot (Gollancz) London 1953
The Pilgrimage (Gollancz) London 1955
Victors and Vanquished (Gollancz) London 1958
The Angels of Providence (Gollancz) London 1959
Black List, Section H (Carbondale Southern Illinois University)
1971 (Martin Brian & O'Keefe) London 1974
Memorial (Martin Brian & O'Keefe) London 1973
A Hole in the Head (Martin Brian & O'Keefe) London 1977
The High Consistory (Martin Brian & O'Keefe) London 1981
We Have Kept the Faith: New and Selected Poems (Raven Arts Press) Dublin 1982

States of Mind (Raven Arts Press) Dublin 1984
Faillandia (Raven Arts Press) Dublin 1985
The Abandoned Snail Shell (Raven Arts Press) Dublin 1987
Night Pilot (Raven Arts Press) Dublin 1988
A Compendium of Lovers (Raven Arts Press) Dublin 1990

SHORT STORIES

The Isles of the Blest English Review 59 December 1934; *The Bandit* Cornhill 157 February 1938; *Minou* Good Housekeeping 75 no 3. March 1959; *Jacob* Irish Press 9.10.71; *The Stormy Petrel* Atlantis 1 no 6 Winter 1973-4; *2016* Cork Review 1 no 1 November-December 1979; *Nocturne at the Cable Shop* Cork Review no 2 January-February 1980; *The Water Garden* Firebird 2 ed T.J. Binding 1983.

POEMS

"Two Poems" Aengus 1 no 2 December 1919, "Criminals" Aengus New Series 1 no 4 July 1920, "Poems" Poetry: A Magazine of Verse ed.Harriet Munro 22 no 1 April 1923, "Introduction to a Spiritual Poem" Transatlantic Review 2 no 4 October 1924, "By the Waterfall" Poetry: A Magazine of Verse ed. Harriet Munro 29 no 1 October 1926, "At the Races" Motley: The Dublin Gate Theatre Magazine 1 no 1 March 1932, "The Outcasts to the Smug and Respectable" Motley: The Gate Theatre Magazine 1 no 5 October 1932, "Ireland" The Capuchin Annual (Dublin 1944), "Three Poems" The Capuchin Annual 1945-1946.

SHORT PROSE PIECES

"A letter to a young lady, more sincere than most letters, yet not entirely so" Aengus New Series 1 no 4 July 1920, "In Church" Aengus New Series 1 no 4 July 1920, "A Note on Jacob Boehme" Tomorrow ed H. Stuart and Cecil Salkeld 1 no 1 August 1924, "In the Hour Before Dawn" Tomorrow ed H. Stuart and Cecil Salkeld 1 no 2 September 1924, "President de Valera" Great Contemporaries: Essays by

Various Hands (Cassell) London 1935, "Frank Ryan in Germany" The Bell 16 no 2 November 1950, "Frank Ryan in Germany part II" The Bell 16 no 3 December 1950, "Selection from a Berlin Diary 1942" Journal of Irish Literature 5 no 1 January 1976, "Introduction" After the War is Over: Irish Writers mark the visit of Ronald Reagan (Raven Arts Press) Dublin 1984.

PLAYS (Unpublished)

Men Crowd Me Round Presented at the Abbey Theatre Dublin 1933, *Glory* Presented at the Arts Theatre Club London January 1936, *Strange Guest* Presented at the Abbey Theatre Dublin December 1940, *Flynn's Last Dive* Presented at the Pembroke Theatre, Croydon March 1962, *Who Fears to Speak* Presented at Liberty Hall, Dublin December 1970.

BOOKS AND THESES ON FRANCIS STUART

Isaacson, Helen *Women and God: A Study of Francis Stuart* Unpublished University M.A. dissertation New York University 1956; McCormack, W.J. *A Festschrift for Francis Stuart on his Seventieth Birthday,* 28 [sic] April 1972 (Dolmen Press) Dublin 1972; Natterstad, J.H. *Francis Stuart* (Irish Writers Series), (Associated University Presses) New Jersey and London 1974; Natterstad, J.H. Irish Journal of Literature (Francis Stuart number) 5 no 1 January 1976 (Delaware) 1976; Wheale, John *Redemption in the work of Francis Stuart* Unpublished Ph.d. thesis, The University of Warwick.

SELECTED ARTICLES ON FRANCIS STUART

Garfitt, Roger "Outside the Moral Pale: The Novels of Francis Stuart" London Magazine New Series 16 no 4 (October-November1976; Greene, David H. "The Return of Francis Stuart" Envoy 5 no 20 April-June 1951; Kiely, Benedict " Modern Irish Fiction- A critique" (Golden Eagle Books) Dublin 1950; Molloy, F.C. "Francis Stuart's Australian Connection: The Life

and Death of Henry Irwin Stuart" Irish University Review
Vol 16 No 1 Spring 1986 Dublin; Murphy, Daniel
"Imagination & Religion in Anglo-Irish Literature 1930-1980
(Irish Academic Press) Dublin 1987; Murphy, Hayden "Case
for the Cause of Francis Stuart" New Edinburgh Review
Spring 1984 6-14; O'Brien, R.J. "Francis Stuart's Cathleen
Ni Houlihan" The Dublin Magazine VII Summer 1971;
Rafroidi,P. and Harmon, M. eds "The Irish Novel in our
Times" (University of Lille) Lille, 1976.

SELECT BIBLIOGRAPHY

Campbell, Christy: *The World War II Fact Book 1939-1945*
(Macdonald) London 1985; Cardozo, Nancy: *Lucky Eyes And
A High Heart* (Bobs-Merrill) New York 1978; Carter J.: *The
Shamrock and the Swastika: German Espionage in Ireland
in World War II* (Pacific Books) Paolo Alto, California 1977;
Cole, J.A.: *Lord Haw-Haw:The full Story of William Joyce*
Faber & Faber London 1987; Cooke, John Ed: *Murrays
Handbook for Travellers in Ireland* seventh edtn.(Stanford)
1906; Cronin, Sean : *Frank Ryan: The Search for the
Republic* (Repsol) Dublin 1980; *Documents on German
Foreign Policy 1918-1945 Series D Vol IX* (HMSO) London
1956; *Documents on German Foreign Policy 1918-1945 Series
D Vol IX* (HMSO) London 1956; Ellmann, Richard: *Yeats, The
Man and The Masks revised edtn.* (Penguin) Harmondsworth
1971; Farago, Ladislas: *The Ganes of Foxes (*Pan) London
1973; Finneran, Richard J., George Mills Harper and
William M Murphy, Eds.: *Letters to W.B. Yeats (*Macmillan)
London 1977; Fisk, Robert: *In Time of War: Ireland, Ulster
and the Price of* Neutrality 1939-1945 (Deutsch) London
1983; Gregory, Augusta *Journals, Vol 11. Ed. Daniel
J.Murphy (*Colin Smythe) Gerrards Cross 1978; Hone,
Joseph: *W.B.Yeats (*Penguin) Harmondsworth 1971; Jeffares,
A.Norman: *A Commentary on the Collected Poems of*
W.B.Yeats (Macmillan) London 1968; Jeffares, A. Norman:
W.B.Yeats: Man and Poet Macmillan 1949; Kelly, John and
Domville, Eric: *Collected Letters of W.B.Yeats Vol I* 1865-
1895 (Clarendon Press) Oxford 1986; Levenson, Samuel :
*Maud Gonne (*Cassell) London 1976; Mannin, Ethel *German*

Journey (Jarrolds) 1948; Mannin, Ethel: *Late Have I Loved Thee* (Arrow Books) London 1969; MacManus, Francis,: *The Yeats We Knew* (Mercier Press) Cork 1965; O'Malley, Ernie : *On Another Man's Wound* (Anvil) Dublin 1979; O'Malley, Ernie: *The Singing Flame* (Anvil Books) Dublin 1978; Robinson, Lennox : *Curtain Up* (Cape) London 1939; Shirer, William L.: *The Rise and Fall of the Third Reich* (Pan) London 1960; Stephan, Enno: *Spies in Ireland* (Four Square) London 1965; Stuart, Madeleine: *Manna in the Morning* (Raven Arts Press) Dublin (Colin Smythe) Gerrards Cross 1984; Taylor, James and Shaw, Warren : *A Dictionary of The Third Reich* (Grafton) London 1987; Ursa, Theodore,: *Can Allies Lead?* (Pew Press) Glasgow 1943; White, Jack: *Misfit (Cape) London 1930; Yeats, W.B.: Collected Poems* (Macmillan) 1965; Younger, Carlton: *Ireland's Civil War* (Fontana Press) revised edtn. London 1986.